Created and Directed by Hans Höfer

**INSIGHT
GUIDES**

CYPRUS

Edited by Hansjörg Brey and Claudia Müller
Photography by Bill Wassman and others
Translated by Ian McMaster and David Ingram
Managing Editor: Dorothy Stannard

APA PUBLICATIONS

CYPRUS

First Edition
© **1992 APA PUBLICATIONS (HK) LTD**
All Rights Reserved
Printed in Singapore by Höfer Press Pte. Ltd

ABOUT THIS BOOK

Palm-fringed beaches enclosed by rugged cliffs, cool cedar forests, scented orange groves and arid steppes broken by carpets of wild flowers: Cyprus is an island of spectacular beauty. What's more, despite its turbulent history, it can justifiably lay claim to being the most romantic island in the world; according to myth, it was the birthplace of Aphrodite, and, as a token of Antony's esteem for Cleopatra, it played a role in one of history's greatest love affairs.

But Cyprus's special geographical position as the easternmost island of the Mediterranean, straddling oriental and Western civilisation, has also endowed it with a rich cultural legacy. Cupolas, domes, towers and minarets pepper the old quarters of towns and villages. Modern holidaymakers tread in the footsteps of such diverse figures as St Paul, Alexander the Great, Haroun el Rachid and Richard the Lionheart.

However, in many people's minds, the island's fascinating early history is eclipsed by its more recent past. Modern events have badly scarred Cyprus. Since the Turkish invasion of its northern territory in 1974, the island has been divided into two zones: Greek-Cypriot to the south and Turkish Cypriot to the north. This has caused bitterness and misery among many Greek Cypriots, but it has also instilled an iron will to survive and even prosper – a fact reflected in the booming economy of Southern Cyprus since partition.

All these aspects made Cyprus a challenging destination for Insight Guides, a series of travel guides which prides itself on its frank approach to travel writing. The first of many difficult tasks was finding a suitable editor – someone who knew the island inside out and who would also be sensitive to, and honest about, the political situation.

In the end, two people were enlisted for the job. The first, **Hansjörg Brey**, knows the country and its people like the back of his hand; his knowledge of the historical and political development of the island was acquired during his work as the vice-secretary of the Sudosteuropa-Gesellschaft (Southeastern Europe Society), based in Munich, and while editing the magazine *Sudosteuropa-Mitteilungen*. Brey is currently working on a scientific study of Cyprus.

His co-editor was **Claudia Müller**, who was a regular visitor to Cyprus even before she embarked on her studies of archaeology and Byzantine art. Cyprus has now become her second home. Her special interest is in the island's cultural diversity and vivacity.

The Authors

The project editors' first task was to assemble a team of expert writers and photographers, who shared their own passion for Cyprus. One of their first appointments was **Klaus Hillenbrand**. After completing his studies in political science and sociology, Hillenbrand worked as a freelance journalist in Nicosia, feeding stories to newspapers and magazines in his native Germany. His articles have appeared in a number of German publications, including the progressive Berlin daily *taz*, which he now edits. For *Insight Guide: Cyprus*, he shares his intimate knowledge of Nicosia, guides us through the minefield of modern history and writes about Cypriot crafts.

After studying as a journalist, Munich-born **Barbara Walz** moved to Cyprus to

Brey *C. Müller* *Hillenbrand* *Walz*

work at the Goethe Institute. She stayed in the job for 16 years, a lengthy stint that gave her a deep insight into both sides of the island and its people. For the purposes of this guide, she took to the road in the Turkish-occupied north and also examined Cyprus's thriving modern art scene.

Joachim Willeitner works as managing editor of the magazine *Antike Welt*. Since 1980 he has organised study trips to the Near East and the Mediterranean. His valuable experience as a tour guide is reflected in his chapters on the Larnaca area. He also compiled the book's Travel Tips section, which contains detailed information about travel, accommodation and restaurants.

Another vital member of the team was philologist and historian **Günter Weiss**. His interest in the historical development of the eastern Mediterranean region made him an obvious candidate for tackling the history section. Likewise, another specialist, **Eckehard Willing**, who has an honorary post at the Botanical Museum in Berlin, wrote the feature on Cyprus's abundant flora.

The youngest member of the team was **Alexander Laudien** from Munich. While still a student of art history and German literature, Laudien contributed articles to a number of magazines and books. His interest in Cyprus stems from his love of Byzantine Art, the subject of his contribution.

Angelika Lintzmeyer, an inveterate globe-trotter, is another contributor who knows Cyprus intimately. She was of indispensable assistance in the editing of the texts and wrote the feature on Zeno, the founder of Stoicism, who was born in Citium (forerunner of modern-day Larnaca).

The Photographers

The Insight Guide series is celebrated for its stunning photography. For this reason, the project editors of *Insight Guide: Cyprus* enlisted the talents of the American photographer **Bill Wassman**, an Insight Guide regular renowned for his remarkable "people" shots. Also well represented in the book is the work of **Gerhard P. Müller**, a freelance photo-designer since 1983 who specialises in the Mediterranean area, and **Bodo Bondzio**, a graphic artist from Cologne who has travelled the world for over 20 Insight Guides.

Thanks are due to **Cyprus Airways** for the invaluable support they have given the project.

The guide was translated into English by **Ian McMaster** and **David Ingram** under the direction of **Tony Halliday**. **Susan Sting** translated the Travel Tips section.

The English edition was masterminded in Insight Guides' London editorial office by **Dorothy Stannard** and editorial director **Brian Bell**, and was proofread and indexed by **Carole Mansur**.

Willeitner

Weiss

G.P Müller

Wassman

History

Features

Places

Maps

TRAVEL TIPS

Compiled by Joachim Willeitner

**For detailed information
see page 289**

ΕΚΤΗСΤΗ·ΕΝ
ΕΝѠΚΕΡѠΫΕΓΛ
ΧΙΑ·ΚСΕΗΔΕΛΠΕ
ΤΟΠΑΧ̄ΟСΛΟΠΖѠΛ
ΛΛΗ·СΠΥΔΗ·ΠΙΕΓ
· ΙΟΑΝ

Sunshine, blue sky and beaches are the criteria that determine many people's choice of holiday destination, and in summer months Cyprus scores a hat-trick. But the island is not only a paradise for indolent sun-seekers: archaeological finds dating back to 7,000 BC, medieval castles, remote mountain villages, and inviting cedar forests, orange groves and vineyards attract more adventurous travellers too.

Cyprus, the easternmost island of the Mediterranean, is engirdled by the Near East, yet Eastern culture is matched by a large dose of European. Rome and Byzantium, the crusaders and the Venetians, the Turks and the British have all left traces. The English writer Robert Byron, in *The Road to Oxiana* (1937), said of Cyprus: "History in this island is almost too profuse. It gives one a sort of mental indigestion." But a man with a heartier appetite for history, Lawrence Durrell, in *Bitter Lemons,* his impressionistic account of his life on Cyprus between 1953 and 1956, rejoiced in "the confluence of different destinies which touched and illumined the history of one small island in the eastern basin of the Levant, giving it significance and depth of focus."

Compared with the surrounding countries of Syria, Lebanon and Turkey, Cyprus is prosperous. Evidence of new industry and development is everywhere (though not always agreeable to the eye). But the thin veneer of prosperity hides deep cuts. The war of 1974, which resulted in the Turks occupying almost 40 percent of the island and every third Cypriot becoming a refugee in his own country, is still fresh in local minds. Many islanders still live in the hope of returning to their former homes.

So Cyprus is much more than sunshine, blue sky and beaches. This Insight Guide is intended to acquaint you with the many different aspects of the island, both positive and negative – to provide you, in other words, with a true insight into the nature of the place and its people.

Preceding pages: the Orthodox face of Cyprus; writing on the wall, Kolossi; Limassol's castle; the church of St Paraskevi, Yeroskipos; holiday homes, Ayia Napa. Left, proud to be Cypriot.

Cyprus has four main topographical regions: the Kyrenia range of mountains to the north, extending from Cape Kormakiti to Cape Andreas; the forested Troodos massif; the hilly landscape to the east and southwest of the Troodos massif; and the Mesaoria Plain, once covered by sea.

The Kyrenia range, with its rough rock walls and steep precipices, is largely formed of hard, compact thrust masses of whitish-grey limestone. On both sides of the limestone are sandstone, clay, calciferous breccia and conglomerate.

To the north and south the range divides into numerous small valleys and ravines, which on the south side are extremely dry and rather bleak. On the north side, the hard limestone is covered by much softer strata consisting of varying types of clay soil, resulting in a very varied coastline.

Deep river valleys, swollen in spring with mountain torrents, lead from the Kyrenia range to the coast. The isolated villages on the slopes are linked by narrow roads, some of which climb right up to the mountain ridges. Beyond, forest tracks lead across nearly the entire length of the massif, affording varied and magnificent views of the steep limestone walls, fabulous rock formations and forests. Clear paths pick their way through bright, dry pine forests, which rarely become dense and dark. Walks across the heights of the Kyrenia range provide many visitors with their most memorable experiences of Cyprus.

The other mountainous region of the island, the Troodos massif, stands in stark contrast to the northern range. The central part, roughly 18 miles (30 km) long, consists of igneous rock. Mount Chionistra or Mount Olympus is composed of dunite, and is surrounded by areas of peridotite, gabbro and dolerite. Over the course of millions of years the dunite gradually changed into serpentine, leading to the mining of asbestos in the Troodos massif. In contrast to the Kyrenia range, the landscape here is more undulating

Preceding pages: the wild shores of Paphos. Left, Pano Lefkara, in the foothills of the Troodos. Right, fertile Cyprus.

and spacious; bright colours and steep, rough rock are nowhere in evidence.

The hill country surrounding the highest mountain in Cyprus could not provide more of a contrast. The predominant colours in the Troodos region are light and dark browns, as well as shades of grey. The hill country is mainly characterised by glaringly white chalk. On sunny days the cliffs can play havoc with photographers' exposure meters. Unsurprisingly, this sun-soaked landscape is covered by extensive vineyards.

The Mesaoria Plain lies between the Kyrenia range and the Troodos massif, between Morphou to the west and Famagusta to the east. It is made up of Pliocene and Quaternary strata composed of sandstone, conglomerate, and calcareous tufa, covered by a further layer of alluvial deposits which have been so eroded in places that the substratum has been exposed. Rivers have carved up the landscape, and water and wind have shaped it. The Mesaoria Plain has been dubbed the bread-basket of Cyprus, but large areas of it frequently lie fallow.

A varied coastline: In the Troodos region and up in the Kyrenia range the land tends to drop down quite steeply before reaching sea-level. Despite this, most of Cyprus is distinctive for its relatively flat coastline. The north-western and southeastern ends of the central plain, i.e. the areas around Morphou and Famagusta, contain broad expanses of flat coastline. To the southwest of the island, too, near Paphos, and also in the Bay of Akrotiri and around Larnaca, the coastline is broad, with smooth, flat beaches. Large salt-water lakes have formed near Larnaca and Limassol. Steep cliffs are a rarity here, but some can be found at the points where the Troodos massif runs steeply towards the coast on its north and south sides: between Pomos and Kokkina in the north, and to the

west of Cape Aspro in the south.

In the extreme northwest of the island, northeast of the Akama Forest, there are further stretches of rocky coastline, but the wide-open expanses of sand unprotected by cliffs are equally attractive. Visually stunning and very varied stretches of coastline occur wherever the chalk of the hill country meets the sea. The hilly landscape near Kourion, for example, drops sharply to the narrow strip of intensively-farmed land along the coast; what trees there are here have been bent inland by the wind.

The coastline of the Kyrenia range is even more varied and interesting. Here, hard lay-ers of limestone lie above softer layers of clay, some of which have been partially washed away. The result is a low and steep coastline with slabs of limestone jutting out above the clay below. It's well worthwhile to visit these coastal areas – which extend from Cape Kormakitis in the northwest to Cape Plakoti – to study the rock formations and characteristic coastal flora.

Lakes and rivers: The map of Cyprus shows a large number of quite small rivers flowing straight into the sea from the hills and mountains. However, most hold water only in the winter and spring, and dry up with the onset of summer. During sudden summer thunderstorms, however, a dusty wadi can turn into a torrent in little under half an hour.

The island gains much of its distinctive appearance from the deep valleys created by these rivers, with their broad gravel beds. The longest river in Cyprus is the Pedhieos, which rises near the monastery of Makheras, southwest of Nicosia, and flows into the sea near Famagusta. Together with the river Yialias, with which it flows parallel, it irrigates the plain. The Yialias has been dammed in two places to form reservoirs.

As far as the island's springs are concerned, two in the Kyrenia range are famous: both are called Kefalovriso, one is near Kithrea and the other near Lapithos. Several more springs, shaded by plane trees, can be found in the Troodos mountains below an altitude of roughly 5,250 ft (1,600 metres) – especially in the countryside around the village of Prodhromos, as far as Kykko monastery and Stavros tis Psokas. Some of them, such as the spring near Kalopanayiotis, are rich in minerals and for centuries have been used for therapeutic purposes.

The only major lakes on Cyprus are the salt-water lakes near Larnaca and Limassol, which were originally lagoons. Over the millennia they became separated from the sea. They are a rich source of birdlife, particularly in December and April when birds migrate between Europe and the Nile Delta, which lies almost directly south. This twice-yearly event has been a dependable feature of Cyprus since the earliest days in the island's history, providing a constant in even the most tumultuous times.

Left, cacti belt. **Right**, splendid cedar in the Troodos mountains.

7000–3000 BC: Neolithic Period. First traces of settlement on Cyprus at Khirokitia.

4500–3500 BC: Traces of Neolithic settlement in Sotira. Ceramic production begins.

3500–2300 BC: Chalcolithic Period. Areas of settlement spread towards the west. Copper is used for making tools and jewellery. Red-on-white ceramics predominate.

2300–1900 BC: Beginning of the Bronze Ages (2300–1050 BC). Copper production increases. First immigrants arrive from Anatolia. Trade with Syria and Egypt. Red polished ware predominates.

1900–1625 BC: First fortifications. Ceramic art developed further (white and red-on-black ware, ceramics with black rim).

1625–1050 BC: Enkomi becomes the centre of metalworking and the export trade.

1500 BC onwards: Cypro-Minoan syllabic script introduced.

1400–1200 BC: Economic prosperity.

1200 BC onwards: Extensive Aphrodite cult in Old Paphos.

1200 BC: Destruction of Enkomi and Kition by "Peoples from the Sea".

1050 BC: Enkomi destroyed again, along with most Late Bronze Age settlements. Salamis is re-founded.

1050–750 BC: The Iron Age. Phoenicians settle the island. Temple of Astarte in Kition. Royal Tombs at Salamis.

750–475 BC: The Archaic Period.

700 BC: Assyrian king Sargon II subjugates the city-kingdoms of Cyprus.

650 BC: Tombs of the Kings at Tamassos.

560–540 BC: Egyptian rule by Ahmose II.

540 BC onwards: Persian rule.

498 BC: Every kingdom on Cyprus except Amathus joins the Ionian Revolt. It fails. The Persians tighten their grip on the island.

480 BC: At the Battle of Salamis, Cyprus joins the Persians against Athens.

475–325 BC: The Classical Period. Cyprus remains a Persian naval base.

411–374 BC: King Evagoras I of Salamis. Evagoras unites the island, despite Phoenician resistance.

333 BC: Alexander the Great, with Cypriot kings' support, defeats the Persians at Issos.

325–250 BC: Hellenistic Period. Cyprus becomes a Hellenistic cultural province, most notably under the rule of Evagoras I.

232 BC: After the death of Alexander Cyprus becomes embroiled in the various fights to succeed him.

312 BC: Zeno of Citium (Kition) founds Stoicism in Athens.

310 BC: Nicocreon, king of Salamis, commits suicide. In 294 BC, Ptolemy I assumes control of the island. Cyprus becomes an Egyptian province.

294–258 BC: Ptolemaic rule. Paphos becomes the capital. Tombs of the Kings at Paphos. Economic and cultural upswing.

58 BC: Cyprus becomes a Roman senatorial province.

50 BC onwards: The beginning of a long period of peace, the *Pax Romana*.

AD 45: Apostles Paul and Barnabas arrive as missionaries. Temples to Apollo Hylates in Salamis, Soli and Kourion are built.

AD 115–116: Major Jewish uprising culminates in the expulsion of all Jews.

313: Christianity becomes the official religion of the Roman Empire.

3rd–4th centuries: Mosaics at Paphos.

332 and 342: Paphos and Salamis destroyed by earthquakes. Reconstruction of Salamis, which, under its new name of Constantia, becomes the island's capital.

395–647: Early Byzantine Period.

5th century: The island becomes *autocephalous* – i.e. independent of the Patriarchate of Antioch.

5th–6th centuries: High point in the construction of Early Christian basilicas.

6th century: Cyprus is an independent administrative unit within the Roman Empire.

648: Arabs occupy the island.

688: Cyprus is forced to pay tribute to both the Byzantine Empire and the Caliphate.

730: Beginning of Iconoclastic Controversy over the use of religious images.

787: The Council of Nicaea condemns iconoclasm and restores iconodule doctrine after much Early Byzantine art is destroyed.

843: End of Iconoclastic Controversy.

965: Cyprus is regained for Byzantium by the emperor Nicephorus II Phocas.

965–1185: Middle Byzantine Period. Cyprus flourishes. Towns founded include Kiti, Episkopi, Lapithos.

1094: Kykko monastery founded. Churches with several cupolae at Geroskipou, Kiti and Peristerona.

11th–12th centuries: The foundation of Makheras and Neophytos monasteries, and castles at Hilarion, Kantara and Buffavento.

1184: Reign of terror by Isaac Comnenos.

1191: Cyprus is captured by Richard the Lionheart.

1191–1489: Rule of the Lusignan dynasty.

1192: Cyprus sold to Guy de Lusignan.

13th–14th centuries: St Sophia in Nicosia

and St Nicholas in Famagusta, and the abbey of Bellapais are built.

1359–69: Rule of Cypriot king Peter I.

1372: War between Genoa and Cyprus.

1374–1464: Genoese occupy Famagusta.

1426: Island is overrun by a marauding expedition from Egypt, and forced to pay tribute to Cairo.

1427: Peasants' uprisings.

1460–1473: Reign of king James II.

1472: King James II marries the Venetian Caterina Cornaro, who becomes queen fol-

lowing the premature death of her husband.

1489: Caterina Cornaro cedes Cyprus to the Venetian Republic.

1489–1571: Venetian rule. Byzantine painting flourishes around the turn of the century.

1517: Egypt is conquered by the Ottoman Turks. Cyprus is forced to pay tribute to the Turks.

1562: Rebellion against Venetian rule.

1570: Ottoman troops invade Cyprus.

1571: Famagusta capitulates.

1571–1878: Ottoman rule, based on the *millet system*, i.e. toleration of religious and ethnic diversity. Christian and Moslem uprisings among the population.

1660: The Sublime Porte bestows the right of independent representation upon bishops.

1750: Aqueduct built near Larnaca.

1774: The archbishop is recognised as the representative of the Christian population.

1804: The Turkish population rebels against dragoman Georhakis Kornesios, who is executed in 1808.

1816: The Sultan Tékké mosque is built near Larnaca.

1821: Mainland Greece's war of liberation against Ottoman rule results in massacres, and looting against the Greeks on Cyprus.

1878: Cyprus is leased to England.

1914: Britain annexes Cyprus.

1930s: Economic boom. Attempts to unify Cyprus with Greece (*enosis*) and to liberate the island from British rule.

1955: Terrorist activities by the right-wing EOKA under the command of General Grivas in order to secure independence.

1959: Makarios III becomes president.

1960: Republic of Cyprus formed. Guarantor powers are Britain, Turkey and Greece.

1963: Fighting between Greek and Turkish Cypriots, who begin to form enclaves.

1964: United Nations peacekeeping force is stationed on Cyprus.

1967: Military junta takes over in Athens.

1974: Coup carried out against Makarios by the Cypriot National Guard, under orders of the Greek military authorities.

July 1974: Turkish troops invade the north of the island. Exchange of sections of the population according to their respective ethnic groups. *De facto* partition of Cyprus.

Preceding pages: neolithic remains, south Cyprus. **Above,** Steatite idol (3000–2500 BC).

A history of Cyprus usually begins with the description of the island by the Greek historian and geographer Strabo of Amasia. Although his text dates from roughly AD 19, he quotes several earlier sources (for example, Eratosthenes, 3rd century BC), and gives a detailed account of the original state of this fertile, densely-forested island. In the extract printed below, he mentions its important mineral resources and agricultural products, as well as changes wrought by civilisation:

"As a fertile island, Cyprus is unsurpassed, for it produces good wine, good oil and also enough corn for its own use. In Tamassos there are, moreover, a large number of copper mines, containing copper sulphates as well as copper oxide, which is suitable for medical purposes. Eratosthenes tells us that in ancient times the plains used to be covered with dense forest and, as a result, could not be cultivated, but the mines remedied the situation, for the inhabitants chopped down trees in order to smelt copper and silver. Eratosthenes also says that shipbuilding was a further reason for deforestation, for the sea was a traffic route, sometimes for whole merchant fleets. Since the islanders were unable, in spite of this, to master the sheer extent of forest on the island, they allowed anyone who was willing and able to fell trees to adopt the land thus won as their own property, without having to pay any taxes." (*Strabo 14.6.5*)

Earliest history: Strabo's account does not go as far back as the Neolithic Period (7000–3000 BC), to which the earliest known settlements of Cyprus are thought to belong. Archaeologists have discovered finds linking Cyprus with Asia Minor, Syria and Palestine all over the island, many of them in fertile river-valley regions: Khirokitia, Petra tou Limniti, Troulli, Kalavassos, etc. It is evident that the people lived from hunting and fishing, but the existence of primitive forms of agriculture and animal husbandry (sheep and pigs) has also been determined. From roughly 4800 BC onwards, rough brown

pottery was manufactured. The houses, made of rubble, wood and mud-brick, were elliptical in shape, and some were built underground. Religious life featured primitive forms of the Near Eastern "great mother goddess" or *magna mater*, influencing later concepts of God.

During the Chalcolithic (literally, "copper-stone") Period (c. 3000–2300 BC), copper played an increasingly important role, as Strabo stresses, and the metal that proved so plentiful probably gave the island its name.

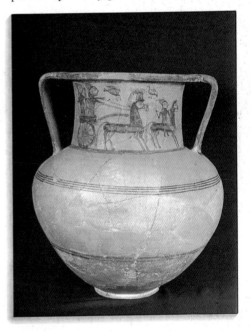

The word "copper" cannot be traced back to Indo-Germanic or Semitic roots (the theory that the island derived its name from the Greek word for the henna-bush or cypress tree has been rejected). One of the first copper implements, a simple chisel discovered in Erimi, is thought to have been imported by immigrants from Asia Minor or southern Palestine.

Soon, however, from the Early Bronze Age onwards (2300–2000 BC), Cyprus was exporting its own copper. It was tempered by a complicated process, and then reduced to metal over a charcoal fire. Tamassos (Politiko), mentioned by Strabo, was the centre of

Left, a smile from former times. **Right**, amphora decorated with chariots and riders, from Marion (850–700 BC).

copper production on Cyprus from the Middle Bronze Age (2000–1600 BC) onwards. The only evidence of settlements from this period are tombs, but it is thought that the island must have been both densely populated and economically prosperous.

It was in close contact with the rest of the region (the earlier advanced civilisations of Mesopotamia were developing fast, and the pyramids were being built in Egypt). In particular, it kept in touch with the coast of Syria and Palestine, and Minoan Crete.

Cyprus retained its political independence and its unique culture based on the production of weapons and other high-quality metal artefacts and ceramics featuring red-on-

Cypriots", or "True Cypriots" (traces of whose non-Greek and also non-Semitic language survived in Cypro-Minoan syllabic script until the 4th century AD, especially in the kingdom of Amathus), resulted in the birth of a Near-Eastern/Aegean/Greek culture unique in the Mediterranean. Vases portraying chariots, ships, bulls, birds and human figures, as well as high-quality ivory carvings and seals, all bear magnificent witness to this period.

Archaic cults and myths: Later records (in particular those of Herodotus) and archaeological finds give us only a vague idea of the sheer profusion of temples and cults on Cyprus, but it seems that many were ecstatic as

black paintings of men and animals. Various fortifications (e.g. in Krini, Hagios Sozomenos and Nitovikla) were built during this period, a sign of the harassment the island was receiving at the hands of the Hyksos Kingdom (c. 1650–1550 BC), although evidence suggests that Cyprus was not subjected to any large-scale raids.

In the Late Bronze Age (1600–1050 BC), Cyprus received a major influx of immigrants, initially merchants and craftsmen and then, by the end of the 13th century BC, refugees: the Greek Achaeans, bearing the Mycenaean culture. Integration with the indigenous population, the so-called "Eteo-

well as mystic: for example, Temple IV at Kition (Citium) contained an opium pipe for religious use. There are few places in the Mediterranean with so many sanctuaries in such a confined area. The goddess Aphrodite alone – symbol of the island for medieval religious travellers and pilgrims – was worshipped at 12 different sites.

The cult of Aphrodite at Paphos is typical of the island's mixed religious culture, a characteristic which has its roots far back in the Bronze Age. In Salamis a male deity was

Above, one of the innumerable fertility symbols.
Right, the Baths of Aphrodite, near Paphos.

APHRODITE

Aphrodite, known as Venus to the Romans, was worshipped by several cultures in the ancient world, and was also associated with Ishtar and Astartes. She originally arrived from the east, as the *magna mater*, or great mother, and was worshipped as the goddess of war as well as the goddess of the sea. Her reputation for valour didn't last, however. She was disarmed by the ancient Greeks and thus reduced to the erotic functions and attributes associated with her today. In *The Iliad*, Homer thus had Zeus, the father of the gods, say: "Fighting, my child, is not for you. You are in charge of wedlock and the tender passions."

In the 12th century BC, long before Homer wrote *The Iliad*, the first sanctuary to Aphrodite was built at Old Paphos. Its high priest was Paphos's founder-king, Cinyras. As Herodotus mentions, the cult in Palea Paphos (Kouklia) included temple prostitution, whereby young women sacrificed their virginity, ostensibly to the goddess though, in fact, to whomever happened to be passing the temple at the time. The usual procedure was for the virgins to go to the temple, hang around until chosen by a man, and then submit to a night of unbridled passion. The proceeds earned from such sacrifice were dedicated to the goddess. In spring, the temple's festival of Aphrodite and her lover Adonis drew pilgrims from all over the ancient world.

Surviving artefacts from the cult include a statue of a phallus with salt, symbolising the birth of Aphrodite from the sea-foam, a myth famously illustrated by Botticelli's *The Birth of Venus*, in which the goddess rises from a vast cockle shell. According to the legend related by Hesiod, Aphrodite was born from the white foam produced from the severed genitals of Uranus (Heaven) when he was castrated by the Titans. (According to some versions of the legend, she originally rose from the waves off the island of Cythera off the Peloponnese but, finding the land there too rocky, sped away on her shell to Cyprus.) The claim that Aphrodite was descended from a man is seen as an attempt to integrate the eastern goddess of fertility into the patriarchal pantheon of Greek gods. She was worshipped as Aphroditos, a bearded man, in many Cypriot towns, particularly at Amathus.

As patroness of love and desire, and as an embodiment of feminine beauty, Aphrodite fea-tures in numerous Greek myths, including the legend of Atalanta, also associated with Cyprus, in which the eponymous heroine is left at birth to perish by her father and must fend for herself in the forests. She grows into a beautiful woman, and offers to marry anyone who can outrun her – but vows to spear those whom she overtakes. Among the suitors is Hippomenes, a great-grandson of the sea-god Poseidon. Just before the contest begins, Eros, son of Aphrodite, shoots one of his famous arrows at Atalanta. Overcome with love for Hippomenes and fearful of his fate, she implores him not to enter the race. Distraught at her inability to change the rules of the contest, which she herself has devised, Atalanta thinks of a trick: she plucks three golden apples from a tree

on Cyprus and tells Hippomenes to drop them as he runs. When he drops them, she stops to pick them up, and thus loses the race to Hippomenes, who consequently wins happiness for them both.

Aphrodite's legendary birthplace, the rock known as *Petra tou Romiou* to the south of Paphos, is bewitching, and especially romantic at sunset. If you have come to Cyprus in the hope of finding something of the Aphrodite spirit, or have brought somebody who might benefit from her influence, it might also help to take a quick swig from the *Fontana Amorosa*, a spring at the northwestern point of the Akamas peninsula, not far from the Baths of Aphrodite. Its waters are said to enamour anyone who takes a sip. ■

worshipped who was subsequently put on an equal footing with Zeus. The Semitic god Resheph, with his two horns, became the mighty Apollo.

According to legend, Cinyras was priest-king of Old Paphos before being driven from power by Agapenor, king of Tegea and leader of the Arcadian troops at Troy. The latter's ship was driven off course after the city had fallen, and he ended up at Paphos. Pindar, who died in 445 BC, refers to Cinyras as "the darling of Apollo, the gentle priest of Aphrodite" (*Pyth. Ode 2.15*), and his forefathers allegedly came from Ashur. Agapenor built a new temple of Aphrodite. *The Iliad* tells us that Agamemnon, the

Cyprus, known as *Alashiya* or *Alasia* in Ugaritic and Egyptian records because of its capital of Alashiya (Enkomi) of that time, and as *Kittim* to the Hebrews (cf. *Jes. 23,1 and 12*), retained its political independence right up to the end of the Late Bronze Age, even when Rameses III (1192–1160 BC) claimed sovereignty over the island.

A dark period – the Early Iron Age: When many Late Bronze Age settlements were destroyed by earthquakes around 1050 BC (e.g. Enkomi and Kition), and while colonisation continued elsewhere (e.g. Palea Paphos, today's Kouklia), the so-called Dark Age descended on Cyprus and Greece. The island became insignificant and pov-

Greek leader at Troy, received a coat of mail from Cinyras as a present – the earliest written mention of Cypriot craftsmanship (*Il. II, 19-23*).

The legend of Agapenor and Cinyras reflects the generally peaceful colonisation by the Greek Achaeans of areas that had often already been settled. The "Achaean Coast", the name given to the northern tip of the island, the Mycenae-like fortifications at Enkomi, Palaeokastro, Maa and Kition, ceramics, and traces of the Arcadian-Aeolic languages in Greek-Cypriot names and inscriptions all provide conclusive proof of Achaean colonisation.

erty-stricken. The only archaeological evidence pertaining to this period comes from family tombs.

But the Early Iron Age (1050–750 BC) did see the arrival on Cyprus of Phoenicians from Tyre. They were experienced merchants and sailors, and introduced their highly sophisticated Semitic-Syrian culture to the island. At first only trading posts were founded on Cyprus, but later on – perhaps as early as the 10th century BC – Kition had become a full-blown colony, independent of the rest of the country, with its own king. After 850 BC, Phoenician temples to Astarte and Melqart were built above the remains of older temples that had probably been destroyed by earthquakes. After taking over Idalium in the Late Bronze Age, Kition then extended its domains to the interior of the island. Lapithos to the north, which had been settled as far back as neolithic times, and Amathus to the south, which was first settled in the Iron Age and bears many Eteo-Cypriot traces, were strongly influenced by the Phoenicians.

The magnificent "Royal Tombs of Salamis", which date from the end of the Early Iron Age, bear witness to the prosperity of the higher social classes during this era. Ceramics dating from this period developed the ideas and designs of the Late Bronze

documents are not quite clear on this) play a more distinct role. Their city-kingdoms were hereditary, and were probably sacred in character too, especially the one at Paphos. In some cities, such as Amathus and Kition, the dynasties were of Phoenician descent, while others were ruled by Greek dynasties, such as the Teucrid dynasty in Salamis and the Cinyras dynasty in Paphos.

Whether the despotic traditions of the Syrian-Canaanite city-kingdoms prevailed over the Mycenean heritage is doubtful. As at Mycaenae, the tombs of the kings at Tamassos, Salamis and Paphos, and the palace at Vouni all reflect self-confidence, wealth and power.

Age, and have been traced to Eteo-Cypriot influences.

The Archaic Period: During the so-called "Archaic Period" of Assyrian domination (c.750–470 BC), seven Cypriot kings were overthrown, as a stele erected at Kition by the Assyrian king Sargon II (721–705 BC) makes clear. The cities were not destroyed, however; indeed, Assyrian influence was probably rather nominal.

It is at this stage that the seven kings of Cyprus (or possibly 10 of them – Assyrian

Left, embossed gold plaques (700 BC). **Above**, gold jewellery (750–600 BC).

Egyptian domination: After the break-up of the Assyrian Empire, there came a brief period of Egyptian domination of Cyprus, under Pharaoh Ahmose II (569–525 BC); politically this period was peaceful and not all that significant, but the influence of Egyptian culture was very evident on the island. Human figures acquired a rigidity, similar to that of the *Kouroi* style of Ancient Greece, and scarabs were copied.

Cyprus under Persian rule: In 545 BC the Cypriot kings transferred their allegiance to the initially very relaxed rule of the mighty Achaemenid (Persian) kingdom, and deferred to a culturally superior power structure that was also open to Greek influence – the greatest structure of its kind, in fact, to have arisen in the Near East before Alexander the Great. Cyprus thus became embroiled in the tensions between Greece and Persia, and in 498 BC it joined the Ionian Revolt in western Asia Minor. Herodotus doesn't mention why they decided to do this; he makes no mention of any Greek nationalist sentiment on Cyprus.

Onesilos, the younger brother of the king of Salamis, persuaded all of Cyprus's major cities to join the Greek side. Only Amathus, with its strong Eteo-Cypriot and Phoenician influence, demurred. Once the ignominious revolt had ended, its inhabitants impaled the

head of Onesilos above their city gates. At the famous and decisive battle against the Persians near Salamis, Stasenor, the king of Kourion, deserted his allies, and the Salaminians followed suit. It was only in Soli that the Persians encountered tougher resistance. Rulers friendly to Persia were installed in power, and supplied with Persian troops for protection.

At the Battle of Salamis in 480 BC, a Cypriot contingent of 150 ships fought on the side of the Persians, alongside Egyptians, Cilicians and Pamphylians. "A bunch of good-for-nothings", pronounced Queen Artemisia of Caria (*Herodotus VIII, 68*).

Greeks against Persians: During this period (470–325 BC) Cyprus continued to be affected by the political tensions between Greece and Persia. Nevertheless, neither Athens nor Sparta succeeded in establishing a firm foothold on Cyprus for any length of time. By now the island had become a highly desirable naval base, as well as a valuable source of wood for shipbuilding, and Cyprus remained Persia's most important Mediterranean naval base; the Persian fleet which put paid to Spartan naval domination near Knidos in 394 BC set sail from Cyprus.

During this period, Cypriot art came under strong Attic influence, as discoveries made in the handsome palace of Vouni reveal. Greek sculpture and vase-painting was widely imitated, but the traditional Cypriot forms held their own against the new trends and influences.

King Evagoras I of Salamis (411–374 BC) became a symbol of Attic influence. He was an adept politician, who had wrested control of Salamis from a Tyrian called Abdemon, under the successful pretext of being descended from the city's ancient kings. He was adept at capitalising on the tensions between Persia and Athens, and despite resistance from the Phoenician-based dynasties of Kition, Amathus, Golgoi and Soli, he succeeded, albeit by force, in uniting the island politically for the first time in its history. His eulogist, Isocrates, portrayed the king's life in terms of Hellenism's struggle against barbarism. According to him, "[Evagoras] assumed control of the government of [Salamis], which as a result of Phoenician domination was run by barbarians; the city despised the Greeks, showed no interest in the arts and had neither a market place nor a harbour; Evagoras remedied all these deficiencies and increased the city's territory still further, surrounding it with new walls and providing it with triremes..." (*Isocrates Evagoras 47*).

Greek artists and politicians frequently crossed the water to visit the home of this philhellenic king. Though still retaining some Near Eastern characteristics, Cyprus had now become a unified Hellenistic cultural province.

Left, limestone head of a general or king. **Right**, Cyprus's most famous figure, Aphrodite, to be found in the Paphos Museum.

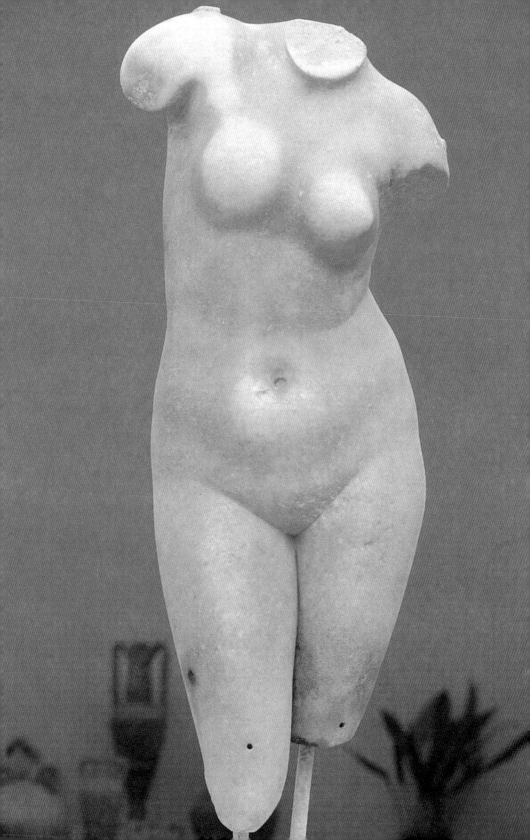

The history of Cyprus is in many ways quite different from the histories of other Mediterranean regions: the island had experienced a special kind of "Hellenism" – an interplay of Greek and Near Eastern influence – in its political, cultural and religious life long before the mighty campaigns of the great Macedonian general Alexander. So when a Cypriot fleet, with soldiers and technicians, fought alongside Alexander's army in his campaign to conquer the east, the island's integration into his enormous empire (356–

Lapithos, Kyrenia and Marion took the side of Antigonus (the rulers of Kition and Lapithos were of Phoenician descent, but spoke Greek).

In 318 BC Ptolemy set out to subdue the cities. Only Nicocles of Paphos tried to oppose him. The consequences were tragic: King Nicocles fell on his sword, together with his wife and family. Inscriptions inform us that he was closely connected with the Hellenism of Argos, Delos and Delphi, and the fabulous luxury and splendour of his

323 BC) was inevitable.

Power struggles: The power struggles that ensued between Alexander the Great's successors – Ptolemy, governor of Egypt; King Antigonus, the governor of Phrygia, whose power base was Syria; and the Seleucid Empire, based in Greece and Asia Minor – proved politically disastrous for Cyprus. The island was a strategic base, and as a supplier of copper, silver, grain and wood (for use in shipbuilding), it acquired vital economic importance. Politically, however, its kingdoms were divided into two camps: Salamis, Paphos, Soli and Amathus lined up strongly on the side of the Ptolemies; while Kition,

court were legendary.

By the beginning of the 2nd century BC an astoundingly diverse assortment of different peoples were living on Cyprus, including a Jewish community, the Seleucids. They ruled the island from 306 to 294 BC, and succeeded in recruiting 16,000 infantrymen and 600 cavalrymen.

The Ptolemaic kings: For the next two centuries (294–58 BC) Cyprus was a province of Ptolemaic Egypt, ruled by a governor-general, or *strategus*. These *strategoi* resided in Salamis, and were often related to the Ptolemaic royal family. The *strategus* of Cyprus was also in full command of the entire Egyptian navy. The local dialect on Cyprus was replaced by the common idiom of Hellenistic Greek, and the island's coins started to bear the heads of the ruling Ptolemies. The cities on the island were ruled by tough garrisons of foreign mercenaries under the command of Greek officers (most of whom were not Cypriots), and by local Phoenician families (e.g. Lapithos and Kition). Local Greek Cypriots started filling important political posts only at the beginning of the 1st century BC.

It was in the more refined realms of culture, arts and religion that the flourishing cities, with their magnificent market-places, gymnasia and theatres, enjoyed most independence. New towns were founded, three of which were all called Arsinoë in tribute to the sister of Philadephus, one of the Ptolemaic rulers of the island). Records document the names of the leaders of the various guilds, in particular those in charge of the gymnasia (gymnasiarchs), and sports (agonothetes). The cities all joined forces to form a new cultural organisation known as the *Koinon Kyprion*.

Egyptian cultural and religious influence, in particular that of Alexandria, the centre of Hellenistic city culture, increased on the island. Serapis, Isis, Osiris, Zeus and the Libyan god Ammon were just a few of the deities worshipped, and the market-places and gymnasia were decorated with sculptures and carvings influenced by Alexandrian craftsmen. The so-called "Tombs of the Kings" at Nea Paphos (Kato Paphos) near Ktima – the most important archaeological find dating from the Hellenistic period on Cyprus – are based on Egyptian designs. Cypriot literature was written exclusively in Greek, and the island produced a modicum of literary talent, such as Stasinos with his epic *Kypria*, and Sopatros,

who wrote comedies.

The philosopher Zeno of Citium (334–262 BC) occupies a central place in the history of European thought. The son of a merchant named Mnaseas – the Greek version of the Phoenician name Manasse or Menahem – he frequented as a young man the philosophy schools of Crates, Stilpon and Xenocrates in Athens. In 308 BC he founded his own Athens school: the Stoic School. His ideas were heavily influenced by Greek tradition.

Roman rule: The transfer of control of Cyprus to the Roman Empire in 58 BC completed Roman domination of the Mediterranean and left Egypt politically isolated. A

Preceding pages: the Battle of Salamis. Left, mosaic in the Cyprus Museum, Nicosia. Above, favoured deities Aphrodite and Apollo.

rather suspect testament legitimated the Senate's decision to take control of Cyprus on a "provisional basis". Although Egypt managed to regain the island twice during the civil wars of the Republic, the Romans held on to Cyprus for good once the Empire was established. The puritanical Marcus Portius Cato tried to persuade the last of the Ptolemaic rulers to relinquish all claim to Cyprus in return for the office of high priest of the Aphrodite cult at Paphos (the unfortunate ruler preferred to commit suicide instead). The orator Cicero was one of the island's first proconsuls, but even he, staunch opposer of corruption and injustice, was noticeably passive in his attitude to-

area around Salamis, which gradually decreased in importance as Paphos grew. Well-preserved Roman theatres can be seen at Soli and Kourion.

The magnificent mosaics at the 3rd-century House of Dionysos, with its 70-odd rooms, near Nea Paphos, as well as the fine mosaics discovered in Kourion illustrate the smoothness of the cultural transition. An oath of allegiance to the emperor Tiberius, dating from AD 14, demonstrates Cyprus's loyalty to Rome:

"By our Aphrodite of the mountains, by our mistress, by our Apollo Hylates, by our Apollo of Kyrenia, by our guardians the Curetes, by all the gods of Cyprus together

wards the various civil servants who bled the island dry with extortionate "loans".

The Romans adopted the original strict administrative structure of the Ptolemies. Cyprus was now ruled by a proconsul, and his officials, from Paphos – or *Augusta Claudia Flavia Paphos*, to give it its full Roman name. The road network on the island was improved, but there were few changes which affected the native population. The Roman contingent on Cyprus numbered only 2,000 men.

Ruins of some of the spacious public buildings *(ager publicus populi Romani)* dating from this period can still be seen in the

with the council, the gods and goddesses of our fathers who belong to this island, the birthplace of Aphrodite, by Caesar Augustus who is our god, by eternal Rome and by all other gods and goddesses, we and our children do hereby solemnly swear... to remain loyal to Tiberius Caesar and to honour him... to have the same friends and the same enemies... to accord holy honours to Rome and to Tiberius Caesar Augustus... and only to the sons of his blood. " (*Rise and Fall of the Roman World* by T.B. Mitford.)

Above, in pursuit of hedonism. **Right**, Zeno took a more sober approach.

WHAT A STOIC

Stoic indifference is an attitude which visitors often need in Cyprus – when their wishes are not answered as quickly or as efficiently as they might be in another country, for example. It is fitting, therefore, that the philosophy of Stoicism dates back to the Cypriot philosopher Zeno, born in 336 BC in Kition (Latin Citium), north of today's Larnaca. In the words of Cyprus expert F. G. Maier, Cyprus's most famous Stoic made "a unique and inestimable contribution to the history of European thought."

Impressed from an early age by the Greek philosophers, and by Socrates in particular, Zeno left Cyprus around 312 BC to go to Athens where he could devote himself to the study of philosophy. He visited various philosophy schools in the city, including that of the famous Cynic, Crates. In contrast to today's definition of this term, the Cynics of ancient times were not bitter and vicious faultfinders but thinkers whose philosophy stressed the benefits of returning to a more "natural" life, free of social conventions.

Around the year 300 BC, Zeno decided to found his own school. Since he did not have the capital to buy a building of his own, and possibly because of his Cynical attitude to property, he gave his lectures in the agora in Athens, in the *stoa poikile*, a colonnade known for its series of paintings depicting the battle of Marathon, and it was this colonnade that gave Stoicism its name (just as the Academy gave its name to the followers of Plato).

The Stoic school was less formally organised than some of its competitiors, such as the Peripatetics or the Epicureans. Zeno was the only philosopher in Athens at that time to run a school of philosophy from a public building.

Zeno practised what he preached: his lifestyle was austere. He said that man's highest aim in life should be to live in harmony with nature. Conscious eschewal of passion and active cultivation of apathy, he maintained, allowed man to develop enough insensitivity to face the fortunes and ills of his life with indifference.

Against the laws of nature, he also maintained, the joys and sorrows of the individual were of no significance. If man lived a life according to rationally established values, one that was in harmony with his own inner being, he would then become insensitive to such things as pain, suffering, love and even death. This philosophy was accompanied by a belief in the divine corporeality of all things.

To begin with, enthusiasm for Zeno's teachings was slow, though his short work, the *Politea,* attracted more attention and abuse than any other work by a Stoic (by the mid-2nd century onwards Stoics were trying to minimise the importance attributed to this work). After Zeno's death, his successor, Ariston of Chios, diverged from Zeno's teachings and brought the Stoic school to the verge of insignificance.

It was only under Chrysippus of Soli (281–208 BC) that the school flourished again: Chrysippus adhered strictly to Zeno's original teachings, but bolstered them with tenets of his own, thereby laying the foundations for Stoicism as understood

ZENO FLORVIT OLIMP. 190.
Exiguo prudens arctatur zeno tabella:
Immensum cuius mentis acumen erat.

today. In the words of Diogenes Laertius, in *The Lives and Opinions of the Philosophers*, "Without Chrysippus there would have been no Stoa."

Zeno's teachings were particularly popular in the Roman Empire, especially since they gave man the possibility of securing a personal happiness quite independent of external circumstances and social conditions. The Roman emperor Marcus Aurelius (AD 121–180), a supporter of Stoicism, illustrated what he called the "trivial nature of life" with the slogan "a drop of sperm today, a handful of ashes tomorrow!"

Zeno died at the age of 72 when he committed suicide. What, one wonders, could have robbed him of his famous indifference? ∎

The decision of the Roman emperor Constantine (c. AD 247–337) to give preferential treatment to Christianity as opposed to the many other forms of religion in the Roman Empire led to far-reaching religious, cultural and political changes across the whole Mediterranean region. The Christians, until then widely persecuted, now became the merciless persecutors of their pagan rivals. A politically and economically powerful ecclesiastical hierarchy arose, a kind of "state within a state". The effects this had on Cyprus, with its strong pagan traditions, were immense.

The spread of Christianity: From quite early on, perhaps even as early as AD 40, a number of Cypriots had been followers of St Stephen in Jerusalem. Some also became missionaries in Syrian Antioch, and on Cyprus itself (cf. *Apostles 11,19 f.*). A few years later, the converted Cypriot Jew Joseph Barnabas (cf. *Apostles 13,14 f.*) began his own missionary work, initially with the Apostle Paul. Travelling from Salamis to Paphos, they came across several Jewish communities. The conversion of Roman proconsul Sergius Paulus (c. AD 46–48) is undisputed, but the story relating to the appointment of bishops in Soli and Tamassos at about the same time belongs to the realms of legend rather than historical fact.

Unlike Asia Minor, Cyprus bears few traces of Christianity before Constantine's time. After the conversion of Constantine, however, there was a swift increase in the number of bishoprics (there were 12 in AD 344 and 15 by AD 400), reflecting the island's intensive Christianisation. The emperor's mother, St Helena, is said to have brought several reliquaries of the cross to Cyprus on her return from Jerusalem (some of them still survive in the island's monasteries, for example at Stavrovouni).

Early Christian basilica construction reached its zenith in the 5th and 6th centu-ries. Two particularly impressive examples are the remains of a three-aisled basilica with mosaic decoration at Kourion, and the extensive church complex (four basilicas with hot springs) at Cape Drepanum. Very little, however, remains of the former seven-aisled basilica at Salamis, a building which broke new architectural ground.

It was in the 5th century that the Church of Cyprus succeeded in becoming autocephalous – i.e. independent of other patriarchates, particularly that of Antioch – thus giving the

archbishop of Cyprus a great deal of political power right up to the present day. It came about when Archbishop Anthemius of Constantia (Salamis), prompted by a vision, found the Gospel of St Mark in the tomb of St Barnabas. He sent it to the emperor Zeno in AD 488, who forthwith granted the archbishop of Cyprus the special imperial privileges of carrying a sceptre rather than a crozier and writing his signature in purple ink. Special status was confirmed at a council held in AD 692, the so-called Trullanum.

The Byzantine Empire: As a province belonging to the Diocese of the Orient, and governed by a consul based in Salamis (which became known as Constantia after AD 342), Cyprus was subject to the Eastern or Byzantine Empire at Constantinople. In the 6th century the island became an independent administrative unit, or *quaestura exercitus* – a sign of its growing importance. It was thus a part of the Roman Empire, and as such gradually dissolved its political and cultural links with the West, and with the capital city of Rome. It was to survive the decline of the western half of the Empire by more than 1,000 years.

Under the tough conditions of the Eastern or Byzantine Empire which was now taking shape, the Orthodox Church, comprising mainly Greek-speaking Christians and with

oped its own system of officials. They were well known for their ruthlessness and the islanders frequently suffered at their hands. Nevertheless, up until the Arab raids of the 7th century – apart from a few attacks by pirates from the mainland around AD 404, and a brief uprising led by a governor – the island enjoyed 300 years of peace, just as it had during pagan Roman times. However, a period of severe drought at the beginning of the 4th century decimated the island's population, and two earthquakes in 332 and 342 destroyed Paphos and Salamis. Only Salamis – the seat of the consul – was rebuilt.

One Jerusalem pilgrim, Antoninus of Placentia, travelled to Cyprus in AD 570,

its own dogma and special liturgical and institutional forms, evolved (in fact, just one of several new church movements to develop at this time). The marriage of priests, the lack of a papal primate and the use of unleavened bread for the Sacrament were major bones of contention, and divided believers when they came up against representatives of Western Christianity, the so-called "Latins", in the 13th century. Orthodoxy remained firm, however, and has exerted a a strong influence on the people of Cyprus to this day.

Taking traditional Roman administration as its model, the Byzantine Empire developed

and wrote: "From Placentia we arrived in Constantinople. We then travelled to the island of Cyprus, to the city of Constantia where St Epiphanius lies buried – a graceful city with many fine palm trees." In the second half of the 4th century, the Roman historian Festus Rufius noted that the island was "famed for its riches".

Cyprus was the first place to be attacked by the Arabs on their astonishingly swift rampage through the Mediterranean in the 7th century. The first Arabian Mediterranean fleet was built in Syria in AD 648, and Cyprus was conquered just one year later in AD 649. The next three centuries, up until the final recapture of the island by Byzantine emperor Nicephorus II Phocas in the year 965, were among the darkest in the entire history of Cyprus: in 688 it was obliged to pay tribute to both the Byzantine Empire and the Caliphate. This unusual state of joint-owned neutrality, unique in the Mediterranean, did not stop either side from pillaging the island's cities, taking punitive action and forcing large sections of the population off the island altogether.

Between 692 and 698, following a new resettlement programme instigated by the Byzantine emperor and yet another Arab invasion, Cyprus became almost completely depopulated. Its inhabitants – most of them

by the Byzantine patriarch Nikolaos Mystikos at the beginning of the 10th century as not raising its hand against either the Byzantine Empire or the Caliphate, and made up of loyal vassals who were "more loyal to the Arabs than to the Byzantines".

Many Cypriots were forced to withdraw to remote areas in the mountains; their cities lay in ruins. Between 911 and 912 the island was pillaged for a full four months by a pirate, Damianus of Tarsus. The Byzantine priests attempted in vain to liberate the enslaved population.

Cyprus in the Early Middle Ages: The period between 965 and 1192, during which the island was ruled by a Katepano and his

Greek-speaking Orthodox Christians – were later allowed to return from Syria and Asia Minor. No evidence remains as to whether the population underwent Islamisation at the hands of the Arabs, nor whether any Islamic families settled on Cyprus on a permanent basis. An Armenian element (over 3,000 Armenians had been transferred to the island in the second half of the 6th century to help guard it) mingled with the militarily weak Cypriots, producing a population described

Left, fresco in St John's cathedral, Nicosia. Above, the legends of the saints provide inexhaustible inspiration for icon painters.

officials, and was subject solely to the Byzantine Empire, was one of economic and cultural prosperity for the ecclesiastical élite, who were busy building monasteries and churches, and the officials who, despite the church's protests, were draining the rural population dry. The law tied most country people to the land; even though some had the status of peasant proprietors or free tenants, they were still subject to ferocious taxation. In a dialogue, part of which is reprinted here, written towards the end of the 11th century, Nikolaos Muzalon, the archbishop of Cyprus, uses such unflattering terms as "Prince of the Evil Spirits" and "Beelzebub" to describe his chief official, and refers to his tax-collectors as "out-and-out robbers":

Questioner: *Does the land (on Cyprus) produce anything?*

Muzalon: *All kinds of fruit grow there.*

Questioner: *Gratifying indeed!*

Muzalon: *It only results in more complaints.*

Questioner: *How do you mean?*

Muzalon: *The tax-collectors devour whatever the farmers produce.*

Questioner: *A tragedy!*

Muzalon: *And they demand even more besides.*

Questioner: *Oh dear!*

Muzalon: *They maltreat those who have no property of their own...*

A class made up of merchants and businessmen, of whom, sadly, very little is known, was responsible for the foundation of several new towns, including Kiti, Lapithos and Episkopi, all of which – as elsewhere in Byzantium – were built at a respectful distance from the coast. It was also at this point that the island's most magnificent monasteries were built, with their wealth of splendid paintings and frescoes: Kykko, under the patronage of emperor Alexius Comnenos, with its famous icon of the Virgin Mary, and later the Makheras and Neophytos monasteries.

The arrival of the crusaders, the proximity of the Christian kingdom of Little Armenia in Asia Minor and the increasing activity of the Italian seafaring towns eventually put Cyprus back on the Mediterranean map. In 1148 Venice obtained numerous and far-reaching trading privileges on the island.

Historically, there seem to be no traces at all of any Cypriot regional or national feeling. The short-lived and bloodily suppressed attempts at independence on behalf of individual Byzantine governors that took place in 1042 and 1092 were probably inspired by demands for a cut in the level of taxation rather than strong nationalist feelings. And when the brutal despot Isaac Comnenos – a relative of the imperial family in Constantinople – finally succeeded in freeing himself from central control in the year 1184, it was a rebellion from above rather than below, with no popular support.

Right, a relic containing fibres from the hemp ropes said to have bound Christ to the cross is kept in Omodhos monastery.

CRUSADERS, LUSIGNANS AND VENETIANS

The 900-year period of East Roman-Byzantine imperial rule came to an end almost accidentally. What ensued was almost half a millennium of Latin rule in the Eastern Mediterranean, a period that even outlasted the crusader states of Palestine. The catalyst in this major power shift was Richard I of England.

Seized by the English: Richard the Lionheart's journey to Palestine in May 1192 was a difficult one: some of his ships sank, and the one carrying his bride, Berengaria, met with only slightly less danger when it limped into port near Limassol and was received by the Byzantine usurper Isaac, mentioned earlier. Isaac hated Latins, and held the lady and her entourage as prisoners, even depriving them of water.

When Richard arrived on the island several days later, he swore revenge and immediately requested reinforcements from Palestine. In the battle which followed Isaac, underestimating Richard's strength, suffered a quick defeat, and went down in history as the last Byzantine ruler.

In general, the Cypriot population, mostly Greek Orthodox and Armenian, watched the collapse of Byzantine rule impassively, though some positively welcomed it. But the Cypriots were soon forced to realise the drawbacks of Norman rule: the population was allowed no say in government, they were obliged to part with 50 percent of their capital, all the island's castles were occupied by Normans, and the men were made to shave off their beards as a sign of subjugation. In a letter written shortly after the arrival of the Normans, the Greek monk Neophytos, said: "Our country is now no better than a sea whipped up by storm winds." The population was still subject to Byzantine law, however, and for the time being at least, ecclesiastical and religious matters were left alone.

The Knights Templar: As far as Richard was concerned, the island was a bonus: Isaac had been an exceedingly greedy despot, and had left considerable riches. Richard tried to trade the island for half of Flanders but, unsuccessful in his scheme, he sold it to the crusading order of the Knights Templar in return for 40,000 dinars and the pledge of a further 60,000 from its future income. (In fact, the Knights Templar never managed to make a profit out of the island.)

At the end of 1191 an uprising by the Armenians and the Greeks was brutally suppressed, and in the spring of 1192 the tyranny of the Knights Templar urged the local population of Lefkosia (which soon became known as Nicosia) to a renewed attempt at resistance. An appalling blood bath ensued. The rebellion was one of the most important uprisings against a foreign oppressor in the entire history of the island. (A guerrilla war flared up once again in 1194, under the leadership of a certain Kanakis, but then the Cypriot population sank into centuries of passive and gloomy resignation, broken only by sporadic and fruitless guerrilla uprisings.)

The Knights Templar, preoccupied with their battles against the Saracens, immediately sold the island for 40,000 dinars – the sum they themselves had paid – to one of Richard's henchmen, Guy of Lusignan, the dispossessed king of Jerusalem, thus introducing the 300-year rule of the Lusignan dynasty. The measures Guy had to take during his two years as king of Cyprus reveal what dire straits the island was in:

"When he took the island as his own property, he sent out messages in order to win back the trust of the inhabitants, and he populated the cities and castles anew; and he sent forth tidings to all the surrounding countries that all the knights, nobles and citizens desirous of fiefs and land should come to him, and he would provide them with it. Thus they came, from the Kingdom of Jerusalem, from Tripoli, from Antioch and Armenia. They were then enfeoffed, and provided with land, and he gave the towns civil rights; many of the new arrivals were from the lower classes, and some of them were non-Cypriot Greeks."

The small governing class in Lusignan's feudal state was almost exclusively comprised of Latins, from the west and from the crusader states. The Greek property-owners and nobles on the island had been largely wiped out during the brutal reign of the Knights Templar.

Only a few Greek Cypriots, among them the chronicler Leontius Machairas (early 15th century), were able to adapt to the crusaders' culture. The Greeks were hardly represented at all in the administration, nor in the ranks of the Italian, southern French and Catalan merchants, who had settled into relatively isolated enclaves in the coastal cities. A deep gulf separated the ruling Latins from the Greek Cypriot population.

Indeed, the social status of the Cypriot population had worsened considerably since

siastical controversy, reduced the number of Greek bishoprics on the island to four, in remote villages. They had to swear an oath of loyalty and according to a remark made in a letter by the Latin archbishop Raphael in 1280, their presence on the island was merely "tolerated".

When 13 Greek monks were condemned to death at the stake by a Dominican padre in 1231, Greek resentment escalated. Luckily, this was the only example of the Inquisition on Cyprus. The remains of the unfortunate monks were mixed with those of animals in order to prevent the possibility of any reliquary cult. The Latin church, its ranks swelled by communities of Augustinians,

the Byzantine era: the peasant proprietors, who on top of paying tax had to provide their overlords with one-third of their income and two days' work a week, had lost most of their rights and were constantly in fear of their rulers, who punished them as they found fit – including mutilating and executing them.

Latin versus Orthodox: Conflict between the Roman Catholic and the Greek Orthodox churches became more critical during this period. Inflexible papal policies and fanatical monks increased the tension. The *Constitutio Cypria* (also known as the *Bulla Cypria*) of Pope Alexander IV in 1260, which was officially meant to end the eccle-

Dominicans and Premonstratensians, maintained its dominant role right up to the Ottoman era: its power was symbolised by the impressive French Gothic structure of the 13th-century cathedral of St Sophia (today the Selimiye mosque), the coronation church of the Lusignans, in Nicosia, the cathedral of St Nicholas in Famagusta and in the mighty ruins of Bellapais abbey, the "white abbey" of the Premonstratensian order, near Kyrenia.

The nobility flourishes: The abject poverty of the Cypriot population stood in stark contrast to the late medieval pomp at the court of the Lusignans and in the castles of the wealthy ruling class. The pilgrim Ludolf von Suchen, from Westphalia in Germany, travelled through Cyprus between 1336 and 1341, during the reign of the Lusignan king Hugo IV (1324–59). It was a period of economic prosperity, especially as far as the two great trading rivals, Genoa and Venice, were concerned, and Ludolf remarks on the wealthy merchants living in Nicosia (he also mentions the cult of Aphrodite in Paphos, in particular its temple prostitution, a source of interest to many pilgrims):

"For the princes, the nobles, the barons and the knights of Cyprus are the wealthiest in the world. Anyone with an income of 3,000 florins treats it as if it were no more men than they do their hunters and falconers... Thou shouldst know that all the princes, noblemen, barons and knights on Cyprus are the wealthiest and most noble in all the world. They once lived in the land of Syria, in the wealthy city of Acre, but when that land and that city were lost to them, they fled to Cyprus and have stayed here ever since."

The history of Cyprus during this period is full of political intrigue. There were enough rivalries in the royal household of the Lusignans and among the island's powerful barons to outdo any play by Shakespeare. Peter I (1359–69) was the last of the fanatical crusaders. He campaigned throughout Eu-

than an income of 3 marks. When it comes to hunting, however, no amount is too high to spend. I know a certain Count of Jaffa; he owns over 500 hounds, and one servant for every two of them, to protect them, bathe them and rub them with ointment; that is how well dogs are treated here. Another nobleman has 10 or 11 falconers, and gives them special wages and special rights. There are certain knights and noblemen upon Cyprus who pay less to keep and feed 200 armed

Left, the coronation of Richard the Lionheart in 1189. **Above**, the castle of Kantara, comfortable base of the Lusignans.

rope and even succeeded in conquering Alexandria in 1365, albeit only briefly and with appalling loss of life. He was brutally murdered in his mistress's bedchamber by the mightiest barons on the island, after revenging himself for the alleged infidelity of his wife Eleonore.

It was not only the barons within who kept the power of the Lusignan kings in check: Genoa and Venice, the increasingly powerful Italian trading powers, formed independent, rival states within the Lusignan kingdom. Peter II's coronation in the cathedral in Nicosia in 1372 turned out very differently from the happy occasion expected when a fleet of seven Genoese warships arrived; a year of war followed, with heavy pillaging. The end result was the 90-year-long (1374–1464) occupation and exploitation of Famagusta and its surrounding area by the Genoese. The extortionate sum of 40,000 florins had to be paid annually to secure the return of the other areas that had been taken.

Cyprus under the Venetians: Venice had been either unable or simply unwilling to prevent Genoa's seizure of part of Cyprus. It was happy to wait until the Lusignans themselves were no longer capable of ruling the island alone. The period of Venetian rule on Cyprus (1489–1571) is yet another dark chapter in the island's history. Cyprus was a strategically important base for Venice in its war against Turkey, but was difficult to defend. In 1507 only one-quarter of Nicosia was inhabited, and the city walls were weak; in 1567, a team of master builders spent10 months trying to improve them. Smaller fortified sites, such as the castles at St Hilarion, Paphos and Kantara, were dismantled. All the island's defences were concentrated in Famagusta, where the city's four bastions, and the walls and towers connecting them, had undergone regular inspection and renovation since 1492. Its force of 800 soldiers was far too small, and typically there was not a Greek among them; this force, whose task was to guard the city and its various nationalities, was changed every few years.

The social stratification remained just as it had under the Lusignans. In order to obtain money and soldiers, the *signori* tried to persuade the peasant proprietors to buy their freedom. The Venetians also had to recover enough money from the population of the island (estimated to be only 100,000 to 200,000) to pay tribute to the Turks.

The island's natural wealth was mined extensively. Venice sought to increase trading in traditional products such as wine, flax, hemp, cotton, wax, honey, sugar, indigo, oil and saffron. The saltworks at Larnaca, too, were important. Grain exports were under strict controls. One 16th-century traveller had this to say: "All the inhabitants are slaves of the Venetians… several times a year some new tax or levy gets imposed, and the poor inhabitants are so mercilessly exploited and plundered that they scarcely have enough left to eke out their miserable existences." Droughts, swarms of locusts and outbreaks of the plague exacerbated the situation.

The most important uprising on Cyprus since the beginning of the Lusignan kingdom broke out in the year 1562. Significantly, the head of a Greek cavalry unit, the *Megadukas*, was involved (proving, perhaps, that the Venetians' distrust of Greek Cypriots soldiers was justified). Frankish noblemen, led by Jacobus, known as Didaskalus, a teacher in Nicosia, also joined the uprising. The Venetians were informed of the rebellion and had the ringleaders put to the sword. Thousands of peasants who had gathered in readiness in Nicosia dispersed.

The Ottoman invasion: In July 1570, after several warnings, 350 Turkish ships landed at Larnaca and the island fell to the Turks. The battle for Nicosia was a catastrophe for the Cypriots: they waited fruitlessly for relief to arrive, and their defence was completely uncoordinated. When the Turks, who brought in reinforcements unhindered from the mainland, sent in an attack force of 16,000 men, the city's resistance crumbled. Another bloodbath ensued. The Greeks fought bravely on the side of their Latin rulers and incidents of open siding with the Turks among the rural population were rare.

The 10-month-long battle for Famagusta raged from 23 September 1570 until 1 August 1571. It was one of several sieges in the struggle for the Mediterranean between Islamic and Christian forces; there were other major ones at Candia (Iraklion) on Crete, in 961 and 1669, and on Rhodes in 1522.

At Famagusta, seven major offensives were warded off; the Turks allegedly lost 80,000 soldiers out of some 200,000–250,000 men, while the defenders had only 3,000–4,000 infantrymen, 200–300 cavalrymen and 4,000 Greeks. When the gunpowder finally ran out, the white flag of surrender was hoisted. In flagrant defiance of the terms of capitulation, the Venetian commander-in-chief Bragadino was taken prisoner; his nose and ears were cut off, and he was flayed alive. Seldom are such injustices redressed historically, but in this case, when the commander-in-chief of the Turkish forces, Mustapha, returned to Constantinople, he was met by the dispiriting news of the Christian naval victory at Lepanto.

Right, Neophytos, hermit, stern critic of Richard I and, later, saint.

بسم الله الرحمن الرحيم

الم ۝ ذلك الكتاب لا ريب فيه هدى
للمتقين ۝ الذين يؤمنون بالغيب ويقيمون
الصلوة ومما رزقناهم ينفقون ۝ والذين يؤمنون
بما أنزل إليك وما أنزل من قبلك وبالآخرة هم يوقنون

صورة فاتحة الكتاب

بسم الله الرحمن الرحيم

الحمد لله رب العالمين ۞ الرحمن الرحيم

مالك يوم الدين ۞ إياك نعبد وإياك نستعين

اهدنا الصراط المستقيم صراط الذين أنعمت

عليهم غير المغضوب عليهم ولا الضالين

The violent battles and subsequent emigration of the Latin-Frankish inhabitants (conversion to Islam was a precondition for remaining) resulted in a catastrophic drop in the population. Of the 200,000 or so recorded in 1570, only 120,000 were left by the year 1600; the figure continued to plummet, and in 1740, after bouts of further emigration and a series of natural disasters, it reached an all-time low of 95,000. The island had now become a poverty-stricken province of the Ottoman Empire.

In the early days of Ottoman rule, relatively few Turks commanded the large and soon-to-be-rebuilt fortresses at Nicosia, Famagusta, Paphos, Limassol and Kyrenia: there were only 1,500–2,000 cavalrymen, or *sipahi*, and the same number of infantrymen, or *janissaries*. In 1590 a contemporary observer (Memmo) estimated the total number of Turkish troops on Cyprus at around 4,800. Six *firmans* (Sultan's decrees) ordered the forcible immigration of workers from Anatolia, including some Greeks. "Islamising" or "Turkifying" the island was not the express intention of these *firmans*.

By 1600 the Turkish section of the population had increased to 22,000, though this growth stagnated during the course of the next two centuries. According to a census taken in 1841, the Turks formed only 31 percent of the island's population. At the beginning of the British Protectorate, there were 45,458 Turks on the island out of a total of 185,630 people.

Christians and Moslems: The Christian population mingled even less with the new conquerors and immigrants than it had during the Lusignan period. Though the Moslems were on a higher level, both administratively and socially, than the "infidels" *(rayas)*, who were the only ones to pay a special, three-tiered tax *(kharadsh)* and sacrifice their most promising sons for the élite troops of the *yeniceri*, the Christians enjoyed a certain degree of self-government. Christians and

Moslems lived alongside one another, but in separate areas, in cities and villages alike. In the middle of the 19th century the traveller-historian Mas Latrie counted 705 Christian and mixed villages, and 130 villages with a Turkish majority. He estimated the population of Nicosia at roughly 11,950; 8,000 were Turks, 3,700 were Greeks and 250 were Armenians or Maronites (a Christian sect that had emigrated to Cyprus, predominantly from Lebanon). Larnaca, the main port on the island, was an important European colony,

and, according to Mas Latrie, the city of Famagusta, much of which lay in ruins, was inhabited only by Turks (the Greeks lived in the suburbs). The main concern of the Turkish administration was to keep the "infidels" as far away as possible from the centres of fortification in the major cities.

Even the biased Archbishop Kyprianus, who wrote an extensive, if very one-sided, chronicle of Cyprus in 1788, was forced to admit that the Greeks were pleased with the change from Venetian to Ottoman rule. The hated Latin priests had fled and the Orthodox Church had regained the status it had enjoyed at the end of the Byzantine period. The

Preceding pages: Cyprus opens up to Islam. **Left**, Ottoman-style salon, House of Haji Georghakis Kornesios, Nicosia. **Right**, the Ottomans changed the Gothic cathedrals into mosques.

slave-like status of the peasant proprietors was abolished, and, although the payments they had to make remained, they were much reduced: people were forced to work only one day a week (rather than two) at the state sugar factories, taxes on earnings were reduced, and market duties were also abolished.

The administrative system: In theory, it was the declared duty of the Sublime Porte to avoid tyranny and suppression, to achieve peaceful coexistence between population groups and secure a just system of administration in order to revive the island's natural riches. At least, this was the substance of the various *firmans* that were issued, and of the

Both Christians and Moslems suffered equally from the pressure of high taxation and its arbitrary nature. Famine, droughts, swarms of locusts, attacks by pirates, and the plague (1641) all contributed to the aforementioned drop in the number of inhabitants, which reached its lowest point at the end of the 17th century. Thus it was that the uprisings, which had been occurring on a regular basis since 1572, were directed at overly high taxation rather than against population groups with different religious beliefs. Both the Greeks and the Turks complained about the *dragoman* Markoulles (1669–73). Turks and Christians also showed solidarity in their rebellions against the unscrupulous

various administrative reforms.

In reality, however, the island was suffering from the same old disease it had inherited from Byzantium: its officials could not be controlled and corruption was rife. As the English captain Savile noted at the beginning of British rule: "What needs to be reformed is not so much the law itself as the application of the law. The Ottoman government is famous for its numerous *firmans*, laws and regulations, which can hardly be bettered for their comprehensiveness or their justice: all the problems of this land have been caused either by a failure to observe these laws, or by their improper application."

governor Chil Osman Agha in 1764 as well as against the illegal rule of the adventurer Hadj Baki (1771–83). Nonetheless it was during this period that the incipient tensions which were later to split the two peoples asunder developed.

The Greek clergy: The power of the Orthodox Church was at its height during this period, exerting crucial influence on both the economy and administration: as early as 1660, the Sultan had recognised the Orthodox archbishop and the three other bishops as spokesmen of the Orthodox population, and they were granted the right to send their petitions directly to the Porte in Constantinople, and even to go there in person. In 1754 a *firman* bestowed the title of "ethnarch" – i.e. head of the autocephalous Church of Cyprus and leader of the Greek Cypriot nation – on the archbishop of Cyprus.

The Church was thus drawn into the corrupt Turkish administration, and as an English diplomat noted in 1792, it was soon practically running the island. The unpleasant task of collecting taxes remained the responsibility of the *dragoman*, or "interpreter" to the Porte, who was very influential and often of Greek descent. In 1814, John Macdonald Kinneir, a "captain in the service of the East India Company", described the wretched conditions on the island, and the

of government are nowhere more evident than on Cyprus, where the governor, appointed annually by the island's official owner, Capudan Pasha, is allowed to employ every method of exploitation. The Turks would thus be subjected to the same wretched conditions as the Christians, had the latter – in addition to the demands made on them by the government – not been forced to lend their support to a number of lazy and greedy monks. Every matter concerning the Greeks is presided over by the archbishop and the dragoman of Cyprus (one of the officials appointed by the Porte), who is responsible to the non-Orthodox community for levies, taxes, and the like."

role of the Church in perpetuating them:

"The soil is naturally fertile; however, only a small part of the island is under the plough. Nevertheless, the merchants in Larnaca export many loads of excellent wheat annually to Spain and Portugal. The population numbers no more than 70,000 souls, and is said to be decreasing daily; half of them are Greek under their archbishop, the rest of the inhabitants being Turks, with the exception of the Franks living in Larnaca.

"The drastic effects of the Turkish system

Left, the minarets of Nicosia. **Above**, wood block engraving illustrating the weaving industry.

The most fertile and also the most pleasant areas of the island were the regions of Cerina (Kyrenia) and Baffo (Old Paphos) where, according to Tacitus, Aphrodite rose from the waves. Here, there were forests of oak, beech and pine, as well as olive and sycamore trees. Cyprus was justly famed for the quality of its fruit, wine, oil and silk; its oranges tasted as sweet as those from Tripoli, and its wines – both red and white – were shipped to the Levant, where they were adapted to suit the tastes of the English market. The island produced two different kinds of silk, yellow and white, but the former was preferred. The corn grown on the island was of excellent quality, and rice was grown in regions where the producers could amass enough capital to prepare the soil. However, the Greek rural population, who constituted the only labouring class on the island, had been under the thumb of Turks, monks and bishops for too long and were now reduced to extreme poverty; many emigrated the moment they got the chance. The governor and the archbishop engaged in extensive grain trading, indeed more so than the rest of the population put together; they often decided to confiscate the entire grain output for one year and then export it, or withhold it at a higher price.

Growing dissatisfaction: Tensions began to

mount between the island's Christians and Turks, who, as a French observer, L. Lacroix, put it, "were reluctant simply to stand by and watch those whom they had vanquished lord it over them now." In 1804 the Turks in Nicosia and in the surrounding villages rose against their governor, who had been a willing tool of the Greek clergy. The fact that two pashas with Ottoman troops from Asia Minor had to quell a revolt by their own people only served to increase the tensions between the two segments of the population.

As Lacroix makes clear, 1804 was a dress-rehearsal for the bloody events of 1821 when the Greek nationalist revolution against Ot-

toman rule on mainland Greece erupted. The strong-willed and highly-educated Archbishop Kyprianus, founder of the famous *Pankyprian Gymnasium* in Nicosia, kept himself aloof from the solicitations of the *Philike Hetaireia* or "Greek Revolutionary Union". As Lacroix observed, the Greek population wanted to be left in peace. However, Governor Kucuk Mehmed had Kyprianus, the high clergy and every educated Greek on the island arrested on charges of alleged conspiracy. A total of 470 people were put to death in Nicosia alone – and Archbishop Kyprianus was one of the first. The Greeks' houses were looted, there were massacres, and property was confiscated. For six long months the Greek population lived in abject terror. Greek notables who succeeded in escaping the massacres fled to European consulates.

Thus, the so-called "rule of the bishops" came to an end in 1821. Tensions remained, however, because of Turkish envy at the prosperity of the Greek population. The education gap between the Greeks and the Turks began to widen too, as new schools were founded, and the island's educated classes came into contact with the intellectual trends of Europe, where nationalist ideas were playing an increasingly important role. Contemporary observers noted a lower level of education among the Turkish community.

But it was neither nationalist ideas nor internal tensions that ended Ottoman domination of the island: instead, it was a country which at that time was the most important power in the Eastern Mediterranean – Great Britain. Her Majesty's diplomats were becoming increasingly interested in the internal affairs of Cyprus, and the Levant Company had become the leading trading company. The political weakness of Turkey in relation to Russia, tension with the second great power in the Mediterranean, France, and the secure passage afforded by the opening of the Suez Canal in 1869 finally led the Porte to hand Cyprus over to Britain, without requesting any payment in return (though the Sultan was to remain the island's official sovereign just as before). On 12 July 1878, British troops arrived on Cyprus.

Left, looking towards Mecca in the Turkish quarter of Nicosia. **Right**, dawn and the minaret beckon the faithful to prayer.

ΜΕΛΗ ΤΗΣ Ε.

PALLIKARIDES, EVAGORA, MILTIAZHOUS
1938 TSHADA 5'5"

VRECU CHRISTOFOROU CHRUOKAN

CHRISTODOULOU, DEMETRAKIS
1936 DHERINIA 5'6"

PRANDPOULOS, TONIS CONSTANTINOU
VAROSHA 5'6"

CHRISTOFOROU KYRIAKOS
KSIPEROUNDA

ARISTIDOU YIANNAKIS, % "DROUSHIOT
IOANNIS" 1932, DROUSHA, 5'8"

PHILIPPIDES ANDREAS CHRISTOU, 1932
VRAHBENMOU, from KTIMA 5'4"

EPAMINONDA YIANNAKIS 1952
PEDHOULAS, YIANNCH NICOSIA 5'10"

PAPAYERKITO A EORKIOU 19
E. PANO ARHODES PAPHO

SICILEBO MIEIS KHOGEN

The Roman ruins of Curium (Kourion) lie on the road that leads from the harbour city of Limassol to Paphos in western Cyprus. The view from the rectangular stadium stretches all the way to the Troodos mountains – but it is marred by several tall radio masts. A few miles further on, a whole series of very English-looking terraced houses are grouped together not far from the roadside; barbed wire separates them from the main road. Heavily-armed sentries stand on duty behind camouflage nets at the entrance to the

settlement. To the left, in the distance, one can sometimes make out the odd aeroplane taking off or landing. Down in the valley, there is a well-tended football pitch, its grass every bit as green as the playing fields of London. Welcome to the British Sovereign Base of Akrotiri.

Akrotiri, along with Dhekelia and a military listening-post at the highest point of the Troodos mountains, Mount Olympus, is one of the remnants of British rule in Cyprus. Inside these autonomous enclaves of Her Majesty, British law applies. The Union Jack, lowered for the last time in Nicosia in 1960, still flutters here. When Cyprus be-

came independent, Britain secured 99 square miles of the island for military purposes, and these bases have remained, the final vestiges of the former Crown Colony.

British rule on Cyprus began on Saturday, 13 July 1878. "In the name of Her Majesty Queen Victoria, I hereby take possession of this island," proclaimed Admiral Lord John Hay before a gathering of the island's notables in Nicosia. "Long live the Queen!" shouted the crowd, and the Union Jack was duly hoisted. British troops had landed near Larnaca on the previous day.

Sir Garnet Wolseley was appointed High Commissioner, but at this stage Cyprus had only been leased out to Britain by the Ottoman Empire, in payment for British help in wars against the tsars of Russia, and was not officially British at all. Britain collected the annual "ground rent" it had to pay Istanbul from its Cypriot subjects.

With the British occupation, the centuries-long isolation of Cyprus from the rest of Europe came to an end. The British began modernising the administration and accurate statistics for the island were obtained for the first time. A total of 186,173 people were living on Cyprus in the year 1881, including 140,793 Greek and 42,638 Turkish Cypriots. A modern education system was introduced, with separate schools for Christians and Moslems. The island's first ever hospitals were also built, and the malaria-infected swamps near Larnaca were drained.

As far as politics were concerned, the British introduced the Legislative Council, a committee (half-Cypriot, half-British) for making joint decisions. This new and – compared with conditions under Ottoman rule – liberal system of government meant that political clubs could be founded. The first newspapers appeared. Trade with Europe increased, and a Cypriot upper class evolved, comprising craftsmen and merchants. This programme of modernisation had a marked influence in the cities, but in the villages, where the great majority of Cypriots lived, conditions barely changed.

However, even in the cities disenchantment with the British soon set in. The hoped-for economic and technological developments were much slower than many had at first assumed, and people continued to labour under heavy taxation (many had hoped, rather naively, that all taxation would be abolished under British rule). Britain invested very little in the island: a few roads were rebuilt, a small railway was constructed and the harbour at Famagusta was dredged. The only jobs to be found were in the asbestos and copper mines, where workers slogged away for 10–12 hours a day under hideous conditions, receiving very lit-

from 1882 onwards the British had Alexandria at their disposal, and, since it enjoyed an even better position for these purposes, the military importance of Cyprus declined. At times the island was manned by as little as a single company, numbering between 200 and 300 men.

Even World War I did little to change things. In fact, the only thing that did alter as far as the Cypriots were concerned was a legal technicality: when Turkey joined the war on the side of Germany in 1914, Britain

tle pay. Most smallholders were hopelessly in debt, and were living on the verge of starvation.

This lack of investment in the island was simply a reflection of British interests: Cyprus was important to the empire only from a strategic point of view. It was from here that sea traffic to India via the Suez Canal could be controlled, and any Russian intervention in the Mediterranean checked. But

Preceding pages: heroes of Cypriot resistance, Omodhos Museum. **Left**, hoisting the British flag. **Above**, ships salute the Duke of Edinburgh's birthday, Larnaca harbour.

formally annexed the island. In 1923, under the terms of the Treaty of Lausanne, Turkey officially confirmed Cyprus as a British possession. In 1925, the island was elevated to the status of a Crown Colony – a mere formality, which did nothing to alter conditions there.

It was only during the 1930s that the Cypriots began to see improvements in their economy. With the introduction of farmers' cooperatives, agricultural production could be stepped up. Craft and trade flourished. With the onset of World War II the island's military importance grew rapidly. More and more troops were dispatched to Cyprus, and the war gave the island's economy a huge boost. When Crete fell under German occupation and Rommel landed in Africa, the entire Near East seemed to be directly under threat. Cyprus was now an important military outpost along with Egypt, Palestine and Lebanon. Around 25,000 Cypriots volunteered to fight, many of them hoping to liberate the Greek "motherland" from the Germans. They made up an entire contingent of their own within the British army. Fortunately, no fighting took place on Cyprus itself during the war. Indeed, former British soldiers posted to the island remember feeling extremely bored.

In 1945, just after the war had ended, the time beach holidays were unfashionable.

In the realm of politics, increased efforts were made by the Greek Cypriots for *enosis*, union with Greece. Britain's reaction to this was cool: "It has always been clear that certain parts of the Commonwealth, because of special conditions, can never expect to be granted full independence," was the message sent to Cyprus by the secretary of state for colonial affairs in 1954. The military importance of the island rose dramatically with the onset of the Cold War.

The British began by using military force to stop the guerrilla struggle for *enosis*, which began in 1955. This was unsuccessful, however, and fighting developed into a full-

The Quay, Lanarca, Cyprus

tourist guide *Romantic Cyprus* went into its second edition. Hotels, in particular those in the mountains, advertised in the hope of attracting tourists. The guide's publisher, Kevork Keshishian, wrote: "The precise nature of post-war transport routes cannot be predicted, but one thing is fairly certain: Cyprus, because of its geographical situation and the excellent opportunities it offers, will play an important role in the forthcoming age of the aeroplane." Sure enough, there was a slight increase in tourism in the years that followed. Unlike today, though, it was almost exclusively the summer spas in the Troodos mountains that benefited. At the

scale civil war between the island's Greek and Turkish populations. This in turn endangered the NATO alliance, still in its infancy, and Britain was thus compelled to negotiate. The military planners in London were satisfied with the result: Cyprus was given its independence in return for allowing three British sovereign bases to remain there. On 16 August 1960 British colonial rule ended, and the last governor, Sir Hugh Foot, handed over his official duties to the government of the Republic of Cyprus.

Above, the quay at Larnaca during the British heyday. **Right**, rural idyll or poverty trap?

LIFE IN THE 19TH CENTURY

While Byzantine churches, Gothic cathedrals and medieval castles are found all over Cyprus and there is a wealth of Greek and Roman amphitheatres and mosaics thousands of years old, ordinary houses that have managed to survive 80 or even 100 years are few and far between. The reason for this anomaly is simple: only sacred buildings and houses belonging to the wealthy classes were made of stone; the simple farmhouses (*katogia*) of 100 years ago, almost always one storey high, were much less durable and showed little resistance to the ravages of time. Covered with earth and straw, the houses were prone to rising damp and if they were not looked after on a regular basis they quickly fell into disrepair. Today most have disappeared.

Life at that time was of a simplicity scarcely imaginable now, and marked by bitter poverty. The farmers could produce only the bare minimum to survive. Farmhouses generally contained one single room, where the family ate and slept. Water, in both villages and cities, was obtained from local wells, and electric light was, of course, unknown. Alongside its combined living, eating and sleeping area, the typical village house had an inner courtyard containing a round clay oven, which was used primarily to bake bread. Next to the house there would be a windowless building used for housing provisions and for drying onions, garlic, mushrooms and various kinds of fruit. Many farmhouses had a small covered veranda in front of their doorways to provide protection against the heat.

Life, from the cradle to the grave, was conducted in the one room. Only the wealthy could afford beds. Poor families slept on a large wooden board, usually fully-clothed because bedding alone was insufficient in winter. Other items of furniture included a table, a few wooden chairs and one or more carved wooden chests in which household necessities and the daughters' dowries were kept.

Every young woman had her own bride's chest, its carvings and the quality of the wood denoting the wealth of her family. Eldest daughters inherited their mothers' dowry chests. Cupboards were unknown; they were first introduced to the island by the British. A single shelf set into the wall was all that was necessary for storing the other household objects. There was next to no crockery: poor families owned only one plate and one mug, from which all their members would eat and drink.

The farmers made their own clothes as best they could: cotton and wool were spun and woven by the women to make simple dresses. The men and the women wore coarse white shirts, and knickerbockers which varied in colour, their material and decoration depending on the region in which they were made, and high boots, too – if they could be afforded. The men wore colourful waistcoats over their shirts. Christians and Moslems wore similar clothing, though Turks tended to wear more white than the Greeks, who preferred colours.

Travelling on the island at that time was difficult. When the British landed on Cyprus in

1878 all they found was a bumpy country road leading from Nicosia to Larnaca. Horse-drawn carriages were introduced around the turn of the century. In the country areas, oxen were harnessed to single-axle wooden carts; an ox-cart journey from Kyrenia on the north coast to Lefkara in the south took roughly four days. The main beasts of burden were donkeys and mules, and both survived the railway – the first major technical advance that the British introduced to Cyprus – by several decades. The narrow-gauge railway built at the beginning of the 20th century between Famagusta, Nicosia and Morphou was taken out of service in the 1950s. Donkeys, on the other hand, are frequently used to this day. ∎

Even during the very first year of the British occupation of Cyprus the Cypriots were urging their new rulers to leave. Kyprianus, bishop of Kition, begged the first crown governor in 1878 to allow Cyprus to be "reunited with the Greek motherland". This, one of the firs t bids for *enosis*, or union with Greece, was followed by countless other requests.

The island's leading clergymen felt closer to Greece and it was not long before Greek Orthodox craftsmen and merchants joined the movement. The few educated Greek-speaking Cypriots saw Greece as the source of their culture, their linguistic and religious brother and their best chance for the long hoped-for economic upswing. Britain was investing little in the island, and the Cypriots were impoverished and starving. The call for *enosis* was the equivalent of social protest.

As far as the Moslem Cypriots were concerned, *enosis* was something to be sceptical about. The minority feared that marginalisation would occur if union with Greece took place. Since there was a disproportionately high number of Turkish-speaking Cypriots working for the administration, and far fewer in trade and crafts, the Moslem Cypriots were in favour of prolonging the island's colonial status, or returning it to Istanbul.

The conflict had no effect on daily life, though. Christian and Moslem Cypriots were still living in harmony with one another. In the mixed villages they sold agricultural produce side by side, and all Cypriots participated in the island's festivals, regardless of their ethnic background.

Economic development and nationalism were the catalysts that changed the island's Greek Orthodox inhabitants into Greek Cypriots. Turkish Cypriots emerged a lot later, for it was only after Turkey was founded in 1920 that Turkish nationalist feeling began to develop on Cyprus (though in 1923, Turkey relinquished all claims on the island). But, in spite of their more clearly defined

Preceding pages: Turkish and Greek Cypriot unity, late 19th century. Left, Ledra Street, dubbed "Murder Mile". Right, EOKA men crowned by laurel wreaths in Rhodes.

aims, the Greek Cypriots were continually thwarted. Instead of *enosis*, Cyprus was developing closer ties with Britain, creating a swelling core of ill-feeling fuelled by the British failure to develop the institutions of self-government.

In 1931 underlying social tensions erupted in a rebellion. Originally planned as a protest against increased taxes and customs duties, it grew into an all-out nationalist demonstration against Britain. A prominent Greek Orthodox priest hoisted the Greek

flag, and declared that the revolution had begun. The governor's house was set on fire. Although most rebels were unarmed, the British were forced to send troops to Cyprus.

More than 2,000 Greek Cypriots were arrested as a result, all political parties were outlawed and censorship of the press was introduced.

After World War II the calls for *enosis* became insistent. In 1950 the young bishop of Kition, Makarios, soon to become archbishop, organised a plebiscite which produced a 96 percent majority in favour of *enosis*. But Britain, aware of the instability in Greece itself and doubtful whether Cyprus would be better off under Greek rule, had no intention of letting the island go – Cyprus, its "unsinkable aircraft-carrier" in the Mediterranean, had by then become far too important militarily.

From 1954 onwards, Greece took the side of Cyprus, and in 1956 Turkey maintained that Cyprus was an extension of the Turkish mainland. Tensions thus developed into an international conflict, and the notorious "Cyprus question" was born.

A crucial factor in the continuing development of events was the decision of Archbishop Makarios III and his close friend, General Georgios Grivas, to use violence to achieve *enosis*. On 1 April 1955, Nicosia, in

particular Ledra Street, dubbed "Murder Mile", was rocked by a series of bomb explosions perpetrated by the National Organisation of Cypriot Struggle (EOKA). This conservative guerrilla movement wanted to achieve *enosis* by force, by "executing" British army officers and by murdering any of their fellow Greek countrymen suspected of having leftist sympathies. The British could not gain the upper hand over the partisan movement. Indeed, the only lasting effect of the search warrants, curfews and mass arrests they imposed was increased interest in the EOKA by the Greek Cypriot population.

The British decided to form an anti-terror unit, recruiting members from the ranks of the Turkish Cypriots. Helped by Ankara, Turkish Cypriot nationalists formed their own terror unit to fight for Turkish interests, i.e. against *enosis*, and in favour of *taksim*, or partition of the island. The bloodshed was a foregone conclusion, and military confrontations between partisans and the British army lead to conflicts between the island's ethnic groups.

On 7 June 1958, a bomb exploded in the Turkish press office in Nicosia. It sparked a civil war. Cypriot fought against Cypriot; churches were set ablaze, houses and apartments looted. Many members of racially mixed communities were forced to leave their homes, a hasty migration that turned several city areas into ethnic enclaves. The island of Aphrodite became a battlefield.

At an international level, NATO partners Greece and Turkey were threatening to go to war over Cyprus, and fearful states sought a compromise. The USA put pressure on Athens and Ankara to abandon their main claims and find a diplomatic solution.

Makarios declared forthwith that he would not insist on *enosis*, and after meetings between Greece, Turkey and Britain the so-called "London and Zurich Treaties" were signed: Cyprus was to become an independent state, but the Cypriots were not allowed to have any say in the drawing-up of their own constitution.

The treaties set the official seal on the division of the two ethnic groups: the island's Greeks and Turks were each given their own presidents, vice-presidents and ministers, as well as separate representation in parliament. Votes were taken separately. To prevent any minority discrimination, the Turkish Cypriots were granted the right of veto as well as over-proportional representation in the administration, the police and the army. The development of a Cypriot nationality was thus effectively blocked; now the island was populated by Greeks and Turks.

Greece, Turkey and Britain declared themselves "guarantor powers", and gave themselves permission to intervene should the Cypriots ever decide to change their constitution themselves. On 16 August 1960, the foreign powers granted Cyprus its independence.

Left, **General Grivas**. **Right**, **Makarios**.

On 16 August 1960 the last governor of Her Majesty's Crown Colony, Sir Hugh Foot, handed over his official duties to Makarios III, who was henceforth President of the Republic of Cyprus. An archbishop was now head of state. The tradition of a religious leader exercising both spiritual and secular power, which had originated in Ottoman times, was thus continued in the newly-formed state. Makarios was the ethnarch and the undisputed leader of the Greek Cypriots.

At Makarios's side stood Vice-President Fazil Küçük, elected unanimously by the Turkish Cypriot minority. After a bloody civil war, during which one side had fought for union with Greece and the other for partition of the island, their task was to build a combined republic. In theory, the political activity would no longer centre on the separate interests of the island's Greeks and Turks, but on the concept of a unified state and one people – Cyprus and the Cypriots.

Relations between the two ethnic groups returned to normal in daily life, and in most cases good neighbourliness was re-established. Inhabitants who had fled now returned to their homeland, and the murders and lootings seemed to be ills of the past.

On the political level, however, sensitive relations were severely tried by the new constitution: because the new Republic's ministers, MPs and bureaucrats were each elected and recognised by only one of the two ethnic groups, they saw themselves as exclusively representing either Greeks or Turks, never both. As quarrels over taxation, development programmes and questions of infrastructure arose, the two sides came into conflict, each bent on keeping the larger slice of the cake for itself.

The government and the executive were preoccupied by endless quarrels over resources. Political representatives of both ethnic groups showed little if any interest in genuine cooperation. Indeed, many of them saw the collective state as only a temporary solution. Greek nationalists continued to demand *enosis*, while more and more Turks called for *taksim*, or partition of the island.

This uneasy peace lasted for three years. In spite of difficulties, the economy managed to recover, and in foreign affairs Cyprus became a committed member of the non-aligned states. But at the end of 1963, President Makarios called for a far-reaching revision of the constitution which would have deprived the Turkish Cypriots of many of their guaranteed rights. He insisted that the minority's right of veto, and the ethnic quota system in the police, army and administration be scrapped. The Turkish Cypriot side refused to support his proposals, and the Turkish government threatened to intervene

if they were introduced unilaterally.

The situation finally came to a head at Christmas 1963: fighting broke out in Nicosia, and soon spread to the rest of the island. Former partisans of the EOKA and the Turkish Cypriot terror unit TMT were reactivated. The police and the army divided into their constituent ethnic groups and Turkish Cypriot ministers and people's representatives walked out of the parliament.

Widespread civil violence ensued, started by the very same nationalists responsible for the bloodshed of the 1950s. To this day, the island's Greek and Turkish communities have been blaming each other for triggering hostilities. According to the Greek Cypriots, the Turkish Cypriots had attempted to achieve partition by starting a rebellion. In the opinion of the Turkish Cypriots, the Greek Cypriots had wanted to exterminate the Turkish minority and introduce *enosis*.

Over 500 people were killed during the summer of 1964. It was only when a United Nations peacekeeping force arrived that the violence was brought to an halt. When the fighting was at its peak, the Turkish air force attacked Greek Cypriot positions and for a

threatening to turn Cyprus into "the Cuba of the Mediterranean".

The conflict ended peaceful coexistence for the island's ethnic groups once and for all. The majority of Turkish Cypriots sought shelter in rural enclaves and urban ghettos. Their leaders, who supported the partition of the island, ensured that no further contact with their former neighbours took place.

The Greek Cypriots, with all the state power to themselves, began a trade embargo. Soldiers patrolled the borders separating the

while it looked as if Turkey was threatening to invade. War between NATO partners Greece and Turkey looked increasingly likely. The USA sought a diplomatic solution to the problem, and suggested that the island be divided between Athens and Ankara, with both zones belonging to NATO. President Makarios, however, rejected this suggestion out of hand. From then on the USA saw him as insecure and unreliable, a kind of "Castro in priest's clothing", who had dealings with communists and was

Left, Sir Hugh Foot, the last British governor.
Above, march for independence.

rival ethnic groups: Greek Cypriots were forbidden to enter Turkish Cypriot ghettos, while Turkish Cypriots suffered harassment if they entered Greek-controlled areas. Closed off and isolated in this way, the minority became dependent on relief packages, and their standard of living worsened.

Hope is dashed: The situation began to relax in 1968, when Makarios lifted the embargo. Turkish Cypriots were once again allowed to work and live wherever they wished. The Greek Cypriots' desire for *enosis* began to fade in the face of a burgeoning economy and the military junta in Athens, and only the most extreme of the nationalists still supported union with the Greek military dictatorship. Talks between the two ethnic groups began, under the auspices of the United Nations. The Turkish-Cypriots wanted a bizonal federation with a weakened central government, but the Greek Cypriots would not comply, fearing that it might help to pave the way towards partition. Negotiations took place nonetheless.

As the situation on Cyprus calmed, tensions rose between the governments in Athens and Nicosia. The Greek military dictatorship felt that Makarios was trying to provoke friction by offering asylum to persecuted democrats and not imposing press censorship. Criticism of the Cypriot president also grew more vocal in the USA. With the help of the 950-strong force of Greek soldiers and officers stationed on Cyprus and a nationalist terror group known as EOKA-B, the Greek junta decided to try to rid itself of Makarios. But its attempts to assassinate the archbishop failed. Police units loyal to the government helped put many EOKA-B terrorists behind bars, and for a while it seemed as if Makarios had gained the upper hand.

On 15 July 1974 the island's capital of Nicosia was rocked by gunfire. The presidential palace went up in flames. Terrorists and soldiers supporting the Greek junta embarked on attacks all over the island. The Republic and its defenders never stood a chance. The soldiers interned thousands of democrats and members of left-wing parties, and murdered their wounded rivals even in hospitals. News of Makarios's death was broadcast over the radio. Only the Turkish-Cypriots were left unscathed by the junta (so as to give Ankara no excuse to intervene). The longed-for *enosis* with the "motherland" had happened overnight, but it was a very different union from the one Greek Cypriots had imagined. The majority supported their elected government, and could only watch helplessly as the Greek military took control.

But one part of the Greeks' plan went hopelessly wrong: President Makarios had managed to escape from the burning presidential palace and find his way to the British Sovereign Base of Akrotiri where he was out of the junta's reach. Nikos Sampson, a right-wing radical who had been involved in the mass murder of Turkish Cypriots during the civil war of 1963–64, was proclaimed president in his place. The coup was announced as

an internal affair of the Greek Cypriots. Athens was convinced that Turkey wouldn't intervene in Cyprus. How such a grave misjudgement could have been made has not yet been discovered. Relevant documentation is still lying inside a safe in Athens.

At daybreak on 20 July, five days after the coup, Turkish motor torpedo boats landed on the north coast. The Turkish air force dropped bombs on the island's capital. This time, unlike in 1964, the USA did nothing to prevent Turkey from carrying out its plans. This "peace operation", as the propaganda termed it, seemed to be quite justified under international law because the Cypriot constitution condoned intervention by the guaran-

tor powers should it be necessary. The troops quickly succeeded in occupying an area to the north of Nicosia where many Turkish Cypriots lived; the Moslems rejoiced at having been liberated from the Greek military dictatorship.

The "mini-junta" in Nicosia was just as surprised by the invasion as the larger one in Athens. Two days later, the Greek military dictatorship fell as a result of the Cyprus fiasco. The chief of the mainland's junta, Ioannides, had tried to force his country to go to war with Turkey, but his own officers had refused orders. In Makarios's absence, the post of president in Nicosia was taken by

Glavkos Klerides, the head of parliament, and Konstantin Karamanlis took over in Athens. Democracy had thus been restored – but the human tragedy on Cyprus had only just begun.

In defiance of the United Nations Security Council resolution, the Turkish army of invasion refused to withdraw, and on 14 August, despite intensive talks held in Geneva, the Turkish soldiers marched onwards. Tens of thousands of Greek Cypriots ran for their lives, leaving all their possessions behind. Thousands were taken prisoner. Any who returned for any reason were shot. Turkish tanks rolled across the island, encountering almost no resistance. Two days later the

after "Operation Attila" (the code name for the Turkish invasion) stood at 39 percent.

As far as the Turkish Cypriots were concerned, a minimum of 55,000 of them fled from the south to the safe haven now provided by the occupied north. Once the invasion had begun, the terrorists and junta soldiers inflicted bloody reprisals on the Moslem communities in the south, and the legal government of the island was in no position to stop them. Paramilitary units massacred the entire male Turkish Cypriot population of several villages, old and young alike. Many Turkish Cypriot males, although obviously civilians, were interned inside football stadiums. Likewise, since 1974, 1,618 Greek

Turks had achieved the objective of their operation: 37 percent of the island was occupied. Turkey's long-cherished ambition to control the island situated just off its coast had been achieved. Partition was a reality.

Nearly 165,000 Greek Cypriots fled from the north to the south. Many of them lived in large encampments for months on end, barely able to eke out a living. For years afterwards they were forced to live in refugee settlements, housed in provisional, corrugated-iron barracks. Unemployment in the south

Left, the flags of Canada and the UN wave over Nicosia. **Above**, a British gunner digs in.

Cypriots, soldiers and civilians have disappeared. Many of them have appeared in International Red Cross lists of prisoners-of-war in internment camps in mainland Turkey.

The war of 1974 radically changed Cyprus. Since that time, an impenetrable line has extended across the island, and Greek and Turkish Cypriots have been living in strict separation from one another. Most of those still living in the "wrong" sector were resettled in 1975. Nearly every family on the island lost at least one of its members in the fighting. Around 6,000 people died in that bloody summer of 1974.

The Cypriots cannot and will not forget the dramatic events of 1974 ."*Den Xechnoume*" – "We have not forgotten" – is flashed every evening on Greek Cypriot television screens. In Paphos it appears in shoulder-high lettering on the facade of a school building.

Despite a few ceasefires, by 16 August the heavily-armed Turkish combat units had advanced as far as the "Attila Line", which today forms the border between the remaining territory of the Republic of Cyprus and the Turkish Republic of Northern Cyprus. In the face of the small, badly equipped Cypriot National Guard, little was required for the military success of the operation.

Driven by terror: However, the long-harboured intention to "purge" the conquered territory of its Greek Cypriot population proved more difficult. Bloody suppression had to be avoided in order to keep protests from the international community to a minimum. A few brutal sorties – the murder and rape of civilians – during the first few days of the Turkish occupation had the desired effect: sheer terror drove most Greek Cypriots from their homes, even before they came into contact with the advancing Turkish troops. They headed south as fast as they could, leaving their personal belongings behind – hardly anyone could have known that their steps were irrevocable.

The number of refugees was estimated at 180,000 during the months immediately following the invasion. At the beginning of September 1974, a US Senate committee of investigation described the situation thus as follows: "Travel along the roads of southern Cyprus and you travel through one enormous refugee camp. The refugees are camping under trees by the side of the road, out in the fields in huts made of pine branches and sticks, and in the tents provided by the international aid organisations. Every available public building is filled with refugees – schools, churches, monasteries and administration buildings."

When it came to material help for the refugees, the international aid organisations acted swiftly. The US government in particular – which had played a highly equivocal role in the Turkish attack on Cyprus – doled out massive financial aid. A twofold plan was embarked upon: on the one hand, the government was totally unflinching in its demands that all refugees be allowed to return home forthwith ("We have not forgotten"), and on the other, it made every effort to secure the maximum amount of aid from Western governments. Even today, the actual figure of 160,000 Greek Cypriot refugees in the southern part of the island is frequently inflated to around 200,000 when politcal points are being scored.

Southern Cyprus was confronted with an enormous task. The refugees had to be provided with housing; farmers needed land, workers needed jobs and the self-employed needed the opportunity to start again. Unemployment in the Republic of Cyprus for the second half of 1974 stood at 59,000 – nearly 30 percent of the working population.

By 1975 almost all of the 45,000 or so Turkish Cypriots living in the southern part of the island had been resettled in the Turkish-occupied zone. They, like their Greek compatriots in the north, left house and home behind. The better homes and the more valuable land were snapped up by the Greek Cypriot refugee families, sometimes after rental agreements had been entered into with their rightful owners. Moreover, all Turkish Cypriot-owned housing and land was officially registered (even today Turkish houses in southern Cyprus can be identified by the registration number painted on their outside walls). To begin with, such accommodation was welcomed and considered preferable to tents and Nissen huts, but as time went on many refugees were forced to realise just how wretched the living conditions of their Turkish compatriots had been.

Legally, the Turkish houses on the island are still the property of their former owners. Unsurprisingly, the refugees have shown little inclination to invest in renovation, and properties are dilapidating fast.

The limited number of buildings available made other, more far-reaching solutions necessary. In 1975 the government embarked upon a large-scale housing programme, and by the end of 1979 more than

14,000 living units had been completed, housing 60,000 refugees. Such programmes were generally based on two models. The first was the so-called "self-help housing scheme", under which the authorities provided areas of land as well as a fixed sum of money to refugees. A refugee would build his house – according to plans provided by the authorities – on a "self-help" basis, i.e. helped largely by his family. The other scheme was based on low-cost government housing estates. Here, the government built

not been created as a final solution, but as places where the desire to return home would be kept simmering. Several construction firms earned quick money with sloppy work. At the receiving end were the inhabitants, forced to cope with broken pipes and crumbling masonry.

The very idea of living in a tenement block is anathema to the average rural Cypriot. Nevertheless, as time went by, the ugly concrete structures in the refugee estates disappeared beneath flowering bougain-

huge estates of prefabricated blocks of flats and terraced housing, sometimes accommodating several thousand inhabitants (e.g. Strovolos and Ayios Eleftherios near Nicosia). They were provided with their own small shopping centres, schools and other amenities. The problem with this scheme was that estates became nothing more than refugee ghettos, and living in a confined area with others in the same predicament did little to help integration into society.

The one thing both these housing projects shared was their impermanence: they had

villaea and vines. Outdoor ovens appeared in the narrow front gardens, along with rabbit hutches and chicken runs – reminders of a fondly remembered rural life.

The problem of unemployment among the refugees in southern Cyprus, was solved efficiently, thoroughly and very quickly – and in an exemplary manner. The task of rebuilding the economy and the various infrastructures, along with the boom in the construction industry, manufacturing and tourism from 1975 onwards, meant that the new labour force could be assimilated quickly. Full employment for all was achieved by 1977. Indeed, the hard work of

Above, emergency housing mushroomed.

the refugees was one of the main factors behind the economic boom of the late 1970s and 1980s; their living standards and the loss of their own land made it essential for them, at least temporarily, to work for low pay and do any job.

But despite everything, many refugees have managed to do quite well in the island's newly affluent society; they have built their own houses, and they have progressed to good jobs. Objectively speaking, some of them are doing better now than they were in the north, and although if you ask anyone if they would like to return to their former home the answer is a resounding "yes", the reality of such a prospect may not be quite so

integrity of Cyprus… (and) demands that foreign military intervention in Cyprus cease immediately," ran the text of the UN resolution of 20 July 1974, the very day the Turkish invasion began. The UN Security Council also condemned the self-proclaimed "Turkish Republic of Northern Cyprus" on 18 November 1983.

These, and many other resolutions, have been quite useless and all talks, direct and indirect, between the Greek Cypriot and Turkish Cypriot sides have so far failed, even though the UN General Secretary, under whose auspices the negotiations are taking place, has tried everything in his power to bring the conflict closer to a solution.

desirable. Quite a few of them would find their former homes in ruins, for many of the buildings left behind in the north have not been occupied since 1974.

Forever divided?: The declared intention of the government of the Republic of Cyprus is the reunification of Cyprus. Greek Cypriot politicians have been proposing far-reaching compromises since 1974, but there have been no breakthroughs in negotiations so far.

UN Security Council resolutions and resolutions by the General Assembly unite in calls for the withdrawal of Turkish troops. "The Security Council requires that all states acknowledge the sovereignty and territorial

Plan for peace: But at least areas where agreement might be found have been identified. The basic outline of a solution to the conflict was prepared as long ago as 1977. In that year the President of the Republic of Cyprus, Archbishop Makarios, met Rauf Denktash, leader of the Turkish Cypriot ethnic group, in Vienna. The talks resulted in the "four guidelines" agreed upon by both politicians, and it is worth quoting them here in their entirety:

"1. We shall strive towards the foundation

Above, the barbs of war. **Right**, patrolling the Green Line.

ALONG THE GREEN LINE

A white jeep, flying the blue-and-white flag of the United Nations, rumbles its way across the broken tarmac of what used to be the city centre of Nicosia and is now a wasteland of overgrown buildings and wrecked cars sprouting flowers in their torn upholstery. Ruined houses contain whole colonies of cats. Barriers of sandbags protect the dug-outs of the Greek and Turkish soldiers. Here, only a few metres from the bustle of the city, the silence is frightening. No Cypriot is allowed to cross this closely-guarded no-man's-land. The burned-out houses lining Hermes Street and melted neon signs remind us that this is the former heart of the city.

A thin, lifeless strip of land, the so-called "Green Line", only 60 ft (20 metres) wide in places, dissects the old part of Nicosia. It crosses the town's ancient fortifications, divides its districts, and then extends to the old airport, today the operational headquarters of the UN troops. The demilitarised buffer zone dividing the island (the "Attila Line") is 112 miles (180 km) long, and extends from Kokkina in the northwest to Famagusta in the southeast.

UNFICYP (United Nations Force in Cyprus) has been a familiar feature of life on Cyprus since as early as 1964. It was originally called in to end the civil war between Greeks and Turks. After 1964, its most urgent task was to separate the Turkish Cypriots and their paramilitary units from the National Guard of the Republic of Cyprus. Since the Turkish army invaded northern Cyprus in 1974, the UN force has ensured that the Greek Cypriot National Guard and the Turkish soldiers have kept to their side of the demarcation line. Roughly 2,100 soldiers from eight different nations are stationed on Cyprus. Troops are provided by Britain, Canada, Austria and Denmark, while Australia, Finland, Ireland and Sweden provide military police. Keeping the peace costs around US$25 million a year.

A dirt track leads over to the inspection post, from which the respective armies' demarcation lines can be easily observed. Here, Turks and Greek Cypriots have dug primitive-looking shelters. The beach, distant and inaccessible for the UN troops, can be seen through binoculars. As seven Austrians sitting in a corrugated-iron shelter on a small rise verify, one of the worst things about their job is the boredom. The blue-helmeted soldiers are on duty 24 hours a day for two weeks at a time, and invariably nothing happens. Elsewhere, though, the buffer zone is not as lifeless as it is in Nicosia. In many areas farmers are still allowed to cultivate their fields. And the Austrians have an entire village to supervise in their zone: in Pyla, a village between the two battle-lines guarded by military police, Greek and Turkish Cypriots still live in harmony.

The UN peacekeeping force has the situation firmly under control. The only danger of military escalation has been in Nicosia, where soldiers on both sides frequently start sparring. But it is seldom that shots are exchanged. "Keep the peace and make the peace" is the troops' motto.

For genuine peace, Cyprus still has a long way to go. Nonetheless, some politicians are begin-

ning to make the right noises. Lellos Demetriades, the mayor of Nicosia, is making plans for the redevelopment of the buffer zone once reunification comes about: "I want to get rid of this scar on the face of Nicosia once and for all. I want this scar to be healed, so that nobody would know it had even been there, so that the city can be put back to its original state." Working towards that aim, he is collaborating with the Turkish Cypriots to turn the main shopping streets on both sides of the border into pedestrian zones. "We want to reach the situation where the area around the Green Line becomes much more lively," he says. That, he feels, will produce a more favourable environment in which to build bridges. ∎

of an independent, non-aligned, bizonal federation.

"2. The size of the territory administered by the respective communities shall be discussed in the light of economic viability and ownership of land.

"3. Fundamental issues such as freedom of movement, freedom to settle, property rights and other specific matters are open to discussion, whereby the fundamental basis of a bizonal federative system and certain practical difficulties that may arise with respect to the Turkish Cypriot population should be taken into account.

"4. The competence and function of the central government will guarantee the unity of the country while taking the bizonal character of the federation into consideration."

These "four guidelines" comprise the most important step so far towards reunification. The document lays the foundations of a future federation. Unlike the stipulations of the 1960 constitution, according to this document, the new federation would be composed of two federal states, a Greek Cypriot one to the south and a Turkish Cypriot one to the north.

The paragraph relating to the size of the respective federal states implies a reduction in the size of the region at present occupied by Turkey; since the Turkish invasion, an 18 percent minority has been occupying roughly 37 percent of the island's surface area. This incongruity is to be corrected.

The third point touches on the question of the provision of basic liberties for all citizens of the Republic in every part of the Republic – a question that is still a bone of contention between the conflicting sides. The final point makes it clear that the aim of these endeavours is not a loose union between two states but a single, joint federation, with a central governing authority representing the whole of the country.

During the years that followed the drawing-up of this document, several ideas were elaborated as to what shape the federal institutions should take, e.g whether a Greek Cypriot and a Turkish Cypriot should take turns as president on a rotational basis or whether, according to a second variation, the Greek Cypriots should always elect the president while the Turkish Cypriots elect his vice-president. It was proposed that the minority would be guaranteed certain ministerial posts just as they had under the 1960 constitution. A bicameral parliament would be set up as a legislative body. In the upper house, Greek and Turkish Cypriots would be represented on a 50/50 basis, while in the lower house the two ethnic groups would reflect their actual strengths in the country. The distribution of power between the central government and the island's various districts remained unclear. The Greek Cypriots expressed their desire for a powerful central authority, while the Turkish Cypriots were in favour of strong district authorities.

The "four guidelines" of 1977 contained two fatal flaws: firstly, they ignored the question of finding international guarantors for the new federation; and secondly, the issues of individual liberties and of territorial rights in general were left open to further discussion.

Overcoming stumbling blocks: The easiest question to resolve is that of the size of the two federal states. Even the Turkish Cypriot leader, Rauf Denktash, is aware that the sector now occupied by the Turkish Cypriots should be reduced in size. Maps showing proposed new borders have already been circulated among diplomats in Nicosia. The latest version provides for a reduction in Turkish Cypriot territory of 14 percent, which would give around 90,000 of the 165,000 Greek Cypriot refugees the chance to go back their former homes.

The question of individual liberties is a lot harder to settle. Here, the Greek Cypriot side insists that unlimited freedom of movement, the right to settle and property rights should be guaranteed to all citizens in every part of the federation, pointing out that such freedoms are an accepted feature of any democratic state. Behind these demands is the desire that all Greek Cypriot refugees should be given the right to return to their home. The Turkish Cypriot side, however, vehemently rejects this right. It argues that if all the refugees were allowed to return, the Turkish Cypriots would become a minority in their own land.

The property issue is a controversial one, for most of the fields and houses presently farmed and inhabited by Turkish Cypriots are actually Greek Cypriot property. In the Republic of Cyprus, by way of contrast, houses belonging to Turkish Cypriots may be lived in only by Greek Cypriot refugees, who need to have a special permit. They are aware that they would have to leave the house should its owners return.

Compensation is probably the only way of achieving a solution in this regard, but even that wouldn't solve all the issues. Closer ties between the wealthy south and the impoverished north would bring other problems. For example, Turkish Cypriot companies would have to compete with their Greek Cypriot counterparts. Salaries in the south are about four times higher than those in the north.

Turkish immigrants: The "four guidelines" agreed on by Makarios and Denktash make no mention of the settlers who have immigrated to the northern sector from Turkey.

of them should be allowed to remain; those in power in the occupied sector treat them as fully-fledged citizens.

A central issue in discussions is the presence of Turkish troops in the north, and the question of international guarantors for such a federation. The Greek Cypriots reject Ankara's guarantor status out of hand. For the same reason they also demand the total withdrawal of all Turkish occupying forces. In contrast, the Turkish Cypriots – including the Opposition – insist on the minority receiving protection from Ankara and reject the complete withdrawal of the Turkish army; at most a reduction in the troop presence is offered. As a compromise, the Re-

They were transferred to Cyprus from Anatolia in order to change the island's demographic character. The plan was to fill the occupied sector (too large for the few people living there), and increase the number of Moslem inhabitants on the island. Between 60,000 and 80,000 Turkish settlers now live in the occupied sector. What is to become of them would be another problem in any peace negotiations. The Republic of Cyprus says that, since they are foreigners, they should leave the island immediately; members of the Turkish Cypriot opposition say that some

Above, Nicosia, the divided city.

public of Cyprus has begun discussing the possibility of giving the UN guarantor status over the new federation and its constitution, but this, too, has so far been rejected by the Turkish Cypriots.

In the opinion of most Cypriots, reunification would pose no problems at all. Meetings held on neutral ground between women's groups and peace campaigners are making this increasingly clear. In the north and south of Nicosia there is little trace of the so-called "hereditary enmity" between the Greeks and the Turks. It is not culture, character, religion or language that divides the population. It is politics.

Economists and travellers alike have remarked on the rapid social and industrial progress of southern Cyprus in recent years. Statistics show that its average per capita income lies above that of Greece, and far above that of Turkey.

In the period after independence, and before the Turkish invasion (between 1960 and 1974), the Republic of Cyprus, operating a free enterprise economy based on trade and agriculture, achieved a standard of living that was higher than most of its neighbours',

flected in the average life expectancy, the infant mortality rate, the number of doctors per 1,000 inhabitants and the standard of education), southern Cyprus stands comparison with any of the wealthy industrialised nations of the Western world.

As recently as the 1950s – the last decade of British colonial rule – the island's economy was underdeveloped. The vast majority of Cypriots eked out a subsistence from agriculture or were employed in mining. Copper and iron pyrites and asbestos were exported

with the exception of Israel. Various international agencies, such as the United Nations, contributed to this, as did the World Bank and the International Monetary Fund, who provided loans.

Comparisons have been drawn with the economies in Asia that have seen equally swift development, such as Singapore, Hong Kong and Taiwan. The social benefits have been immense: today, instead of unemployment there is a labour shortage, and the powerful and well-organised Cypriot trade unions regularly manage to push through generous wage rises for employees. As far as the quality of social care is concerned (re-

more or less untreated. Profits from such exports depended on world market prices, which fluctuated wildly – and most of the profits were made by the foreign-owned companies who controlled the mining.

After independence in 1960, Cyprus's main economic policy objective was to free itself from its heavy dependence on foreign countries. Various improvements were made in the field of agriculture, including the expansion of artificial irrigation facilities. The island also concentrated on creating new manufacturing industries. In fact, as far as the most important consumer goods and a few primary commodities (such as cement) were concerned, by 1974 the Cypriots had gained a large degree of independence from expensive foreign imports.

With the invasion and partition of the island in 1974, all that had been achieved seemed to be rendered meaningless overnight. The losses arising from the partition were catastrophic for the southern part of the island. The most important areas of cultivable land around Morphou and Famagusta were lost, and Famagusta harbour, Nicosia airport and several important through routes were

cut off. Almost all the modern hotels on Cyprus now lay on the other side of the Attila Line. Refugees, without homes or jobs, made up one-third of the population. Economic experts predicted a dire future for Cyprus if partition became permanent. The economy of southern Cyprus since 1974 thus rose like a phoenix from the ashes.

Helped by tourism: Most observers tend to ascribe the economic upswing after 1974 to the sharp rise in tourism, an industry which now draws over one million visitors a year

Left, plush hotel developments spawned along the coast. **Above**, a rainbow over new Nicosia.

and is an indispensable source of hard currency. This income alone made it possible to finance the enormously high expenditure on imports, e.g. foreign cars (these days, a Greek Cypriot family that does not own at least one car is a rarity). But the Cypriots did not make the mistake of relying solely on tourism, a notoriously fickle industry. They invested in a modern infrastructure, a bedrock for further economic development; it included new harbour facilities in Limassol and Larnaca, a well-developed network of roads, and modern telecommunications facilities.

Perhaps the greatest achievement of the southern Cypriot economy after 1974 was its successful industrialisation. To begin with, the refugees provided a cheap source of labour. Most crucial, however, was the fact that Cyprus was now able to take advantage of the increasingly wealthy Gulf states, where industrial products, and especially shoes, clothing, cement, paper and synthetic goods were all finding a ready market. Ironically, it was a quirk of fate – the war and subsequent economic collapse in neighbouring Lebanon – that made success possible. Cypriot exporters were instantly able to fill the void left by the Lebanon as a major supplier to the Arab markets.

Foreign interest: The authorities in southern Cyprus have had a lot of success in promoting the island as an ideal location for business transactions with countries of the Near East. By the mid-1980s, nearly 3,000 "offshore companies" were registered in southern Cyprus, among them banks, insurance companies, architectural firms, real estate companies and consultancy firms.

The southern part of Cyprus – unlike the Turkish-occupied northern part – is no longer an underdeveloped country. Success does have its darker sides, though: the construction boom, steadily increasing industrialisation and intensive farming methods are taking a heavy toll on the environment, and the level of foreign debt has reached dangerous proportions. Several industries continue to operate unproductively, with outdated equipment. Many Cypriots wrongly assume that such problems will go away all by themselves the moment political unity is achieved.

PARTY POLITICS

To the left and right of the main street of Kato Pyrgos, four cafés vie for trade. Chairs stand outside the simple buildings, in the shade of an old oak tree. Men on their way to the fields and citrus plantations stop briefly to take a break, drink a Turkish coffee and chat with their neighbours.

But it is not chance or even habit that makes certain men go to certain cafés (the coffee tastes the same in all four cafés and the chairs are identical), it is politics. The first café, on the left, represents the Socialist EDEK Party. Opposite, is the favoured retreat of the Liberal-Conservative Democratic Party (DIKO). Further on are the preferred cafés of the Conservative Democratic Rally and the Communist AKEL respectively. Each café thus stands for one of the parties represented in the Cyprus parliament.

Politics in the Republic of Cyprus permeates life in many different ways. Products manufactured by the Cooperative movement (which is closely associated with the trade union PEO), are associated with the left-wing of the party spectrum. Thus there is "leftist" brandy (produced by cooperatives) and "rightist" brandy (produced by private firms), and "leftist" (locally grown) and "rightist" (foreign) coffee. Left/right categorisations even extend to sports: no Conservative would cheer any victory by the football club Omonia Nikosia, because the club has political affiliations with the Communists. If Olympiakos wins rather than Omonia, however, it's a victory for the right.

Politics during recent decades has been characterised by sharp antagonism between Communists and Conservatives. On the one side there is the Progressive Party of the Working People (AKEL), formed in 1941 and the successor of the Communist Party KKK, which was forbidden under British colonial rule. AKEL and the trade union federation affiliated with it, the PEO, have traditionally looked after farmers' and workers' concerns, thereby gaining substantial influence. The opposing side was initially represented not by an actual party but by the Archbishop and his followers, the clergy and the business world. When the Republic of Cyprus received its independence in 1960, the Democratic Front was founded as a Conservative collective movement. Only since 1968, when this party broke up as a result of ideological and personal differences, has Cyprus had a modern party system. By that time the Communists, with no Social Democratic opposition, were firmly entrenched.

This very active democracy is the consequence of the relatively small size of Cyprus. Legend has it that Archbishop Makarios III, the first president of the Republic, still revered today, was on first-name terms with every single person on the island. Even now, a politician's place of origin and his family's reputation can be far more decisive than his ideological position when it comes to elections. Also, although interest in politics is considerable, there are few active politicians on the island; politicians familiar to the voters for as long as 20 years dominate the hustings. The close connection between individuals, families and politics is evident when one compares election results in one small area: in some villages, the Communists have been overwhelmingly successful for decades even though the inhabitants do not give the impression of being radical left-wingers at all. The very next village will vote for the far right – but the voters themselves are far from being right-wing extremists.

The political system of the Republic of Cyprus is derived from the London and Zurich Treaties, which formed the basis of the island's independence from Britain in 1960. Under their terms, the Turkish Cypriots were accorded representation in the organs of the state that went far beyond their 18 percent minority status. Greek and Turkish Cypriots were given separate municipal administrations and separate representation in the government and in the law courts. Thus, the president was a Greek Cypriot, while his vice-president was a Turkish Cypriot. However, since the Turkish Cypriots abandoned all organs of state at the beginning of 1964, their posts have remained vacant and the 24 seats reserved for them in the 80-seat House of Representatives have been left empty.

The Republic of Cyprus has a presidential

Left, tea and sympathy.

system. The president can appoint and dismiss ministers without parliamentary intervention and decides policy matters in general. The voting procedure is similar to that of France, where the best-placed candidates after a first ballot go on to face a second one to determine who becomes president. The House of Representatives, elected through proportional representation, has only a legislative function.

Since the election of Independent Liberal Georgios Vassiliou as president in 1988, the National Council, a committee formed by all the parties in parliament, has increased in importance. Leaders from all parties now participate indirectly in government policy, whether or not they support the president.

Pressing question: The Cyprus Question dominates parliamentary discussion just as much as it dominates conversation in the cafés of Kato Pyrgos. It overshadows all ideological debates, often producing extraordinary political constellations. Even though the parties have agreed on a bizonal federation, in accordance with agreements already reached between the Greek and Turkish Cypriots and with the UN security resolutions, dissent remains, not only regarding the finer points of a solution but also on how to force Turkey and the Turkish Cypriot leaders to accept a solution at all.

Disagreement among the Greek Cypriots on how a solution can be reached has produced two factions. On one side are the Democratic Rally (DISY) and the Communist AKEL. Although these parties detest one another on ideological grounds, their policies are similar when it comes to the Cyprus Question: they say they are ready to compromise, and seek dialogue with the representatives of the Turkish Cypriots in the occupied sector.

Ranged on the other side are the Democratic Party (DIKO) and the Socialist Cyprus National Democratic Union (EDEK), who favour an altogether harder line. After the repeated failure of talks with the Turkish Cypriots they have called for an end to negotiations and an internationalisation of the problem, by which they mean bringing the conflict before international organisations such as the United Nations or the European Community.

Runners and riders: The most powerful party in the Republic is the Democratic Rally

(DISY), the bastion of conservatism on the island, run by veteran politician Glafkos Klerides. He chaired the intercommunal talks under President Makarios, who died in 1977. After the coup in 1974, Klerides took over as president until Makarios's return, and in 1988 Klerides was only narrowly beaten in the presidential elections by the current president, Georgios Vassiliou. During the parliamentary elections on 12 May 1991 the DISY gained 35.8 percent of the votes and 20 of the 56 seats in the House of Representatives – its best-ever showing. The majority of its voters are entrepreneurs and businessmen, though quite a few employees also vote DISY. Closely affiliated with the

party is the trade union federation SEK, founded in the 1950s as a rival of the left-wing federation PEO. The main criticism levelled at the DISY by the left is that it has provided a new home for some of those who participated in the coup of 1974. Conservative circles, on the other hand, accuse the party of being soft on the Cyprus Question.

The Democratic Party (DIKO) is led by former President Spyros Kyprianou, who was voted out of office in 1988. Kyprianou, too, is one of Cyprus's "elderly statesmen", having been made Foreign Minister under President Makarios as long ago as 1960. Ideologically, DIKO is not all that different from the Democratic Rally, but it is far more uncompromising in its attitude to the Cyprus Question. The party was forced to concede a sharp defeat in the 1991 elections, and now has only 11 representatives in parliament.

The Cyprus National Democratic Union (EDEK) sees itself as a Socialist party, in the Third World liberation movement tradition. However, its leader Vassos Lyssarides, formerly President Makarios's personal physician, has adopted an increasingly Greek-nationalist policy in recent years. In the 1991 parliamentary elections, EDEK won 10.9 percent of the votes and seven seats.

Unchallenged as representative of the workers and farmers, the Communist Pro-

gressive Party of the Working People (AKEL) is very powerful: with 30.6 percent of the vote, the party has 18 representatives in parliament. Domestically, the party tends to follow a more moderate, social democratic line, for even before the collapse of socialism in Eastern Europe AKEL never had a clear idea of communism. The Communists' popularity can be explained by the party's traditional role of representing the "small man".

Left, Georgios Vassiliou, president of the Republic of Cyprus. **Above**, Turkish Cypriot leader Rauf Denktash.

Northern Cyprus: The Turkish Republic of Northern Cyprus calls itself an independent state. It has a president, a foreign minister and its own flag. However, it has only a very small amount of diplomatic representation abroad: just one "embassy" in Ankara. The similarity between the red-and-white Turkish flag and its white-and-red counterpart belonging to the Turkish Republic of Northern Cyprus suggests who calls the shots.

Turkey has roughly 29,000 soldiers stationed in the north of Cyprus. It pays for about half the government budget of northern Cyprus in the form of non-redeemable loans. It has sent between 60,000 and 80,000 settlers from the mainland to occupy northern Cyprus in order to change the demographic structure there once and for all. Its "ambassador" in north Nicosia has a large say in decisions. In brief: the self-proclaimed Turkish Republic of Northern Cyprus is little more than a province of Turkey.

The Turkish Cypriot strong man is Rauf Denktash. As far back as the 1950s he was involved in founding the terror group TMT. As Turkish Cypriot leader in the 1960s he met up with his old friend Glafkos Klerides, who was representing the Greek Cypriot side, during the intercommunal talks.

Democracy was out of the question among Turkish Cypriots in those days. When opposition politician Ahmed Mithat Berberoglu dared to stand as a candidate against Denktash in 1973, he was placed under house arrest until he came to terms with the prevailing power structure and gave up. After the occupation of northern Cyprus in 1974 Denktash had himself elected president of the Turkish Federated State of Cyprus one year later. In 1983 the name was changed, but the president was the same: Rauf Denktash. In 1985 the constitution was altered so that Denktash could stand once again as a candidate for the post.

During the 1990 elections Denktash – a power politician, a highly gifted diplomat and no stranger to political intrigue – received 67 percent of the vote. How many of those who voted were Turkish Cypriots and how many were Turkish settlers is not known. The settlers are living in expropriated Greek Cypriot housing, and farming Greek Cypriot land. Since 1974, tens of thousands of Turkish Cypriots have emigrated abroad from the northern sector, giving rise to fears that the Turkish Cypriots in northern Cyprus may soon become a minority in their own land.

In his role as president, Rauf Denktash is officially above party interests. The actual business of government is the responsibility of the prime minister, a post held since 1983 by Dervis Eroglu. This, however, has not hindered Denktash in any way from having a firm say in both the domestic and foreign policy of his country. He certainly has the necessary power: the Conservative National Unity Party (UBP), founded by him, has an absolute majority. In the parliamentary elections on 22 April 1990 it received 54.5 percent of the vote.

The combined Opposition, consisting of the social-democratic oriented Communal Liberation Party (TKP), and the left-wing Turkish-Republican Party (CTP), gained 44.4 percent. The Opposition is in favour of the reunification of Cyprus on a federal basis, with emphasis on rights for their own ethnic group. Oddly enough, the UBP gained more than twice as many seats in parliament as the Opposition (34:16). Even before the election, the Opposition had criticised the undemocratic electoral system.

For the Turkish Cypriots, the party system is an even more recent phenomenon than for the Greek Cypriots. For a long time, the activities of groups who disagreed with Denktash were severely hampered. The Opposition has been allowed to function only since 1975. Apart from a few exceptions, there is a free press, and the elections, too, could be termed fair – the one caveat being that settlers have equal voting rights even though they are not Cypriots.

When it comes to political questions of a more basic nature, however, democracy comes up against limits imposed by Turkey and Denktash. For example, it was only after receiving threats of violence that the Turkish-Republican Party (CTP) gave its support in 1983 to the "declaration of independence" by the Turkish Republic of Northern Cyprus. The CTP, founded in 1970, is the only organisation among the Turkish Cypriot parties to object to the alleged independence on principle. It calls for the creation of a federal state together with the Greek Cypriots and accuses Denktash of cementing the partition with his policies. In the opinion of party leader Özger Özg Ür, all those settlers who

have not intermarried with Cypriots, thus gaining the rights of citizenship, should leave the island and return home. The Turkish-Republican Party is left-wing in its ideology and sees itself as representing the workers and farmers. In the 1985 elections, when the Opposition stood separately from Denktash's UBP, it received 25.3 percent of the vote.

The second-largest opposition group, the Communal Liberation Party (TKP), is led by Mustafa Akinci, who as former representative of the Turkish Cypriots in Nicosia has received much praise for bringing the ethnic groups closer together. His party, which received 15.9 percent of the vote in the 1985 elections, has shifted its stance from being a supporter of independence to being an outspoken and unequivocal critic of it. The TKP is particularly critical of the close economic links between Ankara and northern Nicosia. Founded in 1985, the party is social-democrat oriented.

The National Unity Party (UBP) was founded by Rauf Denktash in 1975. Although he is no longer party leader, he still exercises a definite influence. The party leader is Dervis Eroglu, who also functions as prime minister. The UBP has been the sole party in power since the foundation of the Turkish Republic of Northern Cyprus. Like Denktash himself, the UBP is in favour of the occupied sector developing its independence still further. However, at the same time it calls for ever closer ties between the north of Cyprus and Turkey. Various officially independent organisations, such as the Association of Fighters and the War Veterans Group, operate in a grey area between the government and the UBP. They are accused of having connections with the ex-terrorist group TMT, which was active against Greek Cypriots and left-wingers in its own ethnic group right up to the 1960s.

Denktash's only role in the discussions towards solving the Cyprus Question is as leader of his own ethnic group. The UN Security Council strongly criticised the formation of the Turkish Republic of Northern Cyprus as long ago as 1983. No country in the world, with the exception of Turkey, has officially recognised it, and it is considered to be territory under Turkish occupation.

Right, walls invariably carry a political message.

THE CYPRIOTS

"What are the Cypriots? Except in name, they are neither Turks nor Greeks, neither are they an amalgam of these two races. From Larnaca to Kyrenia, from Paphos to Famagusta, you will seek in vain for any sample of these types. In neither face nor figure, in neither speech nor genius, has the Cypriot any resemblance to either Turk or Greek. Nowhere have I seen a Turkish figure, nowhere a Grecian profile. It is safe, I think, to say that not a single Turk exists in Cyprus. not a single Turk lives on Cyprus." So wrote W. Hepworth Dixon in *British Cyprus*, published in London in 1879.

Cypriots are never described simply as Cypriots. The word is always prefaced by the qualification Greek or Turkish, in recognition of the two very different ethnic groups which inhabit Cyprus: the Greek-speaking Greek Orthodox community and the Turkish-speaking Sunni Moslems. The question of whether they exist as a single people is up to the islanders themselves to decide, and cannot be answered by sociological study, by the politicians who so often pontificate on the matter, or by the text of a constitution.

Unfortunately with half of the population looking to Athens and Europe and the other half towards Ankara and Turkey, the gulf between the communities continues to widen rather than close. The slogan "Proud to be a Turk" is picked out in white stones high on the slopes of the Kyrenia mountains, and is visible for miles around. Turkish flags, some of them the original red colour, and others with white additions, flutter all over the northern part of the island, just as the Greek cross of St Andrew adorns every church and town hall in the southern part. Waving from the latter, however, one usually sees the flag of the Republic of Cyprus, white with the island outlined in yellow above an olive branch.

Peaceful coexistence: To begin with, following colonisation by the Ottomans, there

were few incidents of social conflict between the Moslem settlers and the indigent Orthodox Christian population. In fact, the two groups joined forces several times to fight their oppressors in Constantinople.

Marriages between the Moslem and Christian communities were unusual, on religious grounds, but in everyday life it was quite difficult to tell the two ethnic groups apart. It was only the growth of nationalism during the 19th century that produced the social and political conflicts that were later

to erupt so violently.

In 1960, when the British Crown Colony of Cyprus was finally given its independence, the new Republic's constitution defined the Greek and Turkish Cypriots as two separate ethnic groups. At that time the members of both groups still lived in ethnically mixed villages and cities. Purely "Greek" or "Turkish" areas were few. In most cases, neighbours lived together in peace and celebrated their festivals together. Many villages operated communal cooperatives. Agricultural products were marketed on a mutual basis.

Today, these two communities have not

Preceding pages: pause for thought; café pursuits; tying the knot in a folkloric courtship dance. Left, groomed for the part. Above, women still play the traditional role in this conservative society.

laid eyes on each other for nearly 20 years. Their only knowledge of one another's activities is gained via television. Nevertheless, the north and south, the "Greeks" and the "Turks", have more in common than they would care to admit. In their daily life, their food and drink, their gestures and their temperament, Greeks and Turks on either side of the Attila Line are Cypriots. In spite of the propaganda promulgated by both communities, 400-year-old traditions often prove much more influential than a few decades of politics.

Relaxed pace: Anyone familiar with Athens and Istanbul will be amazed at the relaxed pace of life in Nicosia. Despite con-

island close more punctually than the shops in Berlin. For the visitor, Cyprus feels far more like a European country than many other countries of Southern Europe.

Greek Cypriot society, in particular, is more markedly cosmopolitan than it may first appear. Almost everyone has been abroad at some time or other, not least to visit their friends and relatives who emigrated. Until the 1950s Cyprus was still a poor country and thousands emigrated to improve their prospects. Today, there are large colonies of Greek- Cypriots in New York and Australia, and the community in London numbers around 100,000.

Those who remained at home have re-

gested traffic jams, car horns are used far less frequently here than in the capital cities of the respective motherlands, for Cypriots tend to be calmer in their reactions to life's daily irritations than either the Greeks or the Turks. Similarly they follow political developments at home and abroad with less passion, even though they have more than enough reason to get aggravated. What is more, the Greek Cypriot economy and social system is far more efficient than, say, that of Athens. The streets are a lot tidier, and life is far more organised. Standards of hygiene, too, are more in keeping with those of Central Europe, and the shops in the cities on the

tained a strong link with the diaspora. An apparent drawback, the lack of a university, has been another factor contributing to a certain cosmopolitanism. All students have to study abroad, and educational standards are high. Most go to Athens, but many study in Britain or the USA. This has contributed to a keen awareness of what is going on outside the island. A side-effect for visitors to Cyprus is that they hardly ever have problems communicating. Most people have at least a smattering of English.

Indeed, Greek Cypriots consider themselves Europeans as a matter of course, even though their island is, geographically, a part of Asia. They look not to Asia Minor but to Athens, Paris or London for inspiration and orientation.

Still a male society: That said, society is still very traditional in its outlook and Cypriot women are conservative. For centuries fanciful male travellers have liked to ponder on whether they retain any of the characteristics of the goddess Aphrodite. Most decided not. In the opinion of one Charles Lewis Meryon, writing in 1846, "They were not in general beautiful, nor was their dress graceful... Seen from behind they resembled nothing so much as a horse in a mantua-maker's showroom, with a dress appended to it." A more recent visitor, the humorist George Mikes,

The Turkish Cypriots' attitude to life is more Near Eastern than that of their Greek Cypriot counterparts. The inhabitants of the northern part of Cyprus are poor compared with their prosperous southern counterparts. The influx of tens of thousands of Turkish settlers may have achieved the desired effect of creating a stronger relationship with Turkey, but it has also caused a mounting wave of protest against "Anatolisation" among indigent Turkish Cypriots.

The divided capital of Nicosia, with its 210,000 inhabitants, is situated in the middle of the Mesaoria Plain. All the other major centres of population lie on the coast: the two most important harbour cities are both on the

said, "I cannot suppress my feelings that had the Cypriot girls been just a shade less virtuous, the history of Cyprus would be less eventful and much happier."

The cafés are still the domain of the menfolk, and they are the centres of political discussion. In the villages the café is the forum for political decision-making too. As a rule, Cypriot women are unwelcome in such cafés. There are only three female members of parliament (out of 50), and the attitude persists that a woman's main role is to look after the household and the children.

Left, head start. Above, priest cum farmer.

south coast – Limassol (pop. 120,000) and Larnaca (pop. 54,000). The port of Famagusta, in the occupied northern part of the island, now has only around 180,000 inhabitants, as a result of the exodus of its Greek Cypriot population.

Cyprus has a total population of roughly 650,000, 84 percent of whom are Greek Cypriot and 14 percent Turkish Cypriot. The remaining 2 percent comprise a variety of small minorities of Maronites, Armenians and Latins. The new Turkish settlers are not included in these statistics because their precise number is still an official secret in the occupied sector.

In keeping with their love of worldly pleasures, the Cypriots adore celebrations and festivals of all kinds. Each occasion is attended by a feast.

Wedding belles: Witnessing a wedding on Cyprus is a real experience for the traveller, even though only a few of the original customs and rituals are still adhered to (for example, the length of the celebration has been shortened from a week to only half a day, and the stipulation that weddings may take place only on Sunday has been relaxed).

Most couples marry in the summer months; leap years are avoided because they are considered unlucky. The festivities begin with the dressing of the bride and groom in wedding finery, usually to a musical accompaniment. Then it's off to church, the time of the ceremony depending on the number of other weddings taking place that day. The guests attending the one-hour-long ceremony – during which the couple is crowned with pearls – are usually too numerous to fit inside the church.

Afterwards, the festivities begin with the "making of the bed", the symbolic setting up and decoration of a mattress: married women carrying the future couple's bedclothes (an important part of the dowry) dance around the mattress and make the bed. Guests then decorate the finished bed with coins and banknotes.

By around 8 p.m., most of the guests have arrived. Each guest is offered a drink and a plate piled high with the wedding supper – traditionally a range of set dishes: fried slices of potato, cucumber, tomatoes, *kleftiko* (lamb roasted in a sealed oven or sealed earthenware pot) and *pastitsio*. Women carrying large bowls distribute *resi* (crushed wheat porridge, a speciality that no self-respecting wedding omits), and *kourabiédes* (baked almond pastries).

At this point the dancing starts, and lasts until about midnight: there's the *tsifteteli*, a simplified form of the belly dance, which men and women do separately in pairs, or the

rembetiko, a dance dating from the war of Asia Minor, in which a single individual performs to the syncopated clapping of a circle of friends.

Depending on the size of the orchestra, instruments usually include the *bouzouki*, the electric guitar, drums and – replacing the bouzouki and the guitar in traditional wedding music – the violin. The repertoire tends to be similar to that employed at most other festivals and in the bouzouki nightclubs; the latest "hits" are essential.

Once the evening is quite far advanced, it's time for the *choros tou androjinou*, danced only by the bridal couple. This is when the guests shower money on the bride and groom. The couple literally disappear under long chains of banknotes, all pinned together. The song has a number of optional choruses – depending on how long the bombardment lasts. Finally, towards midnight, the guests disperse.

The Christening: Festivities celebrating engagements and christenings are similar, but on a more modest scale and without any dancing. Greek Orthodox christenings differ in many important respects from the common Northern European version. The main difference is that the child is naked and completely immersed in water. He or she is then oiled and dressed in fine clothing. The godfather (only one) provides each guest with a baptismal gift, usually a small doll or animal decorated with sweets, and sometimes even a photograph of the baby. The ceremony is followed by a grand party for at least 100 guests.

Name-day celebrations are also very popular with the people of Cyprus. These are held on particular days each year by many monasteries, and are similar to country fairs (without the roundabouts). A large area in front of the monastery fills up with stalls and booths selling everything from household goods and clothing to souvenirs, cassettes, toys, nuts and honey. Sweets are particularly popular, especially *loukoumia* (a kind of Turkish delight), chewing gum, *daktyla* (almond cakes with syrup), *lokmades* (small round cream puff pastries fried in oil) and the ever-popular *soutsoukos* (strings of al-

Preceding pages: festival in Ayios Neophytos.
Left, the *choros tou androjinou* – donations gratefully received.

monds dipped in grape juice and then dried).

Visitors interested in more than just shopping might try their hand at one of the numerous games, where prizes include live canaries. Festivals like these are a great place for meeting friends and dressing up; the women (who are always dressed in the very latest fashions on Cyprus) are exceptionally eye-catching on these occasions.

City festivals: The most important city festival is the Limassol wine festival, held for 12 days every September. The tradition, started by the wine producers, began in 1961 and was only briefly interrupted for a four-year period by the Cyprus crisis. The entry fee entitles one to sample the various types of

festival, with a procession through the streets and competitions among the children for the best flower arrangements. Before partition, two of the most spectacular festivals were the Orange Festival in Morphou and the Carnation Festival in Varosha; unfortunately they have both fallen victim to the political situation.

Of course, there are also the numerous small harvest festivals and fairs *(panegyri)* in all the larger villages of the island, as well as the Dionysos Festival in Stroumbi and the Cherry Festival in Pedhoulas. On these occasions, old and young alike celebrate in the village square, with music, dancing, feasting and drama.

wine on display and to attend all the theatrical and musical activities. Some 100,000 visitors manage to consume around 30,000 litres of wine.

Excuses for a festival in Cyprus are not hard to find. Limassol – and recently Paphos, too – holds its own carnival celebrations in March every year, complete with parades, parties, music and masked balls, and in the summer the firm of KEO hosts a beer festival, similar to the one organised by Carlsberg in Nicosia. There are also several cultural festivals in the summer, including the ancient Greek Drama Festival.

In May, every town has its own flower

Pagan superstitions: As the Cypriots are a deeply religious people, a great number of church festivals are celebrated, but their significance is rather different from what one might expect, for they feature a fascinating blend of pagan superstition and Christian rites. Families attribute little importance to Christmas, for example, but New Year's Day is celebrated with at least one *vasilopitta*, a cake made of baked semolina. A coin is hidden inside the cake, and whoever is fortunate enough to find it is assured of good luck in the coming year. Another custom is to throw olive leaves on to hot ashes, and watch the way they curl; from this, it is maintained, one can predict whether wishes will be fulfilled. *Lokmades* (doughnuts) are an integral part of the Epiphany celebrations on Cyprus; it is customary to throw the first doughnut out of the frying-pan and on to the roof of your house, in order to pacify any lurking evil spirits.

Pentecost is not generally marked. An exception is the popular religious festival unique to Cyprus known as the Kataklysmos Festival, which coincides with Pentecost and is held in Larnaca. It is a water festival of pagan origin in honour of Aphrodite, but it has developed into a Christian festival to mark the Flood. The whole thing culminates in an enormous fair, with music and dancing and

portant church festival is Easter. Preparations begin a full 50 days in advance with the onset of fasting, and a strictly vegetarian diet. During Holy Week this diet becomes even stricter – just pulses and vegetables. On Orthodox Good Friday, in the villages, the Epitaphios procession (led by a coffin containing a figure of Christ) is held, and every icon is draped in black cloth; then on Easter Saturday preparations get under way for baking *flaounes* (pastries filled with a mixture of egg, cheese and raisins).

In the evening villagers gather in church for the service celebrating the Resurrection. Everyone holds a candle, and children are given sparklers. At midnight the priest an-

readings by local poets.

In May, the towns along the coast celebrate Christ's baptism by lowering crucifixes into the water. And in Larnaca on 18 April, citizens hold a procession headed by the icon of St Lazarus, patron saint of the city. The Assumption of the Virgin on 15 August and the Day of the Holy Cross on 14 September are also important church holidays, when fairs are held at many of the monasteries.

Easter time: Without doubt, the most im-

nounces Christ's Resurrection with the words "*Christos anesti*" (Christ is risen), to which the answer resounds: "*Alithinos anesti!*" (He is truly risen!). Then the candles are lit, and the square in front of the church blazes with light. After the service, Easter soup is served, and many people stay out even later. On Easter Sunday, familes sport new clothes and go to the countryside for a picnic of grilled *souvla* (skewered lamb) and hard-boiled eggs that have been painted red.

Greek national holidays are also observed in the southern part of Cyprus. Greek Independence Day is celebrated on 25 March, and "Okhi" Day (celebrating Greece's defi-

Left, a member of the famous Giorgalleto family.
Above, a lute player.

ant "no" to the Italians in 1940) on 28 October. Cyprus has its own Independence Day too, of course, on 1 October.

In the north of Cyprus the festivals correspond to the main Turkish ones. The two largest religious festivals are the Id-ul-Fitr after Ramadan and the Id-ul-Adha a little later in the year. Here, too, good food plays a central role.

Making music: A few words about music in Cyprus. As mentioned before, the melodies most often heard at festivals are *tsifteteli* and *rembetiko* songs: they are happy, light, rhythmical and generally about romance and everyday affairs, without much depth. But there are other types of music too, ranging

from disco and Greek pop to classical music and traditional folk songs. The latter come in various categories: emotional love songs, working songs, children's rhymes, humorous songs, wedding songs, dirges and laments as well as ballads with mythological, Christian, social or political content. Their most popular rhythm is 7/8 time, the *kalamatianos*. One also comes across 2/4, 9/8, 5/8 and 6/8 time. The tempo tends to vary between *portato* and *presto*, and most of the scales correspond to the various church modes (Aeolian, Dorian) while the metre often betrays its ancient origins (iambics, trochees, etc.). Church music as we know it does not

exist, because the Orthodox liturgy allows only chants; these date back to the fathers of the Early Christian Church, John Chrysostom and Basil of Caesarea.

Musical instruments are equally varied. As well as the common instruments of pop music – the bouzouki, drums, accordion, violin and synthesiser – there are a number of very ancient instruments, some dating back to Byzantine times. Some of these are confined to the Turkish culture, such as the *'ùd* (a short-necked lute), the *zornà* (a kind of oboe), the *davul* (a two-headed cylindrical drum) or the *kàsàt* (small finger cymbals), and others are found only in Greek music, e.g. the *laoudo* (long-necked lute), the mandolin, the *aulos* (reed pipe) and the *tambuchin* (large frame drum), as well as the kettledrum, the trumpet and cymbals used in parades. These traditional instruments are gradually dying out, however, due to the increasing appetite for modern pop music. The Turkish Cypriot music of today is similar to the music of mainland Turkey, with the main instrument being the *sas* (a kind of balalaika).

Attempts have been made by modern musicians to rescue and adapt at least some of the island's old melodies. The Trio Giorgalletto, for example, a male-voice group belonging to a musical family that has been famous on the island for decades, frequently goes on international tours. The group also performs on big festive occasions and for radio and television.

Another person keen to resuscitate Cypriot music is Pieris Zarmas, the Cypriot ambassador in Bonn. He has devoted a major portion of his life to the study of music, and trained as an opera singer in Milan (he sings first baritone in the Bonn Opera). With his extensive scholarly studies (from which the brief summary of Cypriot musical traditions here has been taken), he has done Cypriot folk music a great service.

This research, as well as his various recordings will, one hopes, reassert the importance of the traditional at a time when – as a result of modernisation and various attempts to "fit in" with the industrialised nations of northern Europe – there seems to be less and less room for traditional customs.

Left, a Turkish festival in Bellapais. Right, celebrations in Limassol.

FOOD

Food and drink on Cyprus are an integral part of any and every social occasion. Scarcely a conversation takes place without coffee, beer or brandy being proffered, and invaribaly a small snack too. The Cypriots love food. No surprise, then, that the country's cuisine is so broad. The island's geographical position and its history have resulted in an interesting mix of Greek, Turkish, Arabic and English culinary influences.

It is at the weekend, above all, that fathers take their families out to eat, and groups of up to 15 people are nothing uncommon. These kinds of gatherings are informal, and the table is literally strained to breaking-point under the sheer number of different dishes. Plates are piled high, and everyone tries a little bit of everything (leaving a clean plate is considered unusual).

This style of dining stems from the Cypriot preference for *meze* (meaning "mixture"), usually a little of everything that's available that day in that taverna or restaurant and, on occasion, augmented by ingredients brought by the customer – for example, snails they have selected at the local market. There's no better way of getting a general idea of Cypriot cuisine than the *meze*, because it enables one to sample the widest range of Cypriot food in one sitting. A *meze* always includes a few Cypriot specialities, in particular *halumi* cheese (produced by thyme-fed goats), which can be obtained only on Cyprus.

The dishes are well seasoned, but not over-spicy. No one need fear stomach upsets, and oil and fat are used moderately.

Although Cyprus is an island, the price of seafood here is high: this part of the Mediterranean is not rich in fish, and many species have to be imported deep-frozen. Typical Cypriot seafood dishes include small, deep-fried fish and rings of cuttlefish.

It would take another book to describe all the specialities of Cyprus. However, you will find a list of the most commonly-encountered dishes, each with a brief accompanying explanation, in the Travel Tips section at the end of this guide.

Preceding pages: traditional *meze*. **Left**, making no bones. **Above**, *souvlakia*, always a favourite.

The traditional Cypriot dishes that can be found are often modified, doubtless as a result of English influence which is still so much in evidence all over the island. Unfortunately it's no simple matter to find genuine, unadulterated local food, especially in the more touristy areas. Restaurants in the main resorts tend to offer steaks, cutlets and other international dishes, all of which arrive with the compulsory helping of oversized chips. Most hotels offer cooked English breakfasts. The really simple and delicious

local food (e.g. pumpkin slices fried in butter, wheatmeal pilau, broad bean stew, etc.) remains unobtainable for the majority of visitors, because such dishes are not generally considered to be a "full meal".

Nor, when sitting down to dine, should one expect the food to be all that Greek: the salads rarely contain sliced onion, and the *talattouri* (similar to the Greek *tsatsiki*) contains only a dash of garlic. Unlike in Greece, however, the food does arrive hot.

One particular favourite on the menu with Cypriots is game. Ducks, game birds and rabbits, and also, unfortunately, the *ambelopoulia* – a species of small songbird

– are the usual targets of the island's enthusiastic hunting community.

The food in northern Cyprus is closely related to that served in mainland Turkey, with meat and vegetables much in evidence.

A drop to drink: Unlike the Greeks (and the tourists, too), the Cypriots are not great fans of ouzo. Retsina is drunk rarely. Beer, however, is extremely popular (there are two brands, KEO and Carlsberg), as is brandy. The latter is excellent, and there are various types (see Travel Tips for recommendations). Brandy Sour, a long drink consisting of brandy, lime juice, angostura bitters and soda, is a wonderful pick-me-up after a hard day on the beach.

Cyprus sherry (Emva Cream being the most popular) is well known outside Cyprus. Less familiar to outsiders are the various liqueurs made from the island's fruits. Especially delicious is *Filfar*, made from oranges and reminiscent of Grand Marnier. And to quench the thirst of those not keen on alcohol, the island also stocks the full range of internationally known soft drinks – the empty cans that litter the roadside give a good idea of the range.

But the wines of Cyprus are worthy of particular note. The island was famous for its wine as far back as antiquity (they even get a mention in the Song of Solomon), and it was one of the first countries actively to cultivate the vine. Much written evidence, such as that of Roman author Pliny the Elder, attests to the quality of the grapes, and especially their size. Mark Antony gave Cyprus to Cleopatra, as a token of his love for her, with the words: "Your sweetness, my darling, is like the Nama wine of Cyprus." In the mid-14th century the German pilgrim Ludolf von Suchen wrote: "In all the world there are no greater or better drinkers than in Cyprus." And legend has it that Sultan Selim II ordered the invasion of Cyprus after tasting one of the island's wines.

Another important event in the history of Cypriot wine was the invasion of Cyprus by Richard the Lionheart, and his sale of the island to the Knights Templar; the latter were concentrated around Limassol, notably in Kolossi, where they had their "Grand Commandery", which gave the island's famous Commandaria wine its name. Richard is reputed to have later said: "I must go back to Cyprus, if only to taste its wine once again." It was around that time that the Nama wine was rechristened Commandaria.

Even today, this wine, probably the most famous of Cypriot wines, is produced using the same age-old methods, including fermentation in open jars. The grapes are grown in a restricted area and the wine's special merit lies in the way it is blended and "aged". It is sweet and heavy, tastes rather like Madeira, and should really be classed as a fortified wine. There are so many different types available that it is possible to find a Commandaria to suit every palate.

Today, wine-making is still one of the country's most important sources of income. The sunny, mild climate and the fertile soil make it a natural industry. The main wine areas can be found in the Limassol and Paphos regions, and on the slopes of the Troodos mountains. The large wine factories of the four main producers, Sodap, KEO, Loel and Etko-Hatzipavlou, are all based in Limassol and Paphos. Along with the government, they have encouraged the import of several European grape varieties, in particular several from France. Altogether, some 30 countries import Cyprus wine, but the main consumer remains Great Britain.

Left, produce of the Khryssorroyiatissa monastery. **Right,** Cypriot sherry, a major export.

The twin village of Lefkara (combined population: 1,300) nestles in a picturesque setting at the foot of the Troodos mountains. An attractive village, with its unusual red roofs, it was said to have been a popular summer resort with ladies of the Venetian period. Kato Lefkara, the lower part of the village, is tiny, with narrow, winding streets. It has a shop that provides basic necessities, two *Kafeneons*, where the male population of the village meet, and a small church.

Pano Lefkara, the upper part, is larger. Here, restaurants and shops have sprung up around the market-place where the tourist buses pull up and the side streets are flanked by souvenir shops, selling silver and gold jewellery and tablecloths. These, magnificently embroidered, hang outside nearly every shop. In good weather, the women of the village sit outside their houses and work at their broderie anglaise, embroidering motifs on cotton and linen. The store owners are only too happy to invite any passing strangers to take a look around.

Lefkara is the centre of Cyprus embroidery. The industry has gained a world-wide reputation for its intricacy and beauty. Leonardo da Vinci is said to have purchased some *lefkaritiki* embroidery for the Ayia Trapeza altar of Milan Cathedral (a sample hangs in Lefkara in his memory). At the turn of the century, men from Lefkara were travelling halfway round the world selling embroidery, some of them venturing as far as North America, while their wives stayed sewing at home. Records record that in 1910, some £1,720 worth of Lefkara embroidery was exported, a handsome sum at the time.

The base material for the embroidery is Irish linen. Creating, say, a tablecloth can often mean several weeks' hard work, and so prices can be high – though not prohibitively so. The end product is unique: no piece of Lefkara embroidery is the same as any other.

Four main companies, each employing some 150 workers, look after the manufac-

ture and marketing of embroidery in Lefkara. The village also contains several fine stone houses – one of which, the House of Patasalos, contains a Museum of Folk Art – devoted to the history of embroidery, lace and silverwork of the area.

Thanks to its buoyant embroidery industry, Lefkara has prospered, and there is no danger that the village will decline. Other cottage industries on Cyprus, however, are gradually disappearing. They cannot compete with imported industrial products, and

are rapidly vanishing from the market. In some cases, for instance, the examples of "original Cypriot pottery" you see for sale, are not produced by the island at all, but are manufactured in Greece or Hong Kong.

Official Handicraft Centres have been set up with the aim of keeping the island's handicrafts alive. Their workshops still use traditional methods. The employees, many of whom are refugees from the Turkish-occupied sector, keep old techniques alive which would otherwise have been forgotten. Handicrafts made on a private basis are also sold here. Anyone buying goods at any of the Handicraft Centre shops in Limassol,

Preceding pages: modernisation has brought sweeping changes to traditional crafts. Left, pottery in Kornos. Right, a young practitioner of an ancient art.

A THRIVING ART SCENE

Modern art in Cyprus developed at the beginning of this century. It was then that Cypriot artists began capturing the various moods and nuances of the landscape and the island's continually changing light. Their work is noted for its technical brilliance and sharp sensitivity to colour.

The best works of this period can be seen in Nicosia's recently-opened State Art Gallery, housed in a traditional Cypriot town building. As well as the two rooms dedicated to fine art, the gallery contains an interesting collection of naive art documenting village life and picturing the island's

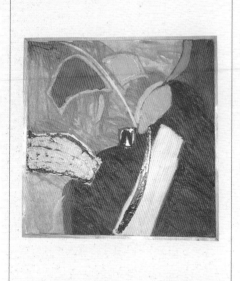

long-standing traditions.

Cypriot artists are as much in touch with the cosmopolitan art scene as artists anywhere else in Europe, and international trends inject local art with fresh ideas. Slowly but surely, new as well as traditional styles are developing into a positive and recognisable national style, with its basis in form and colour. Even though the country is small, Cypriot art goes a lot deeper than handicrafts or the production of kitsch souvenirs for tourists. In small galleries, it is still possible to find a piece of sculpture that is both a souvenir and a work of art, fine landscape paintings, objects and montages influenced, for example, by Joseph Beuys, and modern abstracts that are essentially

Cypriot in their freshness, brightness and arresting colours.

Although in Nicosia galleries tend to open – and close – rather frequently, as in any rapidly changing society, galleries which can be safely regarded as permanent features of the Nicosia art scene include the establishments below:

The Famagusta Gate Cultural Complex, with its large studio, roomy corridors and, on the other side of the street, its small gallery housed in what used to be a bakery, holds frequent exhibitions of contemporary art, many dealing with innovative themes.

The Leventis Museum contains an exhibition of late works by Christoforos Savva, whose post-Cubist paintings reflect the magnificent colours of the island.

The Bank of Cyprus Foundation and the Popular Bank's Cultural Centre put on magnificent exhibitions, both travelling and permanent.

Of the commercial galleries, the Diaspro has the largest selection of contemporary art, while the Gloria Gallery, Apocalypse, Argo and Opus 39 exhibit modern and naive art and traditional arts and crafts.

With its recently-restored Bauhaus-influenced museum, Limassol, too, has become a centre for the arts. Peter's Gallery is a marble-tiled and well-lit modern gallery, built on three levels. Morphi, situated inside an enchanting old building, exhibits both modern and traditional art, while Rogmi, one block further on, exhibits modern art with a distinctly folksy touch. In the rear courtyard of the Odos Athinon, a combined gallery-café, one can listen to music in a relaxed atmosphere, and admire the paintings and sculptures.

In Larnaca, it's worth asking staff at the information office at the harbour whether anything of interest is being shown at the nearby art gallery, which was recently restored by the Pierides Foundation.

One of the finest galleries in Cyprus, the Kyklos Gallery, is in Paphos, not far from the harbour. It is situated in the middle of a meadow full of buttercups and daisies. Here, a fine view of the sea and the unique landscape are complemented by one of the best exhibitions of contemporary art to be found on the island.

Fairs are held by every village from time to time (the Pan Paphian Fair in summer, for example), many of which feature exhibitions by local artists. These are excellent places to pick up Cypriot art at reasonable prices. ∎

Larnaca, Paphos and Nicosia can be sure that their purchase has been hand-made.

Crafts under threat: Indeed, without the Handicraft Centres, production of the handsomely carved wooden bride's chests *(sandouki)*, made of pine, cedar or walnut, would have died out. In the old days these chests used to contain the daughters' dowries and jewellery. These days the Cypriots use ordinary wardrobes, but the old chests – the fronts of which are usually decorated with flower and tree motifs – are still used for ornamental purposes. The town of Lapithos on the north coast of the island, the former centre of chest-making, has been under Turkish occupation since 1974.

wicker plates, with perforated rims, are often used as bowls. The craftsmen tend to be elderly refugees, who want to earn extra money to supplement their pensions.

Embroidery thrives in other villages on the island apart from Lefkara. Colourful cotton embroidery is a speciality of several remote villages, such cloth being the traditional cover for dowry chests. In the wine village of Omodhos, elderly ladies embroider quilts and tablecloths.

Weaving mills were once widespread on the island, but the ancient looms in the remote mountain villages are rarely used these days. In the Handicraft Centres, on the other hand, they are in use daily. Silkworms are bred

GRIGLIA

Another craft that has almost disappeared is the manufacture of gourd flasks, an industry which used to be found wherever bottle gourds grew. Artistically decorated gourd flasks made from the inedible bottle gourd are no longer needed by a world used to canned drinks and glass bottles. Gourd flasks can sometimes be seen hanging outside restaurants, often in the guise of lamps.

Wickerwork and basketry is still being produced. Colourful wickerwork baskets and platters are a very common sight. Decorative

here, too, and their threads are spun into fine cloth for dresses and skirts.

All that glisters: Gold and silver jewellery is still produced today, albeit on a much smaller scale than in years gone by. Most of Cyprus's goldsmiths and silversmiths, whose premises used to share the same street in Nicosia, disappeared long ago.

Copper artefacts are usually antiques, with a correspondingly high price-tag. Small-scale metalworking, however, is still done in the traditional way; here, the piece to be duplicated is placed in a metal frame, which is then filled with a special type of sand on two sides. When the mould is opened the original

<u>Left</u>, modern art flourishes. <u>Above</u>, coppersmith at work.

is carefully removed, and liquid metal is then poured into the sand-mould.

Pottery, made of the local red clay, is still very widespread on Cyprus. Here it's possible to differentiate between larger, simply-constructed pieces and smaller, finer work. The largest specimens, huge round storage jars often measuring up to 3 ft (1 metre) in diameter, are commonly found lying in gardens and outside houses. Called *pitharia*, these jars were formerly used for storing oil, olives, water or wine. The potters who made them were held in high regard, and used to travel from village to village creating them on the spot – without even using a wheel.

Alas, *pitharia* are no longer produced; their enormous size and incredible weight make them unsuitable for modern-day living. Large, simply constructed clay pitchers, however, are still made, and look much like they did in the last millennium. Even in the broiling heat of summer, water stays pleasantly cool in these unglazed containers (which often stand on metal tripods). They are frequently used as flower-pots.

Small pottery ware is a speciality of the Paphos region. Clay figurines, glazed vases, candlesticks, bowls and complete coffee services are all available. Some are colourfully decorated with flower patterns, others are more simple, with geometrical designs. The latter, with their line patterns, are strikingly reminiscent of their ancient counterparts. Some of the decorative forms date back to the Early Neolithic Period. The pots are formed using simple wheels, and are then hand-painted. Beware, however, pottery depicting Greek gods, especially with inscriptions in English – these are usually cheap, mass-produced imports.

Craftsmen are struggling to compete with the cheap, factory-produced equivalents saturating the market: the chairmakers, for instance, who used to make the old wooden chairs with wickerwork seats and arms, are a vanishing breed; their chairs may be hard-wearing, but plastic ones are cheaper. Yet most furniture on Cyprus is still hand-made according to the customer's specifications. But here, too, the competition from industry is gaining ground. With refrigerators available everywhere, who needs *pitharia*?

Right, silver and lace, the filigree products of Pano Lefkara.

925 / 1000
STERLING SILVER
ECHT SILBER
ARGEANT STERLING

Roughly 1,800 different kinds of flowering plant can be found on Cyprus. The most common kinds are the papilionaceous plants (*Leguminosae*), with around 200 different species; the compositae *(compositae)*, some 180 species; grasses, around 170 species; and carnations *(caryophyllus)*, of which there are roughly 90 different species. However, there are a further 46 families that are represented by only one species, e.g. the Agave is represented by the century plant, the walnut by *Juglans Regia*, the birch by *Alnus orientalis*, the laurel by *Laurus nobilis*, the peony family by *Paenia mascula* and the berberis family by *Berberis cretica*.

Unique to Cyprus: Roughly 110 species and 20 subspecies are endemic – that is to say they can be found only on Cyprus. These include the meadow saffron known as *Colchicum Troodi*, with its pinkish-white blossoms, found from the Troodos mountains right down as far as the coast, and the dark-red tulip *Tulipa Cypria*, found predominantly in the Myrtou and Dhiorios areas. Other endemic varieties include *Chionodoxa lochiae* (very similar to scilla) with its bright blue flowers, which blooms in the heights of the Troodos mountains as soon as the snow has melted, the *prius and C. Hartmannius*, which blossoms in winter and is also found high in the Troodos mountains, and the variety of yellow oxtongue known as *Onosma fruticosa*, with its yellow flowers.

Also endemic are various relations of the carnation family, including *Silene, Petrorhagia, Dianthus, Arenaria* and *Minuartia*, as well as two species of buttercup.

In addition to these, are the numerous plants characteristic of the Mediterranean region in general, and especially Greece. Cyprus is of particular interest to botanists because of its large number of species from Asia Minor, such as the buttercup *Ranunculus asiaticus*, the species of clover known as *Trifolium clipeatum* with its ornamental blossoms, and the guinea-hen flowers, *Fritillaria libanotica* and *Fritillaria acmopetala*.

Preceding pages: a wild corner of northern Cyprus. Left, bindweed in the hedgerows. Above, asphodel, a more delicate specimen.

Between March and early May is the best time to study the flora on the hills and plains, and May is the time to appreciate the flowers of the Troodos mountains. Intensive study of flora is well worthwhile on Cyprus, for like so many other areas of the Mediterranean it has still not been thoroughly researched. Surprising floral finds keep on occurring, particularly among the orchid family.

The forests of Cyprus: Cyprus was once rich in forests. Originally they covered the plains as well as the mountains. It was a natural

resource much coveted in the ancient world: wood was needed for smelting copper and silver and, of course, for shipbuilding. The island exported wood to Egypt, for example, and supplied Alexander the Great's fleet.

Within the space of just a few centuries, the island's forests had been seriously decimated, and as early as 400 BC the island's rulers placed its cedar forests under protection. Nevertheless, the island's wood continued to be plundered right up to modern times, and it wasn't until Cyprus fell under the British, during the 19th century, that serious consideration was given to the need for reafforestation and forest protection – far too late, of course, to save the various different kinds of wood on the island. Today, the only forests to be found on Cyprus are high in the mountains, along the Kyrenia range and up in the Troodos massif and its northeastern and southeastern foothills. Only about 10 percent of the island is still covered by forest.

The alder-leaf oak known as *Quercus alnifolia* can be found growing in abundance on the slopes of the Troodos mountains. This oak tree is not as large and sturdy as our Central European oaks: sometimes it is bushlike and only 7–10 ft (2–3 metres) in height, elsewhere it can grow as high as 20–25 ft (6–8 metres), although its trunk seldom grows

sun-drenched slopes just as happily as in shady ravines. On partly grassy or mossy ground, but also in very dry and stony regions, a large number of spring flowers can be found growing in their shade.

Three species of pine tree – the black pine *(Pinus nigra)*, the Aleppo pine *(Pinus halepensis)* and the stone pine *(Pinus pinea)* – comprise most of the forests of the island, from the coastline all the way to the heights of the Kyrenia and Troodos mountains. The Aleppo pine alone constitutes nine-tenths of all the forest on Cyprus, and has always been the main type of wood exported.

The island's pine trees are very hardy, and can resist the greatest extremes of heat and

any broader than a human arm. It is often associated with the strawberry tree *(Arbutus andrachne)*, the turpentine tree *(Pistacia terebinthus)* and the kermes oak *(Quercus coccifera)*. There are some particularly fine stretches of *Quercus alnifolia* to be seen around Kykko monastery.

The cypress tree is a distinctive feature of many Mediterranean island landscapes. Specimens on Cyprus tend to be isolated, though there are a few patches of cypress forest – for example, near the castle of St Hilarion, and Kantara castle, as well as in the southwest of the island. These trees are modest, they need very little humus, and grow on

aridity. Some of them can grow astonishingly high, too. The pine forests are mostly rather sparse-looking, and from a distance it can look as though a hillside is covered by more soil and rock than forest – for example, in the region near Galata on the northeastern slopes of the Troodos mountains, where very sparse pine forests stand alongside brown slopes that are almost devoid of plant life, or in the Asinou area where the light-brown, stony ground lends the pine forests their distinctive colour.

Around the asbestos mines even the sturdy pine forests have been badly afflicted or destroyed. Large black pines stand singly, some distance apart, up near Mount Chionistra on rocky scree-covered ground, and there are magnificent views to be had between the trees into the distance. In the Kyrenia range, too, along the forest road from Klepini to Halevga, there are very sparse pine forests growing on limestone that is almost bare of any vegetation except for small patches of grass containing numerous spring flowers.

In the area around the monastery of Antiphonitis the pine forests give way to expanses of broad, open meadow and limestone formations with sclerophyllous scrub. Thanks to moist sea breezes and frequent low cloud and fog, the pine forests in the

only be spanned by three men. Today's cedars are rather small in comparison, only around 25–30 ft (8–10 metres), and on rare occasions 40 ft (12 metres) in height, and up to 6 ft (2 metres) in circumference. Despite their rather weak and irregular growth, these trees are both impressive and strange with their flat, umbrella-like branches. Beneath the cedars are found the same bushes, herbs and flowers that grow in the island's oak forests.

In the Troodos mountains, above the coniferous forests, there are mountain meadows containing dense clumps of Cretan berberis (*Berberis cretica*) as well as the odd rose and juniper bush. Typical alpine pasture

Kyrenia range often have a luxuriant undergrowth of flowers and bushes.

Dwindling cedars: The most famous tree in Cyprus is the cedar *(Cedrus libanotica subsp. brevifolia)*, but today it grows only within a very small area of Paphos Forest on the slopes of Mount Tripylos. There must have been large expanses of cedar trees on Cyprus in former times, and in antiquity the individual trees must have been much larger. Pliny speaks of trees measuring up to 130 ft (40 metres) in height, with trunks that could

Left, between the blades of grass, you can find jewels like this. **Right**, yellow umbel.

flowers bloom on the stony ground straight after the snow has melted and into early May: violets, forget-me-nots, veronica, crocuses and many other species among them.

Sclerophyllous scrub is found predominantly in low-lying areas which are not used for agricultural purposes. It is composed of herbaceous, bulky, partly thorny and altogether impenetrable bushes, some of which can grow as high as 13 ft (4 metres). Relatively few herbs and flowers grow in these dense areas of scrub, although flowers can often be found along their outer reaches. The sclerophyllous scrub on Cyprus contains fewer species than that in the west and central Mediterranean. The mastic shrub (*Pistacia lentiscus*) is very common, as are the turpentine tree *(Pistacia terebinthus)* and the strawberry tree *(Arbutus andrachne)*. These bushes are rather grey and drab in appearance, but when the broom *(Genista spacelata)* is in bloom the slopes are a magnificent yellow.

The kermes oak *(Quercus coccifera)* and the buckthorn *(Rhamnus oleoides)* are also well-represented on Cyprus. The landscape is lent more colour by the various types of rock rose *(Cistus monspeliensis, salviifolius* and *villosus var. creticus)*. Wherever areas of grass occur in sclerophyllous scrubland it is worth looking for herbs and flowers, even

thin strips separate the terraces in the vineyards, and fill the small, dry valleys. It also covers the hills to the northwest of the island, creating a bleak-looking landscape with just the odd tree here and there, interspersed by small meadows filled with flowers, and small vineyards.

Rock rose bushes grow all over the dry, sun-soaked hills and mountains, up to an altitude of 5,500 ft (1,700 metres). They are impressively colourful in the springtime, when their red blossoms cover large areas. The most noticeable variety is the yellow Parasit *Cytisus hypocistus*. Slopes covered with rock roses can be found high in the Kyrenia range.

when the soil has the appearance of rock or rubble. Nearly every area reveals a different collection of species: numerous monocotyledons of the Allium, Gagea, Lloydia, iris and, of course, the orchid families can be found alongside carnations, buttercups, crucifers and papilionaceous plants.

Sclerophyllous scrub covers hilly areas all over the island. It is particularly impressive in the limestone hills around Lefkara; grey, very dry and bleak, dotted with a few oak trees, it stretches above the green fields and shiny white areas of chalk. Much of this scrub can also be found in the limestone mountains south of the Troodos range; here,

The orchids of Cyprus: Cyprus is a must for all orchid fans. However, at least two if not three trips to the island are necessary to gain more than just a superficial impression of the sheer variety of orchids here. So far, 44 different species and subspecies have been discovered, as well as numerous hybrids, most of them belonging to the family of insect orchids (*Epipactis*). They are mainly found growing on the northern slopes of the Kyrenia range, as well as in the limestone mountains to the south. Some species which have managed to adjust to the landscape and soil can be found in the Troodos mountains. In contrast, a north-south stretch of the

Mesaoria Plain around 18 miles (30 km) long, between Morphou and Famagusta, is almost free of orchids.

Most of Cyprus's orchids also grow in Anatolia, and some grow further west, in Greece, but only a few of the orchids of Cyprus grow in Central Europe; examples include the pyramid orchid *(Anacamptis pyramidalis)*, the cephalanthera *(cephalanthera rubra)*, the small-leafed helleborine *(Epipactis microphylla)*, the bee orchid *(Ophrys apifera)*, the buffoon orchid *(Orchis simia)* and ladies' tresses *(Spiranthes spiralis)*. Endemic varieties which make a trip to Cyprus so worthwhile for orchid-lovers include the insect orchid family, so named because their flowers resemble insects; tactile stimuli by the hairs on the lip operate on the sensory organs of visiting male bees or wasps.

The finest specimens are Bornmüller's insect orchid, which grows in the bushy meadows along the north coast, the Elegant insect orchid, which can be found in the pine forests of the Kyrenia mountains, and Kotschy's insect orchid, with its fascinating black-purple-white labella.

As far as other orchids are concerned, the Anatolian orchid, with its whitish-violet flowers, and the rather inconspicuous Bug orchid also deserve mention; there is also the very rare Dotted orchid with its red-and-yellow flowers. In the Troodos massif, one finds the Cephalanthera, the small-leafed Iberian orchid and Holmboe's wood hyacinth, as well as representatives of the Helleborine family.

For the fauna: One soon notices that Cyprus, unlike Greece, has fewer sheep and goats, a lack which minimises the devastating effect these animals have on plant life. Donkeys can be found everywhere, and oxen still pull very primitive-looking ploughs and harrows. Wild mammals, in contrast, are exceptionally rare. The most interesting specimen here is the *agrino*, a species of wild sheep related to the mouflon, which now has a good chance of being saved from extinction thanks to its strict protection in outdoor enclosures at Stavros tis Psokas and on the western foothills of the Troodos mountains.

Bird life on the island is more varied and interesting. Over 300 different species have been counted, most of them migratory birds that break their journey on the salt lakes to the south. Here, in winter and in spring, one can observe numerous flamingoes, herons, spoonbills, geese and several species of duck. In winter several northern species visit the island, including pigeons, water wagtails, blackbirds, larks and finches.

Among the birds who hatch their eggs here are the rock rose warbler, the Cyprus warbler, various whitethroats, the blackthroat, the blue rock thrush, the blackbird, the great titmouse, the coal tit, the wren, the corn bunting and, of course, the common house sparrow. In the Kyrenia range one continually sees griffon-vultures circling, and the

mountainous areas also contain hawk eagles, peregrine falcons and kestrels.

The fact that the island is a paradise for lizards and snakes becomes readily apparent when one is crossing meadows and mountain slopes off the beaten track. In spring, when shooting herbs and grasses have begun to provide the necessary protection, it is advisable to tread cautiously.

Mating lizards and snakes basking in the sunshine are frequent sights. Unfortunately, the creatures are far more frightened of people than people are of them, and often disappear so rapidly that it is difficult to identify them properly.

__Left__, spring is the most beautiful time in Cyprus. __Right__, agaves blooming at the beach.

Cyprus is characterised by the striking differences between ancient traditions and fast-moving, Western-influenced developments. On the one hand, archetypal Mediterranean landscapes with mountain villages and isolated forest areas; on the other, brand-new farms employing modern methods of agriculture and cosmopolitan cities with seemingly endless suburbs. Sometimes tradition and modernity coexist: not far from the hyper-modern blocks of flats in the city of Nicosia, for example, are the tranquil labyrinths of the old city, full of mysterious impasses.

Some of the island's legendary sites have been victims of earthquakes and art thieves, and their extant remains are thus modest. Yet there are still many spectacular sights, in particular the Byzantine churches and monasteries in the Troodos, with their wealth of frescoes and icons, the splendid Roman mosaics in Nea Paphos and, in the north, the ruins of the Hellenistic-Roman city of Salamis and the Gothic abbey of Bellapais, captured so memorably by Lawrence Durrell's *Bitter Lemons*.

The places section of this guide begins with Limassol, a popular tourist destination and convenient springboard for visiting Kolossi and Kourion, proceeds to Larnaca (ancient Citium) and moves on to the burgeoning resort of Ayia Napa on Cape Greco. It then crosses to the southwest of the island, where Paphos offers the best of archaeological Cyprus, and thence to the island's wilder fringes, such as Polis, and into the Troodos mountains. Lastly, from the divided capital of Nicosia, it hops into northern Cyprus.

Those who want to travel to the north should take into account the political difficulties. The Cypriot population is unable to cross the demarcation line between the two territories, and tourists can only do so subject to considerable restrictions. Normally, tourists are given permission to make only a day trip from Nicosia to the Turkish-occupied part of the island. It is therefore assumed that your journey is of this type, and alternative tours, embracing the main sites, have been devised. Entering northern Cyprus via Turkey is against the regulations of the Government of the Republic of Cyprus and travellers who do so are forbidden from crossing into the south.

Preceding pages: the Petra tou Romiou, mythical birthplace of Aphrodite; on the road in southwest Cyprus; Prophios Elias church, Protaras. **Left**, the harbour at Paphos.

Cyprus

12 km / 7.5 miles

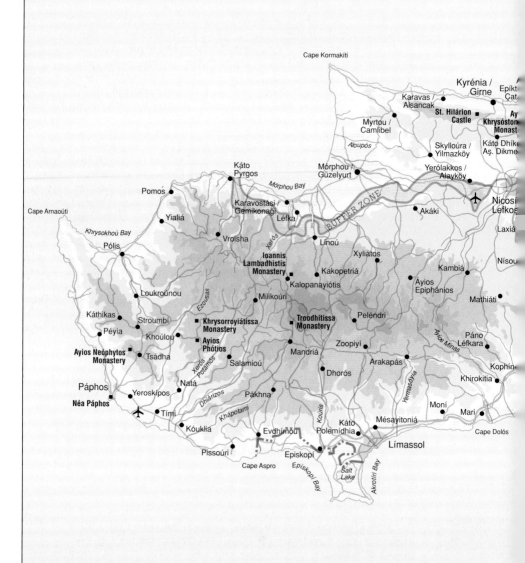

Mediterranean Sea

Cape Kormakíti

Kyrénia / Girne

Epíkt
Çat

Karavas / Alsancak

St. Hilárion Castle

Ay
Khrysóston
Monast

Myrtou / Camlibel

Skylloúra / Yilmazköy

Káto Dhík
Aş. Dikme

Alupós

Káto Pyrgos

Mórphou / Güzelyurt

Yerólakkos / Alayköy

Pomós

Karavostási / Gemikonaği

Mórphou Bay

Akáki

BUFFER ZONE

Nicosi
Lefkoş

Cape Arnaoúti

Yialiá

Léfka

Laxiá

Khrysokhoú Bay

Vroísha

Xerós

Linoú

Xyliátos

Kambiá

Nísou

Pólis

Ioannis
Lambadhistis
Monastery

Kakopetriá

 Áyios
Epiphánios

Loukroúnou

Ezoúsas

Milikoúri

Kalopanayiótis

Mathiáti

Káthikas

Stroumbí

Khrysorroyiátissa
Monastery

Troodhítissa
Monastery

Peléndri

Ayos Minas

Páno
Léfkara

Péyia

Khoúlou

Ayios
Phótios

Zoopiyí

Ayios Neóphytos
Monastery

Tsádha

*Xerós
Potamós*

Salamioú

Mandriá

Arakapás

Kophín

Dhorós

Yermasóyia

Khirokitia

Páphos

Yeroskípos

Natá

Dhiárizos

Pákhna

Kouris

Moní

Mari

Néa Páphos

Timí

Khápotami

Káto
Polemídhia

Mésayitoniá

Cape Dolós

Kóuklia

Evdhímou

Límassol

Pissoúri

Episkopí

Episkopí Bay

Akrotíri Bay

Cape Aspro

Salt
Lake

148

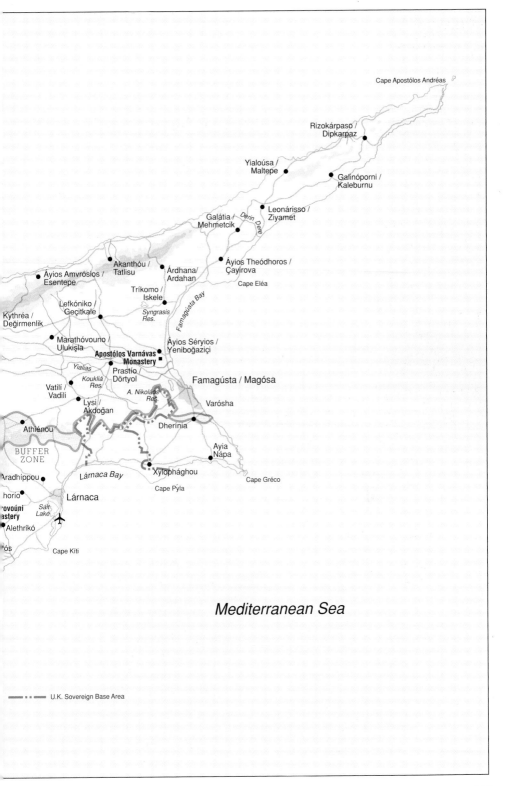

Cape Apostólos Andréas

Rizokárpaso /
Dipkarpaz

Yialoúsa /
Maltepe

Galinóporni /
Kaleburnu

Leonárisso /
Ziyamét

Galátia /
Mehmetcik

Derin Dere

Áyios Theódhoros /
Çayirova

Akanthóu /
Tatlisu

Árdhana/
Ardahan

Cape Eléa

Áyios Amvrósios /
Esentepe

Tríkomo /
Iskele

Syngrasis
Res.

Famagústa Bay

Kythréa /
Değirmenlik

Lefkóniko /
Geçitkale

Marathóvouno /
Ulukişla

Áyios Séryios /
Yeniboğaziçi

Apostólos Varnávas
Monastery

Yialías

Prastio /
Dörtyol

Famagústa / Magósa

Kouklia
Res.

Vatilí /
Vadili

A. Nikoláos
Res.

Varósha

Lýsi /
Akdoğan

Athiénou

Dherínia

Ayia
Nápa

BUFFER
ZONE

Aradhippou

Lárnaca Bay

Xylophághou

Cape Gréco

horío

Cape Pýla

rovoúni
astery

Salt
Lake

Lárnaca

Alethrikó

ós

Cape Kíti

Mediterranean Sea

▬ ▪ ▬ U.K. Sovereign Base Area

LIMASSOL

Limassol, on Cyprus's south coast, has experienced drastic changes as a result of the Turkish invasion of the island in 1974. Virtually all the Turkish inhabitants, who had made up a significant part of the city's population until then, left. Nevertheless, the influx of roughly 45,000 Greek Cypriot refugees from the north of the island led to a near doubling of the city's population, which in 1960 had numbered just 43,600.

Because the Turkish-occupied city of Famagusta lost its position as the island's main port, Limassol took over the role. As a result, the city known to the Greek population as *Lemesos* is now the second largest in Cyprus after Nicosia, with some 120,000 inhabitants, and has turned into an important trading centre. Its newly-built districts now cover the area beyond Makarios III Avenue, which was originally built as a by-pass for the city.

The English soldiers, who are stationed at the military bases on the Akrotiri peninsula to the west of Limassol, and who prefer to spend their free time in the nearby port, are as characteristic of Limassol as the locals who have made their living from trading since time immemorial. Nowadays the export of fruit and vegetables is the most significant branch of the local economy.

In the area around Limassol there are extensive **citrus fruit plantations** of lemon, orange and grapefruit trees. Moreover, KEO, to the west of the city between Franklin-Roosevelt Street and the coast, has established itself as Cyprus's largest manufacturer of alcoholic products. The firm's complex comprises a brewery, wine cellars, and a distillery for schnapps; it is possible to make a tour of the factory during normal shopping hours. Wine-growing has a long tradition; the most important vineyards stretch along the slopes of the Troodos mountains, interspersed with nut bushes and plantations of cherry, apple, pear and peach trees.

Every year, in September, Limassol is the scene of a **wine festival**, whose celebrations even outdo the local spring carnival. The **Arts Festival** in July completes the varied cultural calendar, which is increasingly orientated towards the growing tourist trade.

Every third visitor to Cyprus now spends his time relaxing on the extensive beaches of the **Bay of Amathus**, the "riviera" of Limassol. The approach road from Larnaca is lined solidly with hotels, broken only by restaurants and night-clubs. Limassol has not only taken over Famagusta's role as the main port on the island but also its position as the leading tourist centre.

One of Limassol's fastest-growing communities comprises refugees from the Lebanon, who more often than not belong to the more well-to-do sections of the population. Their business acumen has enabled them to move away from Beirut and set themselves up in Limassol and the capital, Nicosia.

As a result, new business centres and industrial estates have sprung up, actively helped by the government of Cy-

Left, alms-seeker outside a Limassol mosque. **Right**, reminder of the once substantial Turkish population.

prus with tax concessions and ongoing improvements in the infrastructure. Amongst the new ventures are numerous banks – not the usual massive skyscrapers, but buildings which blend discreetly with the surrounding cityscape. Amman is the only other city which has been able to benefit to the same extent from the conflict in Lebanon; Jordan and Cyprus compete to inherit Lebanon's reputation as the "Switzerland of the Near East".

Ancient history: Archaeologists are not able to give a definitive account of the origins of Limassol, not least because of the modern superstructures which have been built over the ancient remains. Various tombs from the Early and Middle Bronze Ages, whose burial gifts – mainly ceramics – can be dated to the end of the 3rd century BC or to the 2nd century BC, are proof that there were settlements in the city around this time (the discoveries are displayed in the local museum).

In the suburb of Ayia Phyla, which lies to the northwest of Limassol, a cemetery was discovered from the Late Bronze Age (around 1300 BC). It has been proved that the ancient coastal settlement of Nemesos, or Lemesos, was situated here, which gave its name to the modern city. At that time, however, the settlement was in the shadow of the more important nearby coastal cities of Amathus (today Amathous to the east of Limassol) and Kourion (further west on the other side of the Akrotiri peninsula), and so played only a minor role.

After a number of severe earthquakes in the post-Christian Byzantine era, the rebuilding of the area under Emperor Theodosius II (AD 408–50) was concentrated on the area of present-day Limassol, to the detriment of the previously more significant settlement at Amathus. The port of Theodosias, named after its builder, was founded anew in the wide bay. In the following period Theodosias was also the see of the bishops, the most significant of whom was Leontius (AD 590–668).

During the Third Crusades King

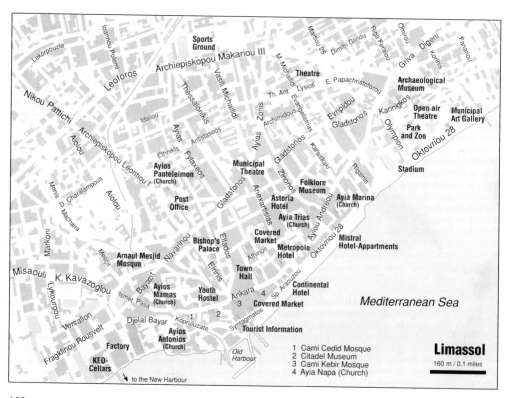

Richard the Lionheart, on his way to the Holy Land, chose Limassol as a landing place for his army and a base for conquering Cyprus. He was also able to free his betrothed, Berengaria of Navarre, from the hands of the Byzantine sovereign, Isaac Comnenos, who had captured the lady when her ship was stranded off the coast of Cyprus. The marriage of Richard and Berengaria took place in the citadel of Limassol, and the Spanish noblewoman was thereby crowned Queen of England.

Before the bridegroom continued his journey to the Holy Land – where, along with Philip II of France, he succeeded in capturing the city of Acre – he sold the island of Cyprus to the crusading Order of the Knights Templar, who subsequently handed it over to Guy de Lusignan.

In the following period the city was fortified, and continued to serve the crusaders as an important base from which they could fend off attacks from the Saracens. It also provided accommodation for the Hohenstaufen emperor

Frederick II, both on his way to the Holy Land in 1228 and on his return in the following year. The Lusignans and the Knights Templar contributed to the economic upturn in the city, as did the Order of the Knights of St John of Jerusalem (the "Hospitallers") later. In 1303 the last Grand Master of the Templars, Jacques de Molay, took his leave from the city, having been ordered back to France by Pope Clement V, where he was burned at the stake six years later.

Limassol itself wasn't always the centre of power: during certain periods this role was enjoyed by the fortress of **Kolossi**, which dominated the Episkopi Plain in the western hinterland of the city. King Hugo I, a member of the Lusignan nobility, handed the fortress over to the Knights Hospitaller during the 13th century.

This area was economically important for a long time as a result of its cane sugar plantations. *Zucchari de Cipro* appeared on European trading documents as long ago as the beginning of the 14th century. Nowadays it is the

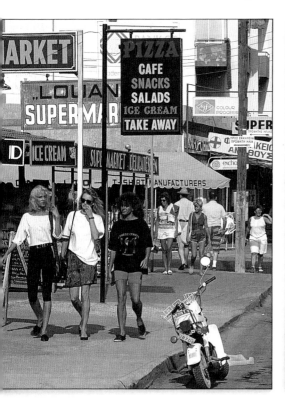

large citrus fruit plantations, known as *Fasouri*, which shape the appearance of the landscape and form the economic backbone of the region.

On the way from Limassol to the castle of Kolossi, west of the famous bathing beach known as **Lady's Mile**, the road crosses the plantations. The cypress avenues which line the journey form the border of the cultivated areas, and provide protection against the wind for the delicate orange and lemon trees. It is hard to imagine that this flourishing region experienced a rapid decline from the Late Middle Ages onwards. Having suffered many severe earthquakes, Limassol was set on fire by the Genoese in 1371 and plundered by Egyptian naval units in the first half of the 15th century. What was left was then destroyed by the Ottoman Turks in 1539.

As early as 1480 the oriental traveller Felix Faber was complaining about the deplorable state of the city. The only building of any consequence left was a single church, and that was virtually ruined (even here the bells had been stolen). The increasing decline of the city and its citadels was described by a succession of European visitors who followed in his tracks.

There were already tensions between the established Greek population and the Turkish-Ottoman newcomers. One traveller who saw Limassol soon after the devastating earthquake of 1584 reported that the entrances to the modest dwellings of the Greeks were so low that you had to bend down to enter them. Their purpose was to prevent the Turkish knights from using them as stables for their horses. As late as 1815 an English traveller described Limassol as a run-down settlement of 150 mud houses, in which the proportion of Greeks to Turks was 2 to 1.

The city's only importance at that time was based on the shipping of wine. In 1881 Limassol had over 6,000 inhabitants. When the export of wine was increased considerably towards the end of the 19th century, and the rebuilding of the harbour had been finished, the city quickly recovered its former pros- **The central market hall.**

perity. The capacity of the old harbour was soon no longer sufficient, and a new complex was built to the southwest of the city, complete with fire-fighting equipment and ship-repair yards.

The coastal road, with its four lanes and green central reservation, starts from the old harbour and runs to the north. The first section is **Spyrou Arouzou** (the Tourist Information Office can be found at number 27). From then on the street is officially known as **October 28th Street**, after the Greek national holiday. Hotels and restaurants serving fresh fish are sprinkled between shops and residential buildings, along with bars and English-style pubs.

Just a little way from the road to the north of the old harbour (but hidden from the road itself) is the **citadel**, in the middle of a small fenced-off area. This now serves as a museum. On the way there from the coast, you pass a small roundabout, near which is a **reptile museum**, run by an immigrant from Pakistan, and an excellent fish taverna, reputed to be the oldest and most tradi-

tional in the whole city. Outside, two live pelicans attract the attention of potential customers. Those of a squeamish disposition should avoid visiting the snake terrarium shortly before the close (7pm), when the animals are fed with small rodents.

The citadel: At the beginning of the 14th century the citadel was built on the ruins of the Byzantine castle. Part of the eastern wall of the castle was still standing and was integrated into the western wall of the citadel. The marriage of Richard the Lionheart and Berengaria took place in the chapel of the Byzantine castle, followed by the coronation of Berengaria as Queen of England by the Bishop of Evreux. Guests at the festivities included representatives from the most important crusader states of the Near East, such as Bohemund from Antioch and Raymond from Tripoli, along with Guy de Lusignan, later to be Lord of Cyprus. From 1291 the Byzantine castle served as the headquarters of the Knights Templar until this Order was banned in 1308.

Night-life on the "Strip".

King Janus (1389–1432) handed the citadel to the Knights of St John of Jerusalem, who had made their headquarters in the castle of Kolossi. Nevertheless they carried out further renovations to the castle of Limassol. After 1570 the Turks moved into the castle and totally rearranged the internal layout (the Great Hall had already fallen in after one of the supporting pillars had collapsed in 1525). Up to 1940 the citadel served as a prison for the British colonial administration, and for a while as an army headquarters. Extensive restoration followed in 1950, including the reinforcement of the vaults.

With the Turkish invasion and the division of the island, the Medieval Museum in Nicosia lay right on the border between the Greek and Turkish halves of the city. As a result the exhibits were moved, with the financial support of the Amathus Ltd shipping company, to the citadel at Limassol and since then have been housed in the new **Cyprus Medieval Museum**.

The entrance of the castle leads into a small ante-room. From here you can enter the lower-lying, almost quadratic Gothic Great Hall to the right. On the left-hand side, spread over two floors, there is a group of smaller rooms, which can be reached via a central corridor. These rooms house various objects from the Byzantine and medieval history of Cyprus.

The most spectacular exhibits are the three silver plates discovered among the famous "Lambousa Treasure" in 1902. Unfortunately a further six from the same collection were smuggled abroad and can now be found in the Metropolitan Museum in New York. The plates, which date back to AD 620, show scenes from the youth of King David. They were discovered in the ancient town of Lapithos, which now lies on the north coast of Cyprus, in the half of the island now under Turkish occupation.

From both the Great Hall, and from the smaller rooms on the left, there are steps leading up to the roof of the citadel. From here there is a good view over **The citadel.**

the port and, above all, over the old city. The two minarets, which tower over the city, provide a lasting reminder that a significant Turkish population once lived in Limassol.

After visiting the citadel you can walk between the two mosques, the **Djami Kebir** ("the large mosque") in the east and the **Köprülü Haci Ibrahim Aga Camii** in the west, and appreciate the typical Turkish architecture of the area, notably the pronounced oriels on the first floors which lean over the street. On some of the houses you can still see Turkish inscriptions, and the further west you go, the more often you come across Turkish street names: Agiou-Andreou Street joins Ankara Street, which at its western end fans out into a mass of small Emirs and Pasas. Here the Köprülü Haci Ibrahim Aga Mosque towers above the river bed of the Garyllis – invariably bone dry.

In the immediate neighbourhood of the Djami Kebir there is a **Turkish bath**, and, just a little further east, the **Ayia Napa church**, consecrated with St Veronica's veil (offered to Christ on his way to the Crucifixion), rises up between the promenade and Agiou-Andreou Street. The present-day church was built in 1903, and a series of icons have been preserved from its early 18th-century predecessor.

The Episcopal **church** and its neighbouring **Bishop's Palace** can be reached via Eirinis Street, which begins at the citadel, crosses Ankara Street and then runs further north. Two turnings further to the east lead to the **covered market**, where fruit, vegetables, meat, and poultry are on sale.

If you follow Agiou-Andreou Street to the north away from the coastline you can make a short detour to the right, to the **Holy Trinity church** (**Ayia Trias/ Hagia Triados**), which can be easily seen from the road. Going back to the turn-off and continuing along Agiou-Andreou Street, leads to a corner house (number 253) standing alone on the left-hand side at the junction of Othonos Street and Amalias Street. Since 1985 this has housed the Folk Art Museum, where agricultural implements and tra-ditional furnishings, ceramics and textiles are on display.

A little further along, on the same side of the street, is the **Cultural Centre**, with rooms for art exhibitions and a library. If you turn into Kanigkos Street at the top end of Agiou-Andreou Street, you reach the northern edge of the **Public Gardens**, which contain an open-air stage and a zoo.

The garden area to the north houses the **District Archaeological Museum**, set up in 1975. Most of the exhibits here are from the discoveries at Kourion and Amathus, along with a number from other sites in the region around Limassol. The exhibitions are organised thematically and chronologically: the first display case documents the history of Cypriot ceramics. Other interesting items include terracotta figures. The larger sculptures nearby reveal both Greek and Egyptian influences, the latter being most obvious in the monumental and ornately decorated capital from Amathus which bears the unmistakable cow-head of the Egyptian goddess Hathor.

The tombs of the citadel's past occupants.

KOLOSSI

About 9 miles (15 km) west of Limassol the **castle of Kolossi of the Order of St John** rises up above the fertile landscape of the plain of Episkopi. Its walls contain not only a fortified tower with living quarters but also a sugar-processing factory for the cane sugar which was grown in the area at the time. The countryside surrounding Limassol was given to the Order of St John by Hugo I (1205–18); in return he received their support in battles against the Moslems.

When the Christians lost Syria to the Arabs following their defeat at Acre in 1291, the Order of St John chose Cyprus as their headquarters. They stayed here until 1310, at which point they founded their own state on Rhodes, where they remained until driven out by the Turks in 1522 and forced to flee to Malta.

On Cyprus they had to compete with the Knights Templar for possession of the castle of Kolossi. It was only after the Templars were banned by the Pope in 1308 that the Knights of St John were able to take proper possession of the castle. In fact they received not only the castle itself but also 60 neighbouring villages, their property and their serfs.

Along with oil, wheat and cotton, the main products were wine and cane sugar. The **Hall of the Sugar Factory** – near the aqueduct used for transporting the water necessary to production – has survived until today. A mill stone with a diameter of 11 ft (3.2 metres), used to press out the juice, also still exists.

The Knight von Gumppenberg mentioned the place in his *Pilgrim's Travels*: "We rode to a house, that of the Knights of St John, and sugar grows there and the house is called Koloss."

But Kolossi was not alone in being a sugar-producing area. There was stiff competition from nearby Episkopi, in the form of the Venetian noble family, the Cornaro. As various historical documents prove, there were continual disputes between the two families over the rights to use the water in the region. In

Hall of the Sugar Factory

the end, Catarina Cornaro, widow of the last king of Cyprus before the island was taken over by the Venetians in 1489, dispossessed the Knights of St John and took possession of the castle and its factory. Moreover her nephew, the Cardinal Marco Cornaro, was then appointed Commander of the Order of St John. An inscription from 1591, which Murad, Pasha of Cyprus at the time, had carved in the south wall, is evidence that the Ottomans, who had conquered the island some 20 years before, carried on this lucrative industry.

Near the sugar factory is the **fortified tower** with its three floors. It rises from a quadratic ground plan whose sides measure 52 ft (16 metres). Its present structure was built in 1454 on the remains of a previous building dating from the time of the crusades. The semi-circular foundations of the original building and a well on the east side of the fortified tower have survived.

A group of coats of arms has been chiselled into the east wall within a cross-shaped frame. In the middle, directly under a crown, is the royal coat of arms divided into four parts and comprising the emblems of the Kingdom of Jerusalem, the Lusignans, the Kingdom of Cyprus and Armenia. This royal coat of arms is flanked by that of the Grand Masters of the Order, Jean de Lastic (left) and Jacques de Milli (right). In the lower arm of the cross is the emblem of Louis de Magnac, one-time Grand Commander of Cyprus and believed to have commissioned the building of the new fortified tower.

At that time, this *donjon* could only be entered via a drawbridge leading to the first floor. After going through a further entrance gate, at one time protected with a machicolation, visitors proceed to a kitchen, with an open fire, and a day-room with paintings of scenes from the crusades. These paintings can be dated from the coat of arms of Louis de Magnac. A spiral staircase leads up to the second floor and two living rooms, one of which has a fireplace (the same coat of arms can be seen on the chimney). The staircase leads up to the roof. Going down instead of up, visitors proceed to three vaulted chambers in the basement, two of which have wells.

Kolossi lies at the northern end of the Akrotiri peninsula. Crossing the peninsula in the direction of the coast to the south, you come to the basin of a **large salt lake**, which is usually dried out. Whole colonies of flamingos can occasionally be seen here, and migrating birds also use the area as a stop-over en route to and from Africa. In contrast to the salt lake near Larnaca, however, no salt is extracted here.

In the immediate neighbourhood there is a British military airport – photography is strictly forbidden – and the small village of **Akrotiri**, which gave its name to the peninsula. On the edge of the village is a modern monastery which has replaced the abandoned monastery of St Nicholas of the Cats, to the eastern edge of the military airport. The eastern tip of the Akrotiri peninsula, "Cape Akrotiri" (Cap Gata), also takes its name from the felines which the monks in the old monastery employed to defend them against snakes.

The castle of Kolossi.

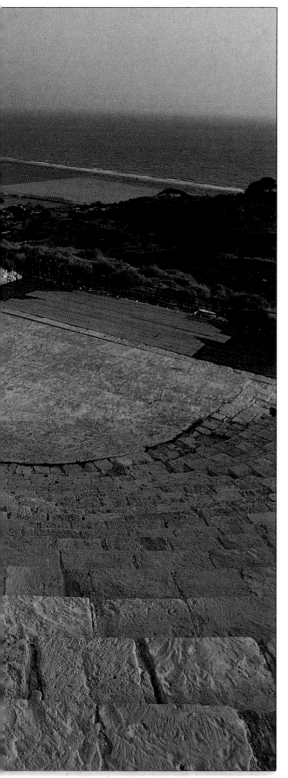

KOURION

If you want to go from Limassol to visit the impressive ruins of Kourion (*Curium* in Latin), which stand in solitary splendour on a massive rock ledge 230 ft (70 metres) above the sea, take one of the public buses which leave the fortress in Limassol throughout the day. What you see on arrival, however, dates only from the Hellenistic, Roman and Early Christian times: the relics of the pre-Hellenistic capital of the local kingdom of Kourion have still to be discovered.

What we know about this period comes from the writings of Herodotus. According to him, the victory of the Persian invaders during the Persian wars in 497 BC, following the suppression of the Ionian rebellion by the Persians, was only made possible by the cowardly retreat of Stasanor, the city-king of Kourion. As a result, Pasicrates, the last king of Kourion, supported Alexander the Great as naval leader in the fight against the Persians during the siege and storming of Tyre from a position off the Lebanese coast.

During the period of the Roman Empire, the city flourished both economically and as a place of worship for Apollo, something which soon gave way to Christianity as the basilica – built in the 4th century after a severe earthquake – eloquently testifies. When the bishop's residence was moved to neighbouring Episkopi in the 7th century, following the Arab invasions, Kourion lost its status and fell into decline.

Today the ruins of Kourion are spread across three areas. Coming from Limassol, you reach the most imposing of the sites first. A gravel path leaves the asphalt road to the left and offers an impressive view over the sea. Following the road up the mountain in the direction of Paphos, you reach the stadium on the right-hand side after half a mile or so. Unfortunately all that remains is an elongated, oval-shaped wall.

Preceding pages: Kourion's Early Christian basilica. **Left**, the spectacular theatre.

Near the stadium is a small basilica. Far more impressive are the ruins of the **Sanctuary of Apollo**, which are slightly off the asphalt road. A sign-post indicates the way.

You have to pay an entrance fee to visit each of the sites, with the exception of the stadium ruins. This means that, although you will already have passed the first of the villa ground plans (with its mosaic-decorated floor) on the left-hand side at the junction of the afore-mentioned gravel road, you have to drive or walk to the little ticket house before gaining access.

Once inside the fenced-off area, if you stay on the inner-side of the fencing, parallel to the approach road, you come to the **House with Wells**, whose water has now run dry, and then to the **House of the Gladiators**, named after its mosaics of armed warriors in action (the names of the villas are inlaid in mosaic). Finally, near the asphalt road, you come to a villa with a mosaic scene (4th-century) depicting the legend of Achilles: in order to prevent Achilles from entering the Trojan War, his mother, Thetis, dressed him in women's clothes and hid him among the daughters of King Lykomedes. However, Odysseus blew his cover by displaying a range of weapons alongside a selection of jewellery and watching Achilles's reaction. Another mosaic in the same villa, showing how Zeus, disguised as an eagle, kidnapped the young Ganymede, has been badly destroyed.

In the area next to these villas, on the same level as the ticket house, is an area where excavations, begun in 1975, are in progress. So far, a longitudinal **stoa** from Roman times has been uncovered, with accompanying rows of columns. The stoa measures 213 ft (65 metres) long and 15 ft (4.5 metres) wide and was built over part of an extensive Hellenistic house of unknown purpose. Parts of a **Roman agora** (market place) have also been dug out. This area can be easily recognised from the columns, whose shafts are not grooved vertically but fluted with winding threads.

Directly northwest of this area, ar-

Sanctuary of Apollo.

chaeologists came across a massive **cistern**, which once fed a nymphaeum measuring 148 ft (45 metres) long and 49 ft (15 metres) wide.

Just behind the little ticket house and restaurant are the remains of a monumental **Early Christian basilica**, thought to have been commissioned by Bishop Zeno, who represented the diocese of Kourion at the Council of Ephesus. The main part of the church had three aisles and the nave included a choir stall, set in front of the apse on a slightly raised level, and at one time separated by a choir screen. On both sides of the aisles you can still see long halls, the so-called *catechumena*.

The entrance hall (*narthex*) in the west, which lies sideways, stretches across the total width of all five aisles. Going further west you come to the deacon's rooms, and the bishop's private rooms. Going north brings you to an **atrium court**, surrounded by columns, with a watertank in the middle and further rooms on three sides. The baptistery used to be on the eastern side.

Christian influence is evident in many of the mosaics.

Inscriptions and the remnants of the mosaic floor can still be seen.

At the southern end of the gravel path you come across the **theatre**, first built in the Hellenistic Period, but whose present size is the result of extensions made in Roman times (2nd century). Despite its size, it remains a rather modest building with just 3,500 seats (the theatre at Salamis can hold an astonishing 17,000 visitors). It was probably not restored by the Christians after the severe earthquake in AD 365 and so fell into decline.

Another complex of buildings worth visiting on account of the mosaics is the **annexe of Eustolios**, next to the theatre. The mosaics are thought to date from the 5th century. Fragmentary inscriptions refer to Eustolios (the builder), and Apollo (the former patron). Originally it was probably a Hellenistic private villa, which was converted into a public baths at the end of the 4th century. Christian influences can be seen in the floor mosaics: floral, geometric (e.g. cross-shaped ornaments) and animal

motifs rather than portraits of people; and one of the inscriptions in the floor mosaic makes it clear that the building did not need defensive features because it was already "surrounded by the most honourable symbols of Christ". The most important motif (in the **frigidarium**) – the bust of a woman holding a measuring rod in her hand, which according to the inscription represents *Ktisis*, the personification of the creation – also reveals the growing influence of Christian thought.

The long oval of the **stadium** (only foundations are extant), which lies between the areas described above and the Sanctuary of Apollo, covers some 750 ft (229 metres), of which the actual arena itself measures 610 ft (186 metres). The rest of the area was occupied by the seven rows of seats, which could accommodate a total of 6,000 visitors.

The **aqueduct pipeline**, which comes from the mountains and provided the city of Kourion with water, goes past the Sanctuary of Apollo and along the southern wall of the stadium. To the

west, a little way back, is the ground wall of an Early Christian basilica, dating from the end of the 5th century or the beginning of the 6th. According to archaeological discoveries, it was built to replace a heathen temple.

The hill is surmounted by the **Sanctuary of Apollo Hylates**, the protector of the woodland. The imported Greek god was merged with a long-established god of vegetation. Two gates, the Paphos and Kourion Gates, lead into the sacred area of this syncretistic deity, who was worshipped only in Cyprus. The passage to the latter is flanked by a bathing area and a square building with a courtyard in the middle (the *palaestra*). The south side of the trapezium-shaped courtyard, into which both gates lead, borders on five right-angled rooms, supported by columns and complete with stone seats.

From here a passage strikes north at a right-angle, past buildings which have a **stoa** in front. The passage is lined by two walled-in **worshipping areas** (so-called *temenoi*) and leads directly to the **Temple of Apollo** itself.

The smaller *temenos* on the eastern side has a small round altar in the middle. Excavations indicate that it was built as early as the 7th century BC. The middle of the larger *temenos* to the west is occupied by a showy circular monument, 59 ft (18 metres) in diameter, dedicated to the "protector of the trees". The whole complex was probably built in the 1st and 2nd centuries AD.

The area around the Temple of Apollo is believed to be the oldest settlement in Kourion, and is said to have been founded by Dorians from Argos in the Peloponnese.

The name of nearby **Episkopi** signifies that this village became the seat of residence of the bishop when the residence at Kourion was abandoned in the wake of the Arabian invasions. The village contains the **Kourion Museum**, containing selected finds from Kourion and its surrounding area, where evidence has been found of Early Stone Age settlements, such as Erimi and Sotira, and the Bronze Age settlement of Phaneromeni.

Left, admiring the Sanctuary of Apollo Hylates. Right, bathed in dawn light.

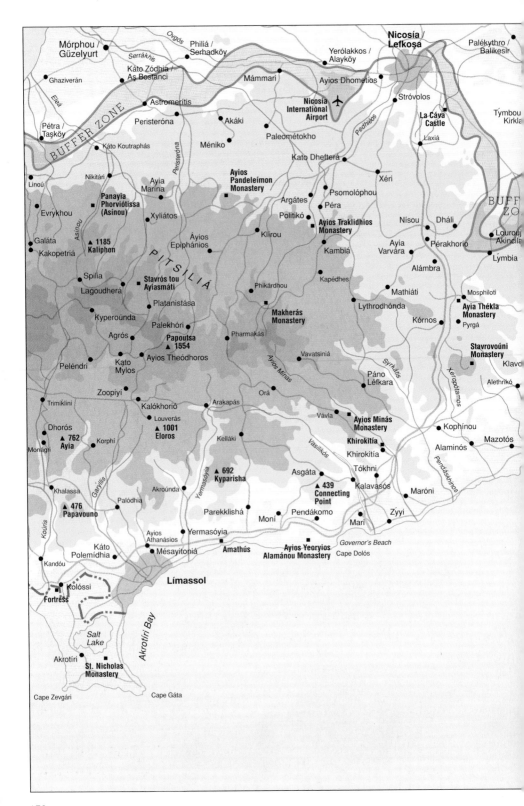

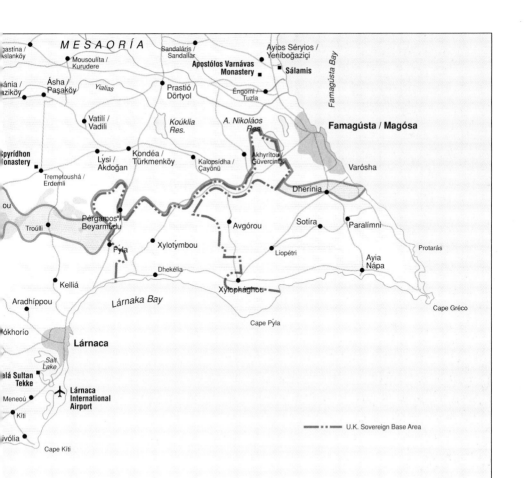

MESAORÍA

gastína /
aslanköy

Mousoulíta /
Kurudere

Sandaláris /
Sandallar

Ayios Séryios /
Yeniboğaziçi

Apostólos Varnávas
Monastery

Sálamis

Famagústa Bay

ánia /
azíköy

Ásha /
Paşaköy

Yialias

Prastió /
Dörtyol

Éngomi /
Tuzla

Vatilí /
Vadili

Koúklia
Res.

A. Nikoláos
Res.

Famagústa / Magósa

pyrídhon
onastery

Lýsi /
Akdoğan

Kondéa /
Türkmenköy

Kalopsídha /
Çayönü

Akhyrítou /
Güvercinlik

Varósha

Tremetoushá /
Erdemli

ou

Pérgamos /
Beyarmúdu

Dherínia

Troúlli

Avgórou

Sotíra

Paralímni

Protarás

Pýla

Xylotýmbou

Liopétri

Ayia
Nápa

Dhekélia

Kelliá

Xylophághou

Lárnaka Bay

Aradhíppou

Cape Pýla

Cape Gréco

ókhorío

Lárnaca

Salt
Lake

alá Sultan
Tekke

Lárnaca
International
Airport

Meneoú

Kíti

━ ━ ■ ━ ■ ■ ━ U.K. Sovereign Base Area

ivólia

Cape Kíti

Mediterranean Sea

Southern Cyprus

8 km / 5 miles

FROM LIMASSOL TO LARNACA

Considering the important role which **Amathus** played in the ancient world, both as a port and the seat of residence of the local kingdom, it is somewhat surprising that archaeologists didn't begin excavating the site until 1980. What has been uncovered so far, on the coast about 5 miles (8 km) east of Limassol, includes an Early Christian basilica, directly on the bumpy coastal road, and the ruins of a sanctuary to Aphrodite on the **Acropolis Hill**, rising behind the road.

Other parts of the lower city, which probably stretched from the foothills of the Acropolis Hill to the south as far as the coast, have still to be excavated. Parallel to a river bed in the west, are the remains of a wall which ran from the southwesterly edge of the Acropolis to the sea. On the other side of the wall, not far from the Amathus Beach Hotel, local archaeologists came across a burial ground from the Cypro-Archaic period. Remains of the old harbour site have been located under the sea.

According to legends recorded by Tacitus, the city was founded by Amathus, the son of Aerias, although Amathousa, mother of King Cinyras from Paphos, is also credited with giving her name to the city. For a time, it was an important trading base for the Phoenicians and during the Ionian rebellion it sided with the Persians. It remained an important port until the time of Richard the Lionheart, who destroyed it. The reason why the ruins give so little impression of the splendour of its ancient past is that, as so often in history, their stone served as building material for the projects of later eras – this time for the Suez Canal.

On the other side of the ruins of Amathus, a side street leads from the main road to Larnaca and Nicosia to the **monastery of St George**. The monastery was founded at the end of the 12th century, but its buildings, built into the side of the mountain, are more recent. Outside the monastery wall a stall offers a selection of icons hand-painted by the monks.

Prehistoric rotundas: The motorway from Limassol to Larnaca crosses an area believed to have been inhabited as early as the Early Stone Age; the rotundas, which are characteristic of this period, have been found in both the village of Kalavassos-Tenta and in the more famous Khirokitia, both of which lie just to the north of the motorway. The motorway also crosses the two Late Bronze Age cemeteries of **Agious and Ayios Dhimitrios**, near Kalavassos. In Ayios Dhimitrios two royal tombs have been discovered – including one belonging to a queen which contained gold-decorated grave goods.

The rotundas of **Khirokitia**, which measure up to 33 ft (10 metres) in diameter, are packed tightly together and stretch over a steep slope halfway between Limassol and Larnaca. They were discovered in 1936, but excavations were halted in 1939 and not restarted until 1975. They are continuing today. This settlement, probably the oldest on Cyp-

riot soil, dates from the 7th or 6th century BC.

Its location was probably selected for its defensive advantages; the Maroni river flows around the hill in a large loop, thereby providing extra protection. The proximity of the river also ensured that there was an adequate supply of water, and its detritus provided building materials for the lower layers of the rotundas. Only the carefully constructed foundations of the rotundas, measuring up to around 3 ft (1 metre) high, have survived. At one time lancet vaults made from air-dried tiles stood on top of them.

Equally conspicuous is a wall-like construction dissecting the settlement. The theory that this is the foundation of a paved way, designed to make the steep climb easier for the people and their animals, has not been confirmed. It seems more likely that the wall marks the extension of the settlement before it expanded. Its people lived from hunting, but also kept sheep, goats and pigs as pets, and carried out a modest amount of farming. Discoveries of the volcanic obsidian rock – not otherwise present on the island – provide proof of trading links with Asia Minor. The dead were buried either in lined graves under the floors of the houses, or outside the houses. The grave goods which accompanied them reveal the religious beliefs of the inhabitants. In the last phase of the settlement, 4th century BC, when the first metal objects (made of copper) made an appearance in graves, the people also produced ceramics with typical "comb" patterns. Most of the discoveries are in the Museum of Nicosia.

Villages and monasteries: If instead of returning from Khirokitia to the motorway you continue north along the approach road (not particularly well-made), you eventually climb up to the village of Favla (after about half an hour). It is not the village, but **Ayios Minas** (St Menas), the convent in the village, which is signposted. it was founded in the 15th century, but owes its present appearance to its rebuilding in 1740. The nuns sell icons, a popular

The remains of Amathus.

honey famous all over the island and grapes, grown in summer houses outside the convent's walls.

Beyond Favla the road meanders gently downhill, passing the picturesquely sited Kato Dhrys, believed to be the birthplace of the Cypriot national hero Neophytos (born in 1134), before joining an asphalt street which leads to the two villages of Lefkara, which are situated at around 1,970 ft (600 metres) above sea-level on the foothills of the Troodos Mountains.

Kato Lefkara is the smaller and lower-lying of the two villages. Most tourists, however, come to visit **Pano Lefkara**, usually to see and buy the elaborate cotton broderie anglaise lace which is produced here. In summer, the narrow streets between the quaint-looking stone houses with red-tiled roofs are open-air workshops, for the women of the village prefer to practise their craft out of doors. The local men sell their wives' filigree products, named *Lefkaritika* after the place of their production, all over the island and beyond.

The local tradition of embroidery is said to have been started by Frankish-Venetian noblewomen who came to spend their summers on Cyprus, and whiled away their time lace-making. Leonardo da Vinci is supposed to have admired their craft and bought an altar cloth for the cathedral in Milan when he visited the village in 1481. In the **House of Patsalos**, a small local museum has now been set up for lace and silver-work (for which the region is equally famous).

The Tou Timiou Stavrou (Holy Cross) church contains an exquisite silver cross, dating from the 13th century, which is the focal point of the annual Festival of the Holy Cross held each year on 13–14 September.

It is worth visiting **Kato Lefkara** to see the 12th-century mid-Byzantine frescoes in the **Archangel Michael church**. In 1865 a cache of sacred objects, including a bishop's mitre, was found in a hiding place under the floor; they date from 1222, when the bishop of Limassol was banished here.

The Monastery of Stavrovouni: A steep,

Bathing below the ruins.

winding asphalt road leads to the oldest monastery in Cyprus – the Stavrovouni monastery (the Mountain of the Cross) – at 2,192 ft (668 metres) above sea-level. Women are prohibited from entering the monastery, as indicated by the sign at the start of the ascent, where the monk Kallinikos paints and sells icons in a little hut. Photographic equipment has to be surrendered at the entrance to the monastery, and the taking of photos is also forbidden on the stretch of the approach road which borders on military territory.

By the last S-bend before reaching the monastery there is a small **chapel.** Beyond the monastery gate, a set of steep steps leads past the gardens to the monastic cells and the main church. Below and to the left of the fortified complex, is the **Constantine and Helena chapel**. This was constructed in the 17th and 18th centuries, virtually on the foundations of the main church which lies one level higher. You have to ask the monks for the key to this chapel.

The Empress Helena, mother of Constantine the Great, is regarded as the founder of the monastery. According to legend, she was stranded here in AD 327 on her way back from Jerusalem, and erected a cross made from cypress wood on the monastery hill. The cross was supposed to contain a nail from the cross of Jesus, and was therefore preserved as a relic. It is is said to have hung freely over the earth, without any form of suspension, until it was stolen by invading Mamelukes. Today a splinter of this cross is preserved in a silver cross in the church. The view on a clear day from the monastery hill to the Troodos mountains and over the extensive Mesaoria Plain to the Mediterranean is magnificent.

The Royal Chapel in Pyrga: It is possible to organise your journey from Larnaca to the Stavrovouni monastery so that you can also visit the Royal Chapel lying just outside the village of **Pyrga**. This small place of prayer, which is dedicated to St Catherine (Ayia Ekaterina) and was extensively restored in 1977, acquired its name when it was **Welcome to Stavrovouni.**

established that it was founded by the Latin king Janus (1398–1423) in 1421. The founder and his spouse, Charlotte of Bourbon, can be recognised on one of the wall-paintings (they are kneeling down on either side of the crucified Christ, and wearing crowns). In addition, the coat of arms of the House of Lusignan appears on the ribs of the vaulting. Other scenes, of Mary and the baby Jesus, the raising of Lazarus, the Last Supper, the washing of Christ's feet, and Christ's Ascension, are all easily recognised. Each scene is supported by inscriptions in old French, spoken in Cyprus at the time. Of the three doors which originally led into the little vaulted building, which had no apse, two were later walled in. On the lintel above the southern entrance is a representation of a wheel, the emblem of St Catherine.

About 4 miles (6 km) southeast of Pyrga on the way to Klavdhia you can see the ruins of a Cistercian monastery.

It is also worth making a detour to **Kornos**, just west of Pyrga and not far from the motorway. Kornos is a centre for ceramic production, in particular the large-size jars known as *pitharia* used for storing water.

In the village of **Kiti**, descendant of the ancient settlement of Kition, you can find the **Panayia Angeloktistos** church (literally "built by the angels"). From an Early Christian basilica, which once stood here, only the apse now remains, on to which a domed cruciform church was added in the 11th century – itself later rebuilt. Amazingly, the 6th-century mosaic decorations in the earlier apse have survived. They show the standing figure of Mary, with the baby Jesus on her arm, flanked by the two archangels, Michael and Gabriel. Although this motif dates from the time when the theological controversy about the worshipping of idols (the "iconoclastic controversy") had been settled, the style of the portrayal of the figures along the arch of the apse (first discovered in 1952) suggest that it came from an earlier period.

Later pictorial representations, such

as frescoes from the mid-18th century, can be found in the church of **Ayios Georgios of Arpera**, 1 mile (2 km) northeast of Kiti, not far from a dam on the river Tremithos. The church's founder, the Greek dragoman Christophakis, has immortalised both himself and his family here, in a picture over the northern portal.

Hala Sultan tekkesi: This *tékké* – the Turkish description for a Moslem monastery – lies within sight of the International Airport at Larnaca, on the southern shore of a large salt lake. The local holy woman is Umm Haram, reputed to have been an aunt of the Prophet Mohammed, on his father's side.

Accompanying her husband on the Arabian invasion of Cyprus in AD 674, she had such a bad fall from her mule that she broke her neck and died. Her tomb made the mosque (constructed over her burial place at a later date) an important place of pilgrimage for Moslems. Umm Haram is known reverently by the Turkish population as *hala sultan* ("great mother").

Another prominent tomb lies in a neighbouring room. Buried under an alabaster cenotaph with golden inscriptions is Chadija, the grandmother of King Hussein of Jordan. Chadija died in Cyprus in 1930. The picturesque mosque, situated in a palm grove and complete with fountains, owes its current appearance to the Turkish Governor of 1816.

In the salt lake, which borders the mosque to the east, you occasionally see whole colonies of flamingos and migrating birds, particularly in winter. Fortunately the birds remain unaffected by the salt-mining practised here – a state industry – as extraction is confined to the period from the middle of summer to the onset on the autumn rains. Then the fierce summer heat causes the water to evaporate and the level to fall so low that a salt-crust is left, which can be mined. The export of salt was already a flourishing business in the time of the Franks in the Middle Ages; nowadays it is carried out on a much more modest scale, supplying only the needs of the local population.

On the left, after a few hundred yards along the extension of the approach road from the airport to the *tékké*, is an enclosed area where archaeological excavations have been underway since 1972. A team of Swedish workers is uncovering the remains of a Middle and Late Bronze Age settlement, thought to have rivalled Kition in importance. Among the most interesting discoveries so far is a bathing area, otherwise unknown in Cyprus in this period, and Cypro-Minoan inscriptions.

In 1978 a treasure trove containing 23 objects of solid gold came to light. Some of these pieces – into which agate, carnelion and rock crystals had been intricately worked – show distinct Egyptian influences. Informative documentation of the archaeological findings is provided in the fort in Larnaca. According to this, the area was settled around 1600 BC and developed steadily until its abrupt destruction in the early 12th century BC, when it was swallowed up by the same severe earthquake which destroyed Enkomi and Kition.

Left, try the local transport – but expect traffic jams (**right**).

178

LARNACA

Larnaca, Cyprus's third-largest city after Nicosia and Limassol, became known by its current name around 1600. Its origins, however, can be traced back to pre-Christian times.

The important port of Kition (Citium in Latin, and Kittim in the Old Testament) is known to have occupied the same site, though extensive urban development has prevented archaeologists from uncovering more than a small part of Kition's remains. The ancient tombs which were found here seem to be the source of the city's modern name: Larnaca comes from *larnax*, a Greek word for sarcophagus. During the period of Frankish rule, when the salt mines in the large salt lake to the west of the port were its main source of industry, the town was known as "Salines" or "Salina".

Today oil is the city's main export product. Being the second-largest port on the island, Larnaca is an important berth for tankers. In addition, there are regular ferry crossings to the Lebanon. Larnaca is also popular with yacht owners on account of its relatively cheap charges for winter mooring.

The city reached its peak under Ottoman rule in the middle of the 19th century. Although Nicosia was the capital, most of the consulates and embassies were based in Larnaca, along with representatives of foreign trading companies. With 13,000 inhabitants, Larnaca was even larger than the capital for a short period. Reminders of that period are the two arches on the arterial road to Limassol. They originally formed part of an aqueduct built between 1746 and 1750 by the Ottoman governor. This 6-mile (10-km) pipeline, fed by a number of springs not far from the river Tremithus, supplied water to Larnaca until 1939.

The Turkish invasion of 1974 brought profound changes to the city. The international airport was moved from Nicosia to Larnaca, and thousands of Greeks arrived, fleeing from the oc-cupied north of the island. Despite the migration of the city's Turkish people in the opposite direction, the net effect was to treble the population of Larnaca, bringing it to 60,000. Before the division of the island the Turkish communities had settled mainly in the coastal areas in the southern parts of the city, as the street names here testify. The fort marked the northern boundary of this area. Opposite the fort, you can still see the **Djami Kebir**, the "large mosque", which had previously been a Latin Holy Cross church.

The city's main thoroughfare is the wide coastal road (known at its beginning as Leoforos Athinon Street, and further up as Ankara Street), which stretches southwards from the port and the marina to the fortress. Parallel to the coastal road is an inviting (but usually crowded) sandy beach. Also here, standing on a plinth, is a marble bust of the Athenian commander Kimon, who, in 450–449 BC, tried to regain Cyprus for the Greeks. He died on the island during his campaign.

The southern end of the beach and the promenade is marked by a small **Turkish fort**. According to inscriptions above the entrance, this fort was constructed in 1605. Much later, during the period of British rule, prisoners were interned here. In one of the buildings there is a small **museum**, whose exhibits include documentation on the Swedish excavations from Hala Sultan tékké. The inner courtyard of the fortress sometimes serves as an open-air theatre.

If you make your way to the north of the fort, away from the coastal road and towards the centre of the city, you will come to the **church of Lazarus (Ayios Lazarus)** after a few hundred yards. The extension of this street past the church to the west leads to **Faneromeni church**, built in 1907 (its two ancient stone graves are likely to interest only real fanatics of antiquity).

In the former, the Lazarus whom Christ resurrected from the dead is supposed to be buried in an accessible crypt to the right of the main altar. After the miracle, the resurrected Lazarus is said to have travelled to Cyprus where he was ordained as bishop by St Barnabas, an office which he is claimed to have held for 30 years.

Icons of the saint are carried through the streets in an annual procession on the Sunday before Easter. The sacred building over the tomb, a multi-domed mid-Byzantine church, was founded by Emperor Leo VI (AD 886–912), following the discovery, in 890, of a stone sarcophagus bearing the name "Lazarus". The relics of the saint were immediately transported to the capital, Constantinople. From there, in 1204, they were taken by plundering crusaders to Marseille, a town which also claims Lazarus as a former bishop.

After the Ottoman conquest of Cyprus, the Christians succeeded, in 1589, in buying the church back. It underwent extensive restoration in the 17th century, and was extended by the addition of a bell-tower. Among the most notable features of the church are its baroque wood-carved iconostasis, and the

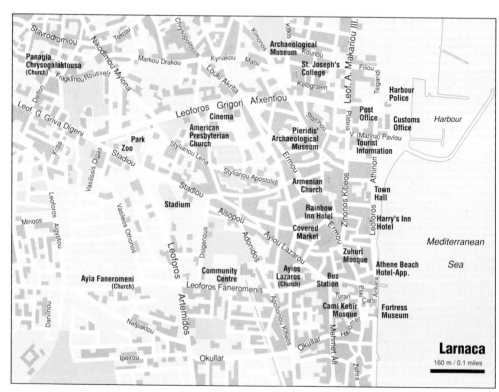

Corinthian capitals at the base of the vaulted roof.

Behind the church is a small cemetery in which privileged 19th-century European diplomats and businessmen lie buried. One of the most notorious foreign representatives, holding the offices of both American and Russian consul at the same time, was Luigi Palma di Cesnola. This accredited diplomat, who had been working in Cyprus since 1865, robbed a number of ancient graves in Larnaca and the surrounding area with the full permission of the Ottoman authorities. He exported his valuable discoveries abroad, mainly to the United States. The Cesnola collection now forms a large part of the stock of the New York Metropolitan Museum of Art.

A local amateur archaeologist and art collector, Demetrios Pierides (1811–95) created a remarkable private museum in Larnaca, the **Pierides Collection**, which is also open to the public. The exhibits, which extend from the Early Stone Age to medieval times, are housed in the family's private house, one of the few remaining examples of resplendent 19th-century villas.

The **Larnaca District Museum** at Kalogrenon Square is hard pressed to compete with the rich and representative collection in the Pierides Museum. Nevertheless it is still worth a visit. Among the ceramics and smaller items in the display cases on the right of the entrance room, and the free-standing statues to the left, are a number of exquisite exhibits.

To the right of the museum is the Catholic **convent of St Joseph**, built in 1848, with an impressive wrought-iron fountain. In the open-air area behind the museum remains from the ancient city of Kition have been excavated. Archaeologists believe they have discovered the acropolis of the city, although only a few relics have survived. Unfortunately the British occupying forces levelled the hill of ruins – known to the locals as Bamboula – in 1879 in order to obtain filling material with which they could reclaim a marshland area.

The tomb of St Lazarus.

Excavations at other sites in the northern part of Larnaca have led to the discovery of a number of remains from the ancient city of **Kition** – for example, at the junction of Ayou Epiphaniou Street and Kimonos Street. The main archaeological area, however, lies further north, and includes, along with the foundations of an important temple, a bronze-processing factory.

Cyprus was an important supplier of copper during the 2nd century BC, particularly for the Hillite Empire in Asia Minor, in whose cuneiform script the island appears as Alaschia. However, the bronze-processing factory in the north of Kition is more recent.

The excavation area is very confusing for visitors as a result of the various building phases from different historical periods which lie next to and over each other. For example, the original shrine from the Bronze Age was replaced by a temple for the goddess Astarte when the Phoenicians settled here in the 10th century BC and developed the city as an important export harbour. The new temple quickly acquired importance well beyond the region. After being rebuilt a number of times it finally burned down in 312 BC.

The Phoenicians extended their power over the island, from Kition outwards, and in the 5th century BC were able to conquer a number of other local city-kingdoms such as Idalion, Tamassos, Golgoi, Amathus and, between 450 and 411 BC, Salamis. Their success was due not least to the support of their allies the Persians. Zeno the younger (c. 336–264 BC), the founder of Stoicism, was also born in Kition (*see page 45*).

Archaeologists distinguish between three main periods in the history of Kition. The first phase, characterised by two temples with altars, separated by an artificially watered **Holy Grove**, probably began in the early 13th century BC and ended with the city's destruction around 1200 BC. The city was then rebuilt by the Mycenaeans. On the site formerly occupied by the shrine a large **temple complex** was built, measuring

Larnaca is a city on the move…

186

110 ft (34 metres) by 72 ft (22 metres), thereby making it one of the largest of the Late Bronze Age temples in Cyprus. Between the temple and the nearby city wall there were extensive copper and bronze-processing plants which were directly accessible from the temple. In other shrines, which have been excavated a little to the east of the main temple, ivory carvings and bull-skulls have been discovered. The seafaring population, who lived from the export of copper, also presented a stone anchor as an offering.

Although the city was rebuilt after severe damage, following the earthquake around 1075 BC it was virtually depopulated. The third and last phase of the city's history was heavily influenced by the Phoenician invaders, whose large **Astarte temple** has already been mentioned. They took advantage of the favourable location of the city and turned it into a naval base. The extent to which the Assyrians had previously influenced the history of Kition can only be guessed: a basalt stele of the Assyrian king Sargon II (721–705 BC) was discovered here, on which he boasts about his power over the island. This now lies in the Near East Museum in Berlin.

Byzantine frescoes: The **Ayios Antonios church**, which lies on a hill to the north of Larnaca, is worth a visit on account of its mid-Byzantine frescoes. The oldest of the wall paintings date back as far as the early 11th century, making them some of the earliest Byzantine frescoes in Cyprus.

If you travel along the bay of Larnaca from the main city to the east, you come to **Cape Pyla** on the other side. The city of the same name can be reached by leaving the coastal road at the vertex of the bay and turning to the north. **Pyla** has achieved a degree of fame since the Turkish invasion in 1974: here, right on the Greek-Turkish demarcation line, is the only place on the whole island where the Greek and Turkish Cypriot populations still live side by side, albeit under the supervision of the UN peacekeeping force.

...but older residents prefer a quieter pace.

The Cypriots call the very flat expanse of land south and southwest of Famagusta Kokkinochoria, "the red land". Nowadays, the name tends to conjure thoughts of sunburnt tourists who populate its beaches, but initially it was the fertile *terra rossa*, the red soil, which made Kokkinochoria into one of the richest agricultural regions on the whole island.

For many years now the area has reaped the added benefits of artificial irrigation. Most of the windmills which used to force the ground water to the surface have long since been replaced by motor-pumps. Today water is received mainly via a monstrous pipeline from a new dam upstream from Limassol. The farmers of Avgorou and Xylophagou have specialised in growing potatoes and now harvest up to three crops each year. More than anything else, the growing demand from Britain has made the Cyprus potato into one of the island's most important exports.

At the beginning of the 1970s there was little here apart from the potato crops. Visitors might have explored the coast to the west and north of Cape Greco with its string of idyllic sandy bays, and those interested in religious art would have found the 16th-century monastery at **Ayia Napa**, the pretty village churches of **Liopetri**, **Sotira** and **Phrenaros**, the 16th-century church of **Ayios Angonas** (near Ormidhia on the road to Avgorou) and the basket-making community of **Liopetri**. The southeast corner of the island was at taht time little more than an unexciting hinterland for *the* tourist centre of the then undivided Cyprus, the hotel city of **Varosha** in the south of the port of Famagusta.

A twofold invasion: None of the other formerly rural areas was turned so completely upside-down by the events following the Turkish invasion of 1974. The strengthening links with the urban

Preceding pages: Ayia Napa monastery. <u>Left</u>, Nissi beach, near Ayia Napa.

centre of Famagusta were suddenly impeded by an impregnable demarcation line. The hotel city of Varosha (which can be seen from the hill near Dherinia) is today a ghost town, serving only as a pawn of the Turkish Cypriots in their negotiations with the Greek Cypriots. Its buildings are falling to pieces after two decades of neglect.

By far the most important result of the invasion and division of the island, however, was the influx of refugees from the area around Famagusta. It led to a sudden quadrupling of the resident population. Large refugee settlements were created near the formerly rural villages and in the open countryside, for example in **Vrysoules**. Within sight of their former home of Akhyritou, now on the Turkish side of the border, nearly 2,000 refugees were given new detached family houses. Yet Vrysoules, an enormous village by any standards, is still nowhere to be seen on Cypriot road maps.

Many of the refugees were soon able to find work. To compensate for the demise of Famagusta and Varosha, hotels sprang up like mushrooms in the latter part of the1970s, in particular in Ayia Napa, Paralimni and Protaras.

Migrant workers: The tranquil fishing village of Ayia Napa has been turned into a hotel city of similar ilk to other Mediterranean resorts. The largest tourist region of the whole island arose virtually from nothing. With some 14,000 beds, a third of Cyprus's tourist capacity is concentrated here. The booming construction and tourist industries have long since absorbed all the local workers and consequently the town must draw on a daily influx of commuters from the economically depressed Turkish-occupied part of the island. Nobody knows exactly how large the number of commuters is, but what is clear is that a situation which both sides originally recognised as an emergency has led to the strictly guarded border becoming much more porous – at least in one direction – than officials like to maintain.

Tourists who stay in the area sur-

No longer a little-known backwater.

rounding Ayia Napa can enjoy a sun and bathing holiday with every possible amenity. There are good sandy beaches and plenty to occupy children. However, those who are looking for isolated bays, traditional villages and typical Cypriot cuisine shouldn't choose this area for their stay.

Holidaymakers staying in Ayia Napa or **Protaras**, immediately to the east of Ayia Napa along the coastal road, will, however, find other things of interest, both locally and in the surrounding area. Ayia Napa's chief attraction is its 16th-century **monastery**, sandwiched between pizza parlours and boutiques, and attendant **Folk Museum** containing examples of prehistoric threshing boards.

There is hardly anywhere better than the surrounds of Ayia Napa to appreciate the division of Cyprus, especially if you take a journey along the demarcation line on the former connecting road between Larnaca and Famagusta, now little used. Anyone making this journey should take a look (from a distance) at the deserted village of **Ahna**, immediately behind the Turkish positions. Near Ahna, the Turkish "Green Line" borders directly on the territory of the British base of **Dhekelia**, one of the two British military bases on the island. Here is a miniature Britain, complete with a military hospital, housing estates built of brick, a golf-course, a gliding field, clubs and pubs.

Travelling on further in the direction of Larnaca, it is worth making a detour to **Pyla**. Because it borders directly on the British bases, Pyla was spared conquest by the Turkish troops and it became the only village on the island where the Greeks and Turks continue to live together.

The village square has both a Greek and a Turkish *kafenion*. In the upper floor of a restaurant a blue-helmeted member of the UN peace-keeping force keeps guard, whilst on a rock spur directly above the village the Turkish military have set up a colossal silhouette of a Turkish soldier ready for battle with fixed bayonet.

Home of Cyprus potatoes.

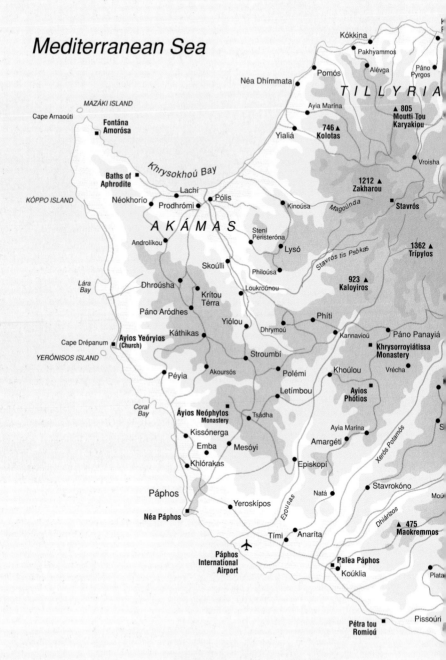

Mediterranean Sea

Kókkina
Pakhyammos
Pomós   Alévga   Páno Pyrgos
Néa Dhímmata

TILLYRIA

MAZÁKI ISLAND
Cape Arnaoúti
Fontána Amorósa   Ayia Marína   ▲ **805 Moutti Tou Karyakiou**
746 ▲ **Kolotas**
Yialiá

Vroisha

Khrysokhoú Bay
Baths of Aphrodite   1212 ▲ **Zakharou**
Lachí
KÓPPO ISLAND   **Néokhorío**   **Pólis**   Stavrós
Prodhrómi   Kinoúsa   *Magoúnda*

A K Á M A S   Steni Peristeróna
Androlíkou   **Lysó**   1362 ▲ **Tripylos**
Skoúlli   Philoúsa   *Stavrós tis Psókas*
Lára Bay   **Dhroúsha**   Loukroúnou   923 ▲ **Kaloyiros**
Krítou Térra
Páno Aródhes   Yiólou   **Phíti**
Dhrymoú
Cape Drépanum   **Ayios Yeóryios**   Káthikas   Kannavioú   Páno Panayiá
(Church)   Stroumbí   **Khrysorroyiátissa Monastery**
YERÓNISOS ISLAND   Akoursós   **Polémi**   Khoúlou   Vrécha
Péyia   Letímbou   **Ayios Phótios**

Coral Bay   **Ayios Neóphytos Monastery**   Tsádha   Ayia Marína   *Xerós Potamós*
Kissónerga   Amargéti
Emba   Mesóyi
Khlórakas   Episkopí

Páphos   Natá   **Stavrokóno**   Moú
Néa Páphos   Yeroskípos   *Eroúsas*   *Dhiárizos*   ▲ **475 Maokremmos**
Tími   Anaríta
Páphos International Airport ✈   **Palea Páphos**   Plata
Koúklia

Pissoúri
Pétra tou Romioú

Mediterranean Sea

Western Cyprus
8 km / 5 miles

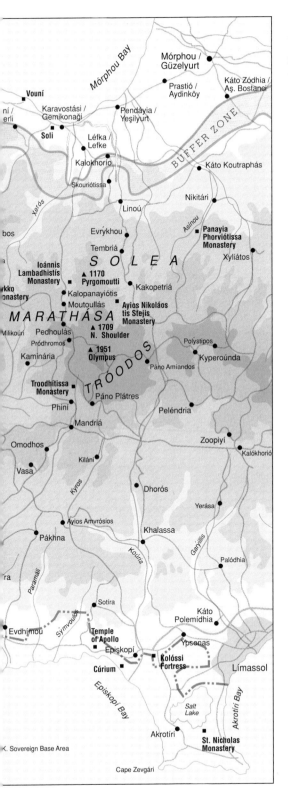

PAPHOS:
THE WILD WEST

The Paphos district, in the west of Cyprus, can look back on a truly glorious past: in the ancient world **Paphos** became a place of pilgrimage for the whole of the Hellenistic cultural area, being a centre for the fertility rituals of Aphrodite. "The Paphian" was one of the names given to the goddess Aphrodite, who according to mythology rose out of the foaming waves off the coast. Here, more than in any of the other areas of Cyprus, you are continually encountering spectacular evidence of the past, and no doubt the earth is hiding further treasures for archaeologists to discover. Those who want to trace the Hellenistic and Roman worlds of Cyprus will experience some of the highlights of their tour here.

Paphos is also an area of considerable scenic beauty. Its particular attraction lies in the dramatic changes between its craggy coastline, steeply terraced vineyards, and the thick pine forests on the slopes of the Troodos mountains. As the moist west winds from the sea get trapped on the edges of these mountains, this part of Cyprus gets far more rainfall than the eastern or central areas. Bizarre cloud patterns decorate skies even in summer. The sea wind brings a very warm and even climate to the coastal region, so bananas and other tropical fruits thrive.

The Troodos mountains also form a natural barrier with the rest of the island. As early as the 19th century the Troodos region had a reputation for lawlessness; livestock rustling in particular was common, sometimes leading to bloody family feuds.

The region remained virtually untouched by the modernisation and industrialisation which happened around Nicosia and Limassol in the past few decades. Instead it continued to be a peripheral area, a somewhat backward, poor hinterland, from which the population began to migrate. Paphos became

Preceding pages: grape harvest in the west.

the most sparsely populated district in Cyprus: in 1982 it contained just 9 percent of southern Cyprus's population.

However, all that changed with the building of an airport in 1984 and the rapid development of tourism. Nowadays Paphos ranks third behind Ayia Napa/Paralimni and Limassol in terms of the number of hotel beds.

A journey through the Paphos area provides insights into the variety of settlements in Cyprus, and into modern-day rural life. Nowhere else on the island is as interesting in this regard: rich agricultural villages, dilapidated mountain settlements, communities destroyed by earthquakes, Turkish Cypriot villages, refugee settlements and smart holiday villages are all here.

The city of Paphos: Paphos is one of the smallest of the Cypriot district capitals with just 13,000 inhabitants. The urban communities in the surrounding countryside amount to a further 7,500 people. Paphos itself is divided into two distinct parts: the lower city of Nea Paphos, with its little harbour, and the upper city of Ktima, once the original town centre, which lies to the north on a 557-ft (170-metre) high rocky edge.

Nea Paphos, also known as **Kato Paphos** (Lower Paphos) was founded around 320 BC. Nikokles, the last ruler of the city kingdom of Paphos, had the capital moved here from Old Paphos (Kouklia). After 58 BC, when the period of Roman rule over the island began, Nea Paphos became the seat of the Roman proconsul.

One important event which is said to have taken place here, and which was to be of lasting significance for the Christian world, concerns the missionary work of the Apostles Paul and Barnabas: on their visit to Paphos in AD 47 they converted the proconsul Sergius Paulus to Christianity. If this is correct, then Cyprus was the first Christian-ruled area. The archaeological treasures of Nea Paphos also date from Roman times. They include the splendid mosaics in the Houses of Dionysos, Theseus, Aion and Orpheus *(see also "Archaeological Cyprus", page 211).*

Coral Bay, a short hop from Paphos.

The focal point of life in Kato Paphos is the little **harbour** with its string of fish restaurants. The catches of the fishing cutters in the harbour basin are among the largest on the island. Across the harbour lies the **fort**, built in 1592 by the Turks. The new tourist zone of Kato Paphos, complete with hotels, restaurants and discotheques, stretches inland from the coast southeast of the harbour, as well as along the road to Peyia. The barren, rocky coast makes swimming less than ideal. All the same, the relatively late development of tourism has meant better planning. Unlike in Limassol, here building is subject to strict control.

The town's Department of Antiquities is permanently holding its breath, for excavators on the building sites are constantly making valuable discoveries which have to be brought to safety.

Away from the hustle and bustle of the tourist trade, the upper city of **Ktima** offers the essential charm of a lively Cypriot town. Its function as a trading and supply centre for the surrounding area, which is still rural in character, ensures plenty of activity. Saturday – market day – is the best time to get the flavour of the place.

Arriving in Paphos from the east, from Limassol, the first thing you encounter is a series of impressive buildings on Yeoryios Grivas Avenue. Particularly striking are the buildings of the **Gymnasium** (a grammar school built in 1960), the **Academy of Economics** (formerly a school and built in 1928) and the portal to the stadium.

The school buildings – extraordinarily grand for a small town like Paphos – reflect the high value which Greek Cypriots continue to place on classical education. Educational institutions here have always been central to Hellenistic thoughts of liberation. One of the reliefs in the courtyard of the **Gymnasium** shows a schoolboy trying to kill a wild lion with a stone, symbolic of the heroic struggle of the young Cypriots against the British colonialists towards the end of the 1950s.

If you turn off towards the town park and the town hall, you come to the **Bishop's Palace**. Archbishop Makarios fled here after the putsch by Greek officers on 15 July 1974. It was from here, over the radio, that he denied the reports disseminated by the leaders of the putsch that he was already dead. Near the palace is the **Folk Art Museum of Professor Eliades**, housed in an interesting-looking town-house. The polyglot professor takes visitors through his collection of exhibits from the Stone Age to the present day. One highlight is the house's own **chapel** – in a Hellenistic rock tomb discovered in the basement.

On Nicodemou-Mylona Street, which lies further to the northwest, are the buildings of the **Post Office** and the **District Administration** including the district court, built in classical style at the beginning of the 20th century. Near the court, a veritable forest of metal plaques indicate the lawyers' offices. According to the Greeks' conception of education, the legal profession enjoys very high status and in Cyprus's "Wild West" there are plenty of disputes requiring legal answers. In one of the little

Paphos
160 m / 0.1 miles

Map labels: Athinas, Ayia Sofia Church, Fellahoğlu, Bus Station, Thermopylon, Boumboulinas, Marias Sygklitikis, Palikaridi, Evagorou, Agoras, Cinema, Leoforos Evagorou, Tepeleniou, Covered Market, K. Karnavalou, Andrea Geroudi, Martiou 9, Leoforos, Turkish Bath, Ch. Mouskou, Post Office, Archepiskopou, Sports Ground, Ayios Kendeas (Church), N. Antoniadi, Grigoriou Afxentiou, M. N. Mylona, Information, Makariou III, Stadium, G. Christoforou, Gladstonos, Leoforos Yeoryios Griva Digeni, Classical Buildings, Ayios Ioannis (Church), L. Apostolou Pavlou, Ivis Maliotou, A. Ioannou, Town Hall, Park, Bishop's Palace, Martiou 25, Exo, Ayios Theodoros (Church), Vrysis, Ilysion, G. M. Savva

streets behind the court, a coffin-maker busily works away.

A little further to the north on a slope below a parking place is the newly renovated **Turkish bath**. Until around 1955 this *hamam* was used by both Greeks and Turks. In later years such peaceful coexistence was destroyed: on 7 March 1964 heavy fighting broke out between Greek and Turkish nationalists. There were deaths on both sides and hundreds of hostages were taken. As a result of the battle, the Turkish Cypriots were forced to withdraw to a heavily protected area. A mosque which stood on the square above the Turkish bath was pulled down by the Greeks after Turkish fanatics had fired on civilians from the tower of its minaret.

To the east of the covered market, you come into the new **Greek city of Ktima**, with its main shopping street, **Makarios III**. North and northwest of the market the Turkish street signs indicate the former Turkish area. The narrow streets, with their many nooks and impasses, have a timeless appeal. This was how the old Cypriot cities looked at the beginning of the 1960s. The 2,900 Turkish Cypriot inhabitants were all resettled in the northern part of the island in August 1975. There are still many reminders of their presence: the Turkish street names, a large expanse of red graffiti – *Denktash* – written on one of the houses, a plinth once topped by a statue of Atatürk. Greek Cypriot refugees, in particular the older, poorer ones, have taken the place of the Turkish population.

In the extreme west of the area you proceed from the **Main Square,** with its clutch of coffee houses, through a triumphal arch from the Turkish period. Under the Turkish half-moon is a slogan in Turkish: "What good fortune it is to be Turkish." Further below in the new-Greek script it reads: "We'll never forget our enslaved homeland." A few steps further on a beautiful view opens up from the edge of a rocky plateau to the archaeological sites of Nea Paphos and the new hotels in the east.

Between Paphos and Petra tou Romiou: The road from Ktima to Limassol goes

Paphos harbour.

through the southern coastal plain, now the most fertile region of the whole area. Fields of bananas, citrus fruits, avocados, grapes, early potatoes, sesame and peanuts flank both sides of the road. All these crops need considerable irrigation, and the water is brought from a dam on the lower reaches of the Xeros Potamos to the west of Kouklia, part of the Paphos Irrigation Project, one of the largest irrigation projects on the island, covering 12,500 acres (5,000 hectares). This ambitious project was completed in 1974. The profits from the area's production – devoted mainly to export – have made a substantial improvement to the living standards in this economically backward region.

Directly beyond the last house of Paphos is the sign for **Yeroskipos**. The name means "Holy Grove". What was once a tranquil garden on the pilgrimage route from Nea Paphos to Aphrodite's shrine at Palea Paphos (Kouklia), is now a busy suburban village. Only a few decades ago numerous mulberry trees stood in the area, and

until 1950 one of the largest silk-spinning mills in Cyprus was situated here. Stools are still produced from the wild fennel in Yeroskipos. Other specialities of the area are the sweet *loukoumia*, made from grape syrup, and *halumi*, a cheese made from the milk of sheep and goats, which feed on the thyme-rich pastures.

Near **Akhelia** a sign points the way to one of the experimental farms run by the Cypriot Ministry of Agriculture. Current projects centre on pig-rearing and attempts to produce exotic fruits. The areas of cultivation formerly belonged to a feudal estate dating from the Lusignans. Later, in the middle of the 15th century, a Venetian firm commandeered large areas for growing cane sugar. According to one legend, sweet-toothed buffalos swam here from Egypt, attracted by the exquisite juice of the sugar cane.

The **Museum of Palea Paphos**, near the ruins of the **Sanctuary of Aphrodite**, is housed in a restored castle, which served as a form of administrative head-

A surfeit of souvenir shops.

quarters for the sugar industry of the area. In 1861 the Latifundium of Kouklia became the centre of the so-called "Kibrisli Empire". Lord of the Manor was the Cypriot Mehmet Ali Kibrisli, previously prime minister to the Sublime Porte.

A few miles after the turn to Palea Paphos (Kouklia) the fertile coastal plain comes to an end. The road now runs through an area of deserted, barren land along the edge of an imposingly steep coast. A number of massive boulders appear below, as if tossed up by a raging sea. It is here that Aphrodite, born from the foam of the sea, is supposed to have stepped out of the waves. The view to **Petra tou Romiou** can be enjoyed from the tourist pavilion lying just inland.

From Paphos to Cape Drepanum: From Kato Paphos and from Ktima roads lead north to the cove of Coral Bay and Peyia. The villages of Khlorakas, Emba and Kissonerga, near the road going from Ktima, have already been swallowed up by the outskirts of Paphos. Extensive developments of holiday homes and apartments sprawl inland, their charms advertised to sun-hungry Europeans by means of massive hoardings. Beyond Kissonerga, the road passes through banana plantations.

The beautiful sandy cove of **Coral Bay** is likely to satisfy those disappointed by the quality of beaches near Kato Paphos. However, you can't expect to find peace and tranquillity: Coral Bay is popular with locals and tourists alike, and is served by a public bus to and from Paphos. Indeed, Coral Bay is another place where a large tourist complex has recently been built, between the beach and the main road, with apartments, shops and restaurants, some of which are very good.

The other side of Peyia, around **Ayios Yeoryios**, you can find quieter beaches and tavernas, some of which have simple private rooms to let. At **Cape Drepanum** you can visit a modern church and the ground plan, complete with floor mosaics, of a 6th-century basilica . The most interesting features, however, are the little **Byzantine chapel** and the new church dedicated to St George. Small strips of material hung on a nearby tree are an indication of the church's importance in the beliefs of local people. Lovers are supposed to come here to discover the outcome of their attachments. St George is also said to help shepherds and goatherds whose animals have gone astray.

Ayios Yeoryios is a good starting point for a tour of the uninhabited **Akamas peninsula**. This journey is best undertaken on foot. A bumpy dust track leads along the coast as far as Lara Bay.

Between Paphos and Polis: From Ktima the road winds upwards in a northerly direction, climbing into the wonderful landscape of the Paphian hill country. Wine is the main product of this area's light marlacious soil. Every turn-off to the left or right along the road to Polis produces its own special reward: there is nowhere better on Cyprus to see authentic rural life, which is now dying out. Be prepared, however, for a degree of adventure – some of the "roads" turn out to be no more than tracks strewn with pot-holes. Often the only alterna-

St George and the Dragon, church of Ayios Yeoryios.

202

tive is to walk. The connecting road from Paphos to Polis wasn't built until the beginning of the 20th century when the British constructed a route for carts. Up until then the only possible means of transport were donkeys, mules or, more usually, camels. The village of **Mesa Khorio** (to the east of the main road by the turn off to the monastery of St Neophytos) was famous for its magnificent camels. Wine and sultanas were transported to the coast and shipped to Egypt, right up until World War II.

At the large village of **Stroumbi** you reach the ridge of the range of hills separating Paphos from Polis. The wine from Stroumbi has a particularly good reputation and is mentioned in Lawrence Durrell's *Bitter Lemons*. Stroumbi was also near the epicentre of an earthquake which destroyed large parts of the Paphos district in September 1953. After the earthquake the British colonial administration erected simple prefabricated shacks for the homeless. In recent years the inhabitants who still remained in these huts were given detached family houses by the Cypriot government.

There are two possibilities for continuing to Polis; they can also be combined to make an interesting circular tour. The first variation is via the main road to Polis, which follows the fertile valley of the river Khrysokhou, descending all the way. Adventurous travellers may want to make a detour from this route to the east in the direction of Lyso. In this area of barren but nevertheless dramatic-looking landscape you will come across a series of Turkish settlements which were abandoned by their inhabitants in 1975. Slowly but surely, the empty houses are falling into decay.

The second alternative leads from Stroumbi via Kathikas through mountain vineyards to the ridge of a further range of mountains which enjoys excellent views over the Akamas peninsula and the western foothills of the Troodos mountains. The beautiful village of **Arodhes,** with its two communities (Kato and Pano), traces its name back to

Birthplace of Aphrodite.

the medieval feudal rule of the Knights Hospitaller. They named the village after the island of Rhodes, the headquarters of the Order.

The village of **Drouscha** reflects on an even earlier history: the ancestors of the current inhabitants came here from Arcadia in the Greek Peloponnese. This wave of Arcadian immigrants is responsible for the remnants of Homeric Greek in the Paphian dialect. *Drouscha* is the dialect word for "cool, fresh", and indeed a cool wind from the Akamas blows almost constantly through the bizarre rock formations above the village. In the Drouscha Heights Hotel it is possible to enjoy this rural idyll in comfortable accommodation.

Hikers are recommended to take the little stony road which winds its way from Drouscha into the eastern part of Akamas via the deserted Turkish villages of Phasli and Androlikou, and down to Prodhromi and Polis.

The villages which lie on the southern end of the Akamas peninsula have suffered a massive wave of emigration as a result of the meagre living conditions in the area. An "Agro-tourist" project set up by Friends of the Earth is hoping to open up new horizons for communities such as Kathikas, Kritou Terra, Theletra and Akourdhalia.

The aim of the project is to promote "gentle tourism". For example, the inhabitants of the villages have been given special low-interest loans to renovate their houses in traditional style so that one part of the renovated building can then be rented out to tourists. By such methods Friends of the Earth hopes, on the one hand, to encourage a form of tourism which will harmonise with the structure of the growing settlements, and, on the other, to ensure that the financial benefits of tourism are available to as many people as possible.

The village of **Pano Panayia** and the nearby monastery of Khryssorroyiatissa make enjoyable day excursions from Paphos or Polis. The journey ascends to more than 2,600 ft (800 metres), to the western edge of the forest belt circling the Troodos mountains.

The Gymnasium, Paphos.

204

Each of the possible routes to Pano Panayia passes through extraordinarily beautiful landscapes. The shortest way from Paphos is via Polemi and past the pretty village of Kannaviou. More impressive, however, is the journey winding from the southern coastal plain in the direction of Timi. There are fantastic views over the Xeros Potamos valley, whose river is one of the few Cypriot rivers not to turn into a desiccated wadi in summer. The villages of **Nata**, **Axylou** and **Eldhiou** further to the north were destroyed by the devastating earthquake of 1953. Only a few old people are still living in the new settlements which the British erected following the disaster: the yields from the vineyards, carob trees and olive trees are too meagre to support much of a population.

Birth of an archbishop: The village of **Pano Panayia** has a particular claim to fame. Here in 1913 a certain Michalis Mouskos was born, the eldest son of a simple farmer and goatherd. His entrance as a novice into the monastery of Kykko was the first step in his extraordinary career, during which he was to become "Makarios III", Archbishop of Cyprus and, from 1960 until his death in 1977, the president of the island republic.

Metal signposts in the village point the way to the house of the parents of Makarios III. The key to the house is guarded by an old neighbour. The traditional architecture of the house, characteristic of the area, makes a visit especially worthwhile. Both animals and people entered the house through the single door at the front. The whole family lived in the large front room, where you can see a collection of old furniture and ceramics. The smaller room at the rear was used as a stall for the animals. The reasoning behind this design was to make it more difficult for rustlers to steal livestock.

A new **museum** and a larger-than-life sculpture of Makarios are further proof of the pride which the inhabitants of Panayia have for their famous son. The important landmarks in the life of this charismatic church leader and statesman are documented with the aid of photographs, mementoes and insignia.

The founding of the **monastery of Khryssorroyiatissa** in 1182 followed the discovery of an icon – as in the case of many other monastic buildings in Cyprus. This one is reputed to have been painted by the Apostle Luke himself. The current monastery church was built around 1770, and its splendidly carved iconostasis contains the miracle-working icon of *Panayia Khryssorroyiatissa*. This somewhat unpronounceable name means "Our Lady of the Golden Pomegranate" and symbolises the nurturing breast of the Virgin Mary. A devastating fire in 1966 made it necessary to rebuild a large part of the monastery.

One of the main reasons for visiting Khryssorroyiatissa, aside from its art-historical importance, is to enjoy the monastic grounds and their setting. The monks tend their own vineyards, pressing the grapes themselves. It is highly regarded by connoisseurs; you can buy it either in the monastery itself or in the adjoining taverna.

The monastery of Khryssorroyiatissa.

THE RURAL EXODUS

In the Paphos district alone 14 villages have become deserted settlements since 1960 – ghost towns, whose houses and meadows are no longer used except as shelters by wandering herds of goats. Souskiou, Zaharia, Akoursos, Fasli, Maronas – are all villages which have fallen into oblivion.

A number of other places can expect to suffer the same fate in the near future. An average age of 60 is common in the mountain villages. Like the head of Janus, rural Cyprus has two faces: here decline, there (usually near the coast) the victim of rampant building activity, as holiday homes and apartments spring up like mushrooms.

The farmer's life in the mountain areas of Cyprus has never been romantic. It is a constant struggle with nature. The steep character of the countryside and the barren stony ground make the farmer's life unadulterated hard-work. An antiquated system of land rights, retaining elements from the Ottoman era, provides an additional difficulty: a farmer's tiny parcels of land often lie far apart from each other, for example, and over 100 different farmers sometimes have legal claims to the yield of one single olive tree. What's more, droughts and plagues of locusts can strike at any time.

Of course, the 20th century has brought some improvements for Cypriot farmers: new agricultural techniques have been introduced and the feudal system of tributes, under whose yoke generations of farmers had laboured, was abolished in the 1920s. The British were responsible for abolishing the exploitative system of money-lending, and the introduction of a close network of rural cooperatives.

Even today, agricultural life in the mountain areas of Cyprus, where irrigation is impossible, could support a limited number of people. However, people's demands have changed. In former years farmers were content with bread, olives, and wine, and dressed themselves in a single *vraka* (baggy trousers). Any surplus money which they managed to save was invested in the future of their children, in particular the compulsory dowry (*prika*) for their daughters. Today, although people can find a husband for their daughters without a dowry, expectations concerning their own living standards have risen sharply: the material wealth of employees in the cities is demanded in the country too – colour television brings news of the latest products and fashions to even the remotest home.

In the 1950s, when Cyprus was still under British rule, large building projects demanded workers outside the agricultural sector. Since the 1960s industrial and trading companies in the large Cypriot cities have also needed workers, as have the massive hotel developments. The result was a massive migration from the remote mountain areas to the towns and their suburbs.

Villages within a radius of 12 miles (20 km) from Nicosia, Limassol and Famagusta experienced rapid growth. People worked in the cities but lived in the village, where land prices were still affordable. They tended their own vineyard or olive grove at the weekend, and contracted a fellow villager to cultivate the land.

In the Paphos district, things were more problematic. Until the end of the 1970s there was neither industry nor tourism to any significant extent. In contrast to Limassol or Nicosia, Paphos was just a large village without any supra-regional significance. Income supplements were only available to a limited number of seasonal workers in the plantations of the southern coastal areas or in the mines on the edge of the Troodos mountains (these are now exhausted and have been closed). The only possible option for many, especially the young and well-educated, was migration to another region. Between 1960 and 1973 this district was the only one in Cyprus to experience a reduction in the number of its inhabitants – not even the high birth rate amongst the resident population could make up for the loss through migration.

The crisis of 1974 and the division of the island brought the Paphos district further population losses. During the course of 1975 all the Turkish Cypriot inhabitants had to leave their homes to be resettled in the Turkish occupied north of the island. In the space of one year the district lost some 15,000 inhabitants, a quarter of its total population. Only a few of the Greek Cypriot refugees took the opportunity of settling in one of the abandoned Turkish villages or areas (in 1976 there were just 6,500 refugees in the district, with 2,700 in the city of Paphos). The prospects of making a reasonable livelihood from farming were simply too poor to persuade people to start a new life here.

In the past few years, however, with the rapid growth of tourism, the economic conditions in the district have changed fundamentally. The coastal area of Paphos has experienced its first boom since the heyday of the ancient cult of Aphrodite, and now its tourist industry is also suffering from a shortage of workers. There is hardly a single *Paphitis* (as the inhabitants of the district are known) who has to leave his home village to find work.

Yet whilst these newly-created jobs are of enormous significance for the region, the old farmers in the Kafenion of Lyso or Fiti are left pondering an uneasy question: will the young people, who are today working in the hotels as receptionists, bar staff, cooks and chambermaids, be able to maintain their relationship with the rural world of their parents, or will they become irrevocably alienated from their roots?

The way out.

This relationship can only be maintained by continuing the business of farming, even if it is only as a sideline. The old stooped farmer knows the situation better than anyone else: Cyprus's rural communities thrive on village unity. What's more, to many foreign visitors, the whole appeal of Cyprus is its traditional life style and values.

Seen from this point of view, all those projects which are aimed at bringing about fundamental improvements in agricultural life and the rural infrastructure (such as schools, water supplies, etc.) are of enormous importance. Until now the beneficiaries of the new large Paphos Irrigation Project have been mainly the landowners on the coastal plain. But other locations in Cyprus are also benefiting from schemes, in particular the Pitsilia Integrated Rural Development Project on the southern edge of the Troodos mountains.

The achievements of such projects should not be measured in terms of the relationship between the costs incurred and the resulting improvements in productivity. Rescuing Cyprus from the circle of resignation, apathy and rural decline is what matters. ∎

ARCHAEOLOGICAL CYPRUS

The ancient city of **Nea Paphos** is on the southwest coast of Cyprus and covers some 235 acres (95 hectares). The archaeological area lies to the west of Apostolos Pavlos Street, which connects the small town of Paphos (Ktima) with modern-day Kato Paphos.

Nea Paphos was founded at the end of the 4th century BC by King Nikokles. Shortly after its foundation, Cyprus fell into the hands of the Egyptian Ptolemies. Around the time of the 2nd century BC, Paphos became the new capital of the island. In 58 BC, Cyprus fell to the Romans, and thenceforth was ruled by a Roman governor; Paphos nevertheless remained the capital of the island. The public buildings and the luxurious houses which have come to light during the excavations have revealed the important role played by Paphos during the time of the *pax Romana*.

Nea Paphos was affected by a number of earthquakes in the 1st century BC and then again during the 1st and 4th centuries AD. In the 4th century, following a series of devastating earthquakes, the city was razed to the ground, and its inhabitants fled. The city of Salamis was then made the new capital of Cyprus under the name of Constantia.

After the Arab invasions of the island in the 7th century, the decline of Nea Paphos continued at a steady pace, interrupted only by short periods of prosperity during the time of the French Lusignans and the Venetians, when a number of Gothic buildings were constructed. During the Ottoman Period (1572–1878) the inhabitants began to migrate to the hinterland – now occupied by the modern town of Paphos – with the result that the coastal region became almost completely deserted.

Such is Nea Paphos's importance that UNESCO has added the area to its list of world monuments.

The houses of Nea Paphos, with their wonderful floor mosaics, are of particular interest. The most famous are the House of Dionysos, the House of Aion, the Villa of Theseus and the House of Orpheus. These names were given to the houses by archaeologists, and refer to the figures represented in their respective mosaics.

The House of Dionysos: This house came to light in 1962, when a chance discovery of the floor mosaic led to further excavations. It consists of an *atrium* (courtyard), from which corridors lead off in four directions. The other buildings of the house were arranged around this inner courtyard. The most impressive features are their mosaics of mythological scenes and geometric shapes.

Just to the left of today's entrance is a mosaic from the surrounding area, which shows Scylla, a mythological monster that is part woman, part fish and part dog. It is the oldest mosaic to have been found in Cyprus, and is peculiar in that it is made entirely of black and white pebbles. On the western side of the atrium are four scenes from Greek mythology. The first one on the left shows the death of Pyramus and Thisbe. The next scene show Icarus learning the art

of wine-making from Dionysos. To the left of Icarus you can see the nymph Akme, and on the right-hand side is a group of figures drinking wine. The neighbouring scene shows Poseidon and Amymone and in the fourth scene Apollo is pursuing the nymph Daphne.

The large reception or dining hall (*triclinium*) to the west of the atrium shows the reception of the triumphal procession of Dionysos on his return from his Indian campaign. The rest of the room is decorated with scenes from the grape harvest. Other mosaics depict more mythical figures, such as Narcissus, Hippolytus, Phaedra, Ganymede with the eagle, and allegories of the four seasons. The building dates from the end of the 2nd century or beginning of the 3rd century.

The House of Aion: Excavations began on the House of Aion in 1983 and have so far uncovered only a small number of rooms. The largest of them, probably the reception hall, is decorated with one large mosaic depicting five mythological themes. The first picture at the top on the left shows the beautiful queen of Sparta, Leda, with the swan. In the next picture, at the top on the right, you can see the young Dionysos sitting on Hermes's lap, before being handed over to Tropheus, while the nymphs are preparing Dionysos's first bath. The middle – and largest – picture shows a famous beauty competition, known as the Judgement of the Nereidens. The winner of this competition is Queen Cassiopeia, who is being crowned by a winged female figure. The centre of the ensemble is dominated by the figure of Aion, the symbol of eternal life and judge over all people. The picture at the bottom on the left shows the triumphal procession of Dionysos, although only the chariot has survived the ravages of time. The last picture shows a musical competition between the satyr Marsyas and Apollo, god of music.

The Villa of Theseus: This building lies close to the House of Aion. It was built in the 2nd century and has undergone numerous alterations over the course of the centuries. Its mosaics date from the

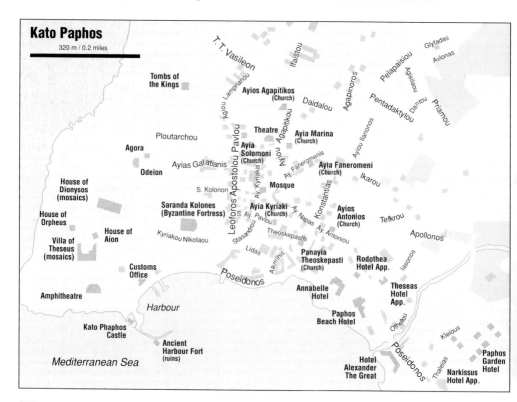

3rd and 5th century. Its size and, above all, its architectural plan have led experts to conclude that it must have once served as the house of a Roman governor. The house consists of a large inner courtyard, from which rooms radiate in all directions.

The most impressive mosaic decorates one of the vaulted rooms on the southern side. The mosaic, which dates from the 3rd century, was restored in the 4th century and has a beautiful geometric motif. The medallion at its centre portrays the battle between Theseus and the Minotaur. Next to this are varied depictions of the island of Crete.

On the floor of the large room on the southern side of the villa is another interesting picture. This shows the newborn Achilles having his first bath. Next to his parents, Thetis and Peleus, are his two trophies and the three Fates. The mosaic dates from the 5th century.

The House of Orpheus: This house is situated to the west of the House of Theseus. Systematic excavations begun in 1982 have so far uncovered a build-

ing with many rooms, which are laid out around an atrium, itself encircled by colonnades (*peristylon*), with baths in the northeastern corner. The original building dates from the end of the 2nd century or the beginning of the 3rd century – when Nea Paphos was at its zenith. Like most of the buildings in the area, the house was decorated with rich floor mosaics and splendid frescoes.

The most important mosaic decorates a room on the northeastern side. This shows Orpheus with his lyre, surrounded by figures, and playing his heavenly music. The inscription under Orpheus is probably the name of the owner or the founder of the house.

Two further mosaics, on the floor of a room to the south of here, are also worth finding. The first shows with impressive simplicity the battle between Hercules and the mythical lion Nemea. The other shows an Amazon standing against a blue background, carrying a horse's bridle in her left hand and a double axe in her right.

The public buildings: The **theatre,**

The Temple of Aphrodite, Palea Paphos.

which lies in the northeastern corner of the old city, above the hill, and which is known nowadays as **Fabrica**, is one of the most important buildings in this region. Although is hasn't been completely excavated, it is possible to visit the upper rows of the *koilon*, which are carved into the rocks. The lower part of the koilon, the *orchestra* and the stage, were all built out of stone. An inscription on one of the stone seats indicates that the theatre dates from the Early Hellenistic Period.

On the western side of the Fabrica Hill you can visit a complex of underground rooms which have been carved into the rocks. The size of some of these rooms is staggering and their original purpose remains a puzzle even today.

Further west still, on the other side of the main road, is the so-called **Guard's Camp**. This consists of two underground rooms, cut out of the rocks, one of which is rectangular and the other circular. It is is thought that they had nothing to do with the camp, but belonged to a subterranean altar from the Hellenistic Period.

On the other side of the main street, on a hill, is the **Northern Gate** of Nea Paphos, whilst a further hill in the west can be identified as the **Northwestern Gate.** These gates probably formed part of the city wall which King Nikokles built at the end of the 4th century BC. The wall began and ended at the harbour, and it is still possible to make out its full length. Close to the sea the wall was built from massive stones, augmented in certain places by rock hewn out of the sea bed. In certain places the wall included multi-sided towers.

Near the northwestern gate you can see both the wall (3 ft/7 metres high) and the towers. Traces of the gate's door have survived until today, together with the ramp, which led to the sea. There are also a number of emergency exits (sally ports), which connected Nea Paphos with the plain outside.

The little hill in the west, where the lighthouse now stands, seems to have been the Acropolis of Nea Paphos. To the south of the lighthouse are the remains of buildings, whilst the Roman

Khrysolplitissa dates from the 4th century.

Odeon, 2nd century, lies on the slopes of the hill. The lower row of *koilon* around the semi-circular orchestra have been restored. Only the foundations have survived from the stage house (*skene*). The audience came into the *odeon* via two side entrances and a corridor to the rear of the *koilon*.

To the south of the *odeon* you can visit the **Asklepeion**, which was the healing centre and altar of Asklepios, the god of medicine. A corridor connects this building to the *odeon*. Its architectural plan consists of a centrally-located arched hall, surrounded by two rectangular rooms. The building dates from the 2nd century.

The surviving foundations of a row of Corinthian columns reveal that the agora, dating from the 2nd century, was located to the east of the *odeon*. It consisted of a courtyard with rows of columns. From this courtyard you could ascend, via three steps, to the stoa and the shops, which lay behind. A number of columns, capitals and other remains have survived.

A little way to the south of the Odeon-Asklepeion complex is evidence of a small **Hellenistic altar**. All that remains now are its foundations, carved into the rock, and the steps which led up to it.

Beyond the city boundaries to the east is the **altar of Apollo Hylates**, from the end of the 4th century BC. It consists of two rooms, both carved into the rocks. Two engraved inscriptions, one over the entrance and the other on the inside, reveal that the altar was dedicated to the god Apollo. From various inscriptions that have been uncovered we know that Aphrodite, Zeus, Artemis and Leto were also worshipped in Paphos.

Also worthy of mention are the remains of the Roman amphitheatre: this consists of a hill with an oval-shaped bowl in the middle, which lies to the northwest of the fort.

Byzantine and medieval monuments: Without doubt the most impressive building of the early Christian period is the **basilica**, known as **Khrysolplitissa** (formerly Panayia Akhroditissa), in the eastern part of Paphos, adjacent to the modern-day church of Ayia Kyriaki.

This imposing building was constructed at the end of the 4th century and has since undergone extensive reconstruction. It is one of the largest early Christian basilicas to be found in Cyprus to date. Originally it had seven aisles, but this was reduced to five during reconstruction in the 6th century. The nave was fitted with a double floor, a characteristic which is unique to Cyprus. Four granite columns still support the eastern part of the roof. In the western part of the church is the **narthex** and the atrium with a fountain in the middle surrounded by rows of columns. A corridor leads in a southwesterly direction to a building which is thought may have served as residence for the bishop of Paphos.

The most important decorations in the basilica are the floor mosaics, which date from a various periods. They comprise mainly plant and geometrical motifs, but near the shrine three pictures have survived from the 4th century depicting inscriptions and stories from the Old Testament. Many of the floors were

Local lamb cook.

provided with new geometrical patterns during the 6th century: the floor of the nave must have been particularly impressive as it was embellished with multi-coloured stone slabs (*opus sectile*).

The basilica survived until the middle of the 7th century, when it was destroyed during the Arab invasions. A small church was then built on the same spot. This was also destroyed in 1500, in order to make space for the current Ayia Kyriaki church.

During the Frankish and Venetian Periods (1192–1489) Nea Paphos was the seat of residence of the Latin bishops and, as a result, a number of important new buildings were constructed. One of them, the **Franciscan church**, lies directly northeast of the Ayia Kyriaki. Here are the remains of the **Franciscan church**, one of the most important churches on the whole island. From the foundations it is possible to recognise a building with three aisles, which was probably constructed at the end of the 13th century or at the beginning of the 14th. The architectural fea-

ture of two arches above a double column is especially interesting.

Just to the west of the church you can see a number of tombstones of Franks who died in the city. According to local tradition, it was upon one of these tombstones that the Apostle Paul was bound and whipped.

On the main road to Kato Paphos are the meagre ruins of the **cathedral of the Latins**, built in the 13th century. All that remains now is its southwestern corner.

On the way to the mosaics – on the right-hand side on a hill – are the remains of a medieval castle, known as **Saranda Kolones**, which means "the 40 columns". It was named after the old granite columns incorporated into the castle which previously lay scattered over the area. The central section of the castle is surrounded by a mighty wall and trenches. The castle has four massive corner towers. In the central courtyard the roof was supported by arches; some of the *pessoí* (the supporting piers) were later converted into toilets.

A large kiln can still be seen. This is said to have served as a heater (*praefurnium*) for water. There are also a number of stalls here. The outer wall was protected by eight towers of different shapes; in the centre of the wall were seven steps which ended in an emergency exit leading to the moat.

We can only speculate about the original construction of the castle, and it is difficult to put a precise date on it. However, we do know for certain that is was devastated by an earthquake in 1222. Later, in the 13th century, during the period of the Lusignans, it was replaced by a smaller fortress near the harbour. What can be seen there today is the remains of a much larger building that was constructed around the core of a Frankish fortress. The Venetians had the fortress extended, but quickly abandoned it when they realised that it was going to prove impossible to defend it against the Ottomans in 1570. An inscription directly above the main entrance shows that the fortress was finally restored by the Turks.

Behind the restaurants at the harbour are the remains of an early Christian

This statuette still bears traces of paintwork.

216

basilica, Panayia Limentiotissa, which was built around the 4th or 5th century. The building was divided into three aisles by two rows of columns; the narthex and the atrium were to be found in the western section. A number of **floor mosaics** can still be seen; in a room in the northeast of the building is a wonderful example of an *opus sectile*. The Arabic inscriptions from the second half of the 7th century indicate that the Arabs made use of this room during their invasions of Cyprus.

The Necropolis: According to ancient tradition, cemeteries (*necropoleis*) were always situated outside the walls of a city. In Nea Paphos the enormous necropolis extends in all directions. The graves of the northwestern necropolis are known as the **Tombs of the Kings** because of their imposing character rather than the regality of their inmates. In fact, they were used by the nobles of the Ptolemies as family graves. The tombs, which are carved into the rocks, were built between the 3rd century BC and the 3rd century AD. They are small,

Byzantine fortress.

cubic graves without any form of decoration. There are over 100 tombs in all and the largest of them display an impressive architectural plan, having been cut into the rocks with the greatest of precision.

The two most important **peristyle tombs** can be reached by going up a flight of stairs leading into an open central courtyard, the atrium. The tombs are arranged around the courtyard and the columns are examples of the Doric style. Traces of a number of frescoes reveal that the rocks were painted at one time. A neighbouring tomb reveals a different architectural form, consisting of a compact cube in the centre, which is surrounded by wide corridors. Unfortunately, only a small section of the decoration and its coloured stucco has survived.

The necropolis served as a place of refuge during the persecution of the island's first Christians. Tomb number 5 was later converted into a kiln and was used for firing medieval ceramics. Tomb number 6, on the other hand, was used

as a chapel, and it is from this that the region takes its name – i.e. *Palioeklissia*, which means "the old church".

Paphos District Museum: The first hall of the **museum** contains finds from the Neolithic and Chalcolithic Periods (8000–2500 BC), the Bronze Age (2500–1050 BC), and metal objects and pieces of golden jewellery from a number of other periods. In the centre of the hall is a mummy of a girl, discovered in the village of Lemba, which dates from the 3rd century BC.

There is also an important collection of ceramics from the Chalcolithic Period in the museum. They have a red pattern on a white background and are among the earliest and most beautiful ceramics which have been found on Cyprus. In addition, a collection of surgical tools from the Roman times is worth seeing. They came from a tomb now lying under the Annabelle Beach Hotel.

In the second hall, finds from the Geometric (1050–750 BC), Archaic (750–475 BC) and Classical periods (475–325 BC) are displayed. Besides the Cypriot vessels with their beautiful paintings and sculptured decorations, you can see the black-on-red receptacles which were imported from Attica. The most significant of the statues are the ones which come from the altar of Aphrodite in Palea Paphos, which display characteristics typical of Archaic-Cypriot sculpture. The Egyptian, Phoenician and Greek influences can be clearly recognised. The wonderful tomb relief in white marble, only parts of which have survived, is of Greek origin, whilst the tomb columns to the side come from Cyprus.

In the same room you can see a row of inscriptions in the Cypriot dialect, as well as the spelling of the Greek language used in Cyprus before the introduction of the Greek alphabet at the end of the 4th century BC. One of the glass display cases contains a collection of bronze and copper coins, most of which come from the mint in Paphos.

In the third hall there are glass and clay pots, along with sculptures and idols from the Hellenistic (325–58 BC) **Peyia basilica.**

and Roman (58 BC to AD 330) Periods. The two rectangular **sarcophagi** in the shape of a house are particularly impressive. Between them is a lion, another Attic work, which was found in Nea Paphos. Amongst the sculptures, the beautiful **head of the Egyptian Queen Isis**, with its characteristic locks of hair, is especially outstanding, as is the **statuette of Asklepios**, the god of medicine, which has survived in perfect condition. Among the lamps (*lynchnas*) is a large lamp modelled in the shape of a ship from the House of Orpheus. It shows the embossed form of the Egyptian king Serapi. In another display cabinet are a number of clay "hot-water bottles", moulded to the shape of the feet, hands and other parts of the body that they might be required to warm.

In the fourth room objects from the Roman and Byzantine Periods (4th–10th centuries) are displayed. The local Roman pottery and the Byzantine amphora come from the House of Dionysos. Particularly worth mentioning are two **trapezophora** made of marble; the first

shows the drunken Hercules surrounded by the Erotidis and the other, which has only survived in part, shows Orpheus and the beasts. A number of Christian inscriptions in marble, and another in the form of a mosaic come from local basilicas. The columns with Arabic inscriptions come from the basilica of Limentiotissa, and are rare evidence of the Arabic presence in Cyprus.

In the last room are discoveries from the Frankish (1192–1489) and Venetian (1489–1571) Periods, including a collection of handsome glazed ceramics. One display case contains examples of glazed Cypriot pottery, which was famous in its time. Another contains examples of imported ceramics from Syria, Italy, Spain and the Near and Far East.

Also from abroad is the **Group of Four Angels**, which was discovered during excavations of the Latin church near the church of Ayia Kyriaki in Kato Paphos. The angels' bodies are made of limestone, whilst their wings are of terracotta and their decorations of multicoloured marble. The Frankish **tomb-**

The swan, a popular motif.

stones are also highly important; their inscriptions reveal vital information about the nobles who died in Cyprus.

Palea Paphos (Kouklia): Palea Paphos is situated 10 miles (16 km) southeast of Nea Paphos and was excavated by the German archaeologist and historian F.C. Maier. According to legend, the city was founded by King Agapenor from Tegea in the Peloponnese. The city owes its considerable fame to the Temple of Aphrodite, which according to various writers – including Homer – was the most revered temple of the world.

The Temple of Aphrodite: The present temple comprises a mixture of buildings from the Late Bronze Age and the Roman Period. From the original buildings it is the enormous stone blocks in the southwestern corner which particularly catch the eye. Most of them have been drilled through at some time in the past by farmers from the surrounding area, searching for the mythical treasure of Aphrodite. A large part of the extant ruins and mosaics come from the construction which took place during the

Roman Period. A number of Roman coins and cameos indicate what the temple could have looked like in its original form; it was divided into three parts, and in the middle there was probably a *baetylos* – an abstract representation of a goddess. According to ancient sources, the cult of Aphrodite was not represented by the statue of a woman. Indeed it is thought that the grey-green conical stone, now in the museum of Palea Paphos, was the symbol of the goddess.

Between the temple and the medieval *kastron* (fortress), a path leads in a north-westerly direction into a small **Roman House**, only a small part of which – a room with floor mosaics, and a bath – has been excavated. In the centre of the geometrical mosaics is a picture of Leda and the Swan. This is, in fact, a copy; the original mosaic now lies in the museum in Nicosia.

Medieval manor house: During the Frankish Period, Cyprus became famous for its sugar production, and the area around **Kouklia** was one of the most important sugar cane and sugar-processing centres on the island. The medieval feudal manor house was the headquarters of the district administration of the sugar-processing industry. It was built in the 13th century, and altered during the period of Ottoman rule. It consists of a large courtyard surrounded by four side buildings. On the eastern side, the large rectangular hall, which is half underground and surmounted by four small cross-vaulted domes, dominates the layout.

The small local museum consists of two rooms. On the ground floor is a mosaic brought here from a Roman building in Palea Paphos. In the upper floor, above the large rectangular hall, the discoveries from the area around Palea Paphos are arranged in chronological order.

In the area around the temple room, but above all in the neighbouring plain (local name Stavros), excavations have brought to light the remains of water-mills which are still in good condition. These water mills were used to power the sugar-processing factory.

Left, enjoying a break. **Right**, market man.

POLIS TO AKAMAS

Polis (meaning city) is the shortened version of **Polis Khrysokhou**, which means "city of the golden land". There are a number of different interpretations of the origin of the eponym golden, all of which probably contain a degree of truth. One cites the extraordinary fertility of the land by virtue of the river Khrysokhou, now augmented by water from a number of dams.

The main product of the Lusignans and Venetians was cotton, obtained from the large feudal estates. But the rich copper deposits in the area, which have been mined since ancient times, are another possible explanation for the name. And it is said that veins of gold really were discovered here during the Ottoman Period, though they were declared as vitriol for export purposes in order to evade Turkish tax laws.

Certainly the region has experienced golden times during its history. The ancient city-kingdom of Marion, founded as a settlement by Ionian Greeks in the 7th century BC, was located just to the east of Polis. But by the time of the British takeover there was little sign of economic prosperity. A report of the District Commissioner of Paphos in 1879 castigated the activities of highwaymen, robbers and murderers in the region. Another type of robbery was also endemic at the end of the 19th century: many thousands of *necropoleis* were opened and robbed – their contents invariably taken abroad.

The English writer Colin Thubron, who visited Polis during his walking tour of the island in 1972, described it as a desolate spot: "I strolled among an unsmiling people down streets lined with deserted shops and houses with damaged roofs which were hanging down… It was the only town I saw in which the owls dared to come in at evening and cry from the rooftops."

Maybe it is precisely the charm of its shabbiness which has made Polis into what it is today: an insider's tip for tourists with rucksacks. The develop-ment of tourism here has followed a very different pattern from that on the rest of the island. There is none of the usual tourist hotels, and no shopping centre with supermarkets and modern fast-food restaurants.

In Polis tourists can find all the things which they know and love from Greece: cosy tavernas with candlelight, music from Theodorakis, and laid-back discotheques which look as though they have been plucked out of the 1960s. On the beach there is still room to move and the hinterland has something wildly romantic about it. Tourism has given the place a modest form of prosperity, and a relatively large proportion of the population has benefited from the purchasing power of the holiday-makers. Many people, for example, rent out private rooms. As a result, Polis now gives the impression of being a pretty up-and-coming town.

A few miles to the west of Polis is the **Akamas** peninsula, the most westerly part of Cyprus. This stretch of land is named after the mythical son of Theseus,

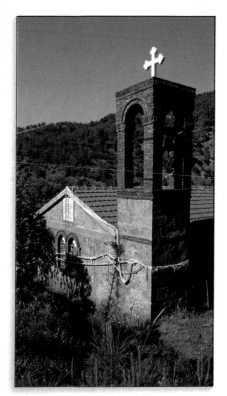

and founder of the later city-kingdom of Soli. The wild landscape, with its steep slopes and deep gorges, is one of the last areas of Cyprus to remain untouched by human hand. Enthusiasts describe it as the last really Homeric landscape of the Hellenistic world.

Its lack of development has made the Akamas peninsula into an important haven for flora and fauna. However, today the Sleeping Beauty quality of the region is acutely threatened. Entrepreneurial Cypriots have long since recognised the potential for tourism – particularly the coastal area with its fantastic sandy bays – and are quickly acquiring the land.

That the further development and eventual destruction of Akamas has so far failed to materialise is due solely to the indefatigable work of the Cypriot environmental campaigners. Groups such as the Friends of the Earth have been campaigning for the Akamas, bringing to the attention of the Cypriot people the danger of further environmental destruction on the island. Other bodies are also concerned. The Council of the European Community has included the Akamas within its Mediterranean protection programme, and the Cypriot government has eventually announced an intention to make the area a national park.

One nature conservation project, with lessons for the whole of the Mediterranean area, has been underway since the middle of the 1970s: the Bay of Lara, which lies on the western coastal edge, serves as a breeding ground for two threatened species of turtle (the green turtle and the hawks-bill turtle). The Cypriot fishing authorities are collaborating with the World Wildlife Fund on the so-called "Lara Project"; its aim is to protect the spawning and newly-hatched young turtles – both from natural enemies and unthinking bathers.

Fish tavernas: From Polis the asphalt road runs in the direction of Akamas via the tranquil fishing village of **Lachi** where there are a number of good fish tavernas. Until recently Lachi was a commercial diving base, in particular

A by-way of Polis.

for diving for sponges. On both sides of Lachi there are beautiful sand and pebble beaches. Further to the west you come to the so-called **Baths of Aphrodite**. Under a rock overhang a cool spring emerges from the rocks and pours into a natural pool. It is here that Akamas is said to have caught Aphrodite unawares as she was bathing naked; the goddess is supposed to have fallen in love with the simple-minded voyeur. Others, however, say that the location of this mythical event was an altogether different spring in the far west of the peninsula. Whichever of the two the *fontana amorosa* is, those who drink from it are supposed to fall head over heels in love themselves.

The asphalt road ends next to a **tourist pavilion** near the Baths of Aphrodite. If you happen to be travelling by a motorbike suitable for cross-country treks, you can drive on to Cape Arnauti. However, those who want to cherish the unspoilt quality of the Akamas should leave their vehicle here and proceed on foot. The scenery is particularly beauti-

ful in spring when the slopes are covered with gorse and sage. For hikers, the Cypriot Tourist Board has designed a nature trail, complete with information boards.

From Polis to Kato Pyrgos: The coast to the northeast of Polis, up to the demarcation line with the Turkish-occupied part of the island near Kato Pyrgos, is the most remote from the cities on the south coast. Before the division of Cyprus it was possible to get to **Kato Pyrgos** relatively quickly from Nicosia via Morphou and Karavostasi, but since 1974 the area of northern Tillyria can be reached only via Polis. The border situation has prevented excessive tourist development – travellers can still find deserted pebble beaches. In Kato Pyrgos there is a small hotel, and in other places private rooms are let.

From Polis you can drive past the now closed administrative buildings and the loading areas of the **Limni mine**. When, in 1979, the supplies of copper concentrates and pyrites were exhausted, the mines were closed down, thus ending a

achi, the
place for fish
uppers.

mining tradition that stemmed back to the Romans.

The road, flanked by the farmhouses, proceeds further along a small strip of irrigated land parallel to the coast. It is hard to imagine that the whole coastal area was virtually uninhabited at the beginning of this century. Until then it was mainly the domain of pirates and slave traders.

The local population preferred to settle further inland, in the area of the modern-day Paphos forest, living from their goats, charcoal burning and other types of forest farming. These ways of earning a living, destructive as they were for the forests, did not meet with the approval of the British Forestry Commission.

Whole villages were moved out, including the 14 families from the village of Dhimmata. In 1953 they were given arable land and British-style brick houses in **Nea Dhimmata**. These houses are still inhabited today.

The last part of the journey on the way to Pyrgos is somewhat difficult but rewarding. The border barricades prevent visitors from travelling further along the coastal road beyond Pakhyammos. The main road now goes in a large arc inland to the mountain region, skirting the village of **Kokkina**. This village was already a refuge for Turkish Cypriots from the Turkish villages of the surrounding area during the Greek-Turkish dispute of 1963–64. The inhabitants of the now empty villages of Alevga, Sellain t'Api and Ayios Yeorgoudhi were evacuated to Kokkina by UN troops, to protect them from the attacks of General Grivas and his national guard. The Turks for their part launched bombing raids.

After the Turkish invasion of 1974 Turkish troops also held the area around Kokkina, even though it wasn't directly connected with the rest of the occupied north. Kokkina has remained a Turkish enclave, guarded by three different border posts of Greek, Turkish and UN soldiers, and the population can be supplied only by sea or by UN lorries.

Right, café society.

THE TROODOS MOUNTAINS

The Troodos mountains rise up like a gentle giant over the western part of the island. The highest peak of this range, Mount Olympus, is also the highest point in Cyprus.

The mass of rock which makes up the central upper Troodos arose 100 million years ago. The oldest part of the mountains, consisting of serpentine and gabbroic rock, is surrounded by a ring of younger rocks (layers of diabase and, further away from the centre, the pillow lava formed from mineral deposits). Vegetation and farming here are determined by the geology of the area and its high-lying location.

The remoteness of the Troodos mountains, together with careful forestry policies, have ensured the preservation of a large forest area in the central part of the Troodos. This forest once extended to the plains, and is unique in the eastern Mediterranean both in terms of its ex-

tent and its beauty. The dominant tree in the Troodos mountains is the Aleppo pine, which accounts for 90 percent of the total stock. Only in the upper reaches, above 4,900 ft (1,500 metres), do the bizarre silhouettes of the black pine predominate.

The inaccessible nature of the mountain area has made it a place of refuge since early times. Byzantine churches and monasteries here survived the period of Ottoman rule more or less undamaged. It is therefore possible to find a wealth of Byzantine art treasures in the Troodos.

In the 20th century the Troodos area has become a refuge of another sort: first as a summer destination for well-off foreign guests and now as a holiday and weekend retreat for the Cypriots themselves. The average temperature on Mount Olympus is around 15°C lower than in Nicosia. In July the maximum temperature is just 27°C. Every year in August whole convoys of cars snake into the Troodos mountains to escape from the sticky heat of the cities. Camping and picnic spots become jam-packed – the Cypriots tending to take a substantial part of their household equipment with them on any outing.

Because it acts as a cloud trap for the prevailing westerly winds the Troodos area receives a relatively high level of precipitation of between 31 and 39 inches (800–1,000 mm) – three times as much as on the plains. In the middle of winter the areas over 4,600 ft (1,400 metres) above sea-level are covered with snow, which in some years reaches a depth of over 10 ft (3 metres)).

Between January and March skiers flit about on the slopes of Mount Olympus. Indeed, even in Ottoman times people knew how to take advantage of the snow, which they transported to Nicosia to sell as a cooling agent.

On the right track: The Cypriot Forestry Commission maintains a network of good (although not asphalted) roads throughout the forest area, most of which are also suitable for walking tours. Those who drive into the remote forest areas (for example the Forest of Paphos) in winter and spring should enquire at the local forestry stations about the state of

Áyios Ioánnis
Lambadhistís Monastery
Kalopanayiótis
Moutoullás
Panayía Podíthou Monastery Galáta
to Nicosía
Kakopetriá
FOREST PATHS
Chromion
Makria Kontarka
Kryos Potamos
Olympus round walk
Pedhoulás
Platania Pine Wood Valley (Hotel)
Forestry College
Pródhromos
Áyios Nikólaos Tis Stejis Monastery
TRÓODOS FOREST
North Shoulder
1709
Pródhromos Res.
Platánia
to Spilía
1112 Koukos
Satellite Station
Trikoukkiá
Olympus
1951
East Shoulder
1739
Paleómylos
Chrome Mine
Youth Hostel
West Shoulder
1710
Tróodos
Páno Amíandos
Asbestos Mine
to Kyperounda
Troodhítissa Monastery
Government Buildings
President's Summer Residence
Káto Amíandos
Phiní
Caledonian Waterfalls
Potamós Mésa
KAKOGYROS FOREST
Páno Plátres
Káto Plátres
MONI FOREST
Saittás

Tróodos Mountains
3.2 km / 2.0 miles

Moniátis
Xi-Lymbos
868
Pérapedhí
to Kiláni
to Kouká
to Límassol

individual roads. Roadworks, landslides or high water level can make even some of the best roads impassable.

Among the particular attractions of the landscape are the cultivated valleys and hills surrounding the high forests. In the middle of the vineyards, orchards, and olive and carob plantations, nestle quiet villages.

Around Mount Olympus: The highest mountain in Cyprus at 6,433 ft (1,961 metres) is **Mount Olympus**, which takes is name from the famous home of the gods in northern Greece. The Cypriots use the more modest name of *Chionistra*, which is a reference to the snow (*chioni*) that lies here in winter. Apart from a fine view on a clear day, the mountain has little to offer. The large white "golf ball" of the radar station near the peak, visible for miles around, has virtually become a symbol of the area. From here the British military authorities eavesdrop on radio communications throughout the Near and Middle East.

The village of **Troodos**, at the foot of Mount Olympus, is not particularly at-tractive. Without a settled resident population, it is just a loose conglomerate of tavernas, souvenir shops, accommodation for visitors and places where the Cypriot civil servants and British soldiers come to enjoy themselves. During the short winter season, from January to March, this is the main centre for skiing in Cyprus, with three ski lifts, a ski school and places to hire out the necessary equipment.

Nearly two miles from Troodos, in the direction of Platres, is the summer residence of the president of Cyprus. The main building was constructed in 1880 under the supervision of the 26-year-old French poet, Arthur Rimbaud (still unknown at the time), and designed as the summer residence for the British governor.

With the aim of providing genuine nature-lovers with more than just holiday camps and fast-food snack bars, the Cypriot tourist authorities, together with the Forestry Commission, laid out a number of nature trails in the upper reaches of the Troodos mountains. The

Venturing into the Troodos.

paths are easy to follow and provide the most vivid and impressive information about the flora and fauna of the area, and also the damage which has been done to the natural habitat. (Individual examples of flora and fauna are described in more detail in a small brochure which is available free of charge in the offices of the tourist authorities.)

The paths take you past strawberry plants and junipers and various evidence of forestry practices and features: places where there have been forest fires, evidence of reafforestation, scarred trees from which resin has been extracted, disused quarries, strange rock formations and impressive views across the mountains, villages and coast.

The nature trails and their starting points (*see map, page 233*) are:

1. **Chromion trail** (6 miles; 10 km): This begins at Troodos. After 2 miles (3 km) there is a spring with drinking water. The destination is the main road from Troodos to Prodhromos, near a disused copper mine.

2. **Makria Kontarka** (2 miles; 3 km):

The starting point is Café Méli on the southern side of the main square in Troodos. The end of the trail enjoys a good view.

3. **Kryos Potamos – Caledonian waterfall** (4 miles; 7 km): This trail begins near the summer palace of the president, and follows the route of a river – water all year round – to a beautiful waterfall. It continues along a small forest road to the Psilodendro restaurant above Pano Platres. The restaurant is popular with tourists (its trout is recommended). This trail gives the best impression of the upper reaches of the forest vegetation.

4. **Around Mount Olympus** (3 miles; 5 km): The beginning and end of this trail is on the Troodos-Prodhromos road, just above the turning which leads to Mount Olympus.

Platres, Prodhromos and Amiandos: The villages of **Pano Platres** (Platres for short) and **Prodhromos** near the summer palace of the British governor were the most salubrious of all the so-called "hill resorts" of the 1940s and '50s (they

were modelled on the hill stations in India, which were built as summer retreats for the British colonial administration). When the British departed, the upper social classes of the Near East started to spend their summers in the comfortable, but expensive, hotels here. Rich traders of Greek origin from Alexandria and Cairo frequented the area, and King Farouk of Egypt once owned a summer villa near Prodhromos. Wealthy Jews from Israel also congregated here, some of whom were said to reminisce about earlier holidays in the Black Forest. At that time, when beach tourism had yet to become popular and mass tourism was unknown, the hill resorts were among the most important tourists centres in Cyprus, in terms of the number of visitors, and the number of nights they stayed.

Coming to Platres and Prodhromos today, you will see only a few reminders of the golden old days. The colonial rulers have long since disappeared from the island, and the development of air travel has opened up other destinations to the upper-crust of the Levant. The once noble hotels are now showing distinct signs of wear and tear, and attract only a run-of-the-mill clientèle during the short summer season. The legendary Berengaria Hotel in Prodhromos – at 4,560 ft (1,390 metres) the highest settlement in Cyprus – is now a ruin. What does remain, however, is the singing of the nightingales in the forests, the groves of fruit trees, and the British character of the buildings. You will still be served with with same formal courtesy which the distinguished British visitors appreciated so much. If you ever run into any kind of problem here, ask advice from Paul, the old man at Hotel Splendid in Platres.

Traces of a very different, less glittering history can be found in **Pano Amiandos**, on the eastern slopes of the upper Troodos. *Amiant* is the local name for asbestos, which was mined here as far back as antiquity. In the past 80 years the mountain has been extensively levelled, first by pick-axes and then by bulldozers, in order to extract the fire-

Workmates.

proof material. The 10,000 men who worked here have turned the mountain in a barren lunar landscape.

The terrible conditions endured by the people who worked in constant contact with the dangerous asbestos fibres was in marked contrast to the luxurious idleness which the visitors to nearby Platres enjoyed. In the end asbestos became as outmoded as summer holidays in Platres: at the end of the 1980s the quarrying was brought to a halt.

Madonna worship: Kykko is the most famous of all the monasteries in Cyprus, being revered all over the Orthodox world. The iconostasis of the monastery church contains an icon of the Madonna, which is supposed to have been hand-painted by Luke. The monk who founded the monastery received this icon in the 12th century from the Byzantine emperor Alexius I Comnenos, after he had cured the emperor's daughter of a severe illness.

Over the course of the centuries the monastery has been destroyed by fire on several occasions; the current building dates from the 19th century at the earliest. There is little historical art to be found here; the monastery is none the less worth a visit on account of the showy extravagance of the monastery church and its grounds. That said, the dazzling marble and gold-plate are no more than modest expressions of the true wealth of the monastery.

At the beginning of the 19th century, when the tax burden on the Orthodox population was particularly excessive, many farmers donated their property to the church to relieve themselves of the tax burden which the land represented. Such donations even brought Kykko property in Russia and Asia Minor. Enormous expanses of expensive land in modern-day Nicosia, which could be used to build on, belong to Kykko.

Numerous pilgrims visit the monastery, particularly at the weekends. They come to worship the icon of Luke and to pay their respects to the tombstone of Archbishop Makarios III. Makarios entered the monastery as a 12-year-old novice in 1926 and was later to become its abbot. After his death in 1977 his mortal remains were buried on Throni Hill, high above the monastery. In recent years the monastic authorities have built a whole series of buildings in which Cypriot visitors (but not foreigners) can stay overnight free of charge.

The monastery of Kykko is also the starting point for a trip to the famous **Cedar Valley**. This type of *cedrus brevifolia*, which can only be found in Cyprus, is larger and more beautiful than the Lebanese cedar, itself a symbol of the Levant state. Cedar Valley, at the foot of Mount Tripylos in the heart of the Paphos Forest, got its name from being the last large natural habitat of this majestic tree.

Saved from extinction: With a bit of luck you may also come across a mouflon in the area around Cedar Valley. This Cypriot species of Mediterranean wild sheep is both rare and shy. Just as the species was on the point of extinction successful attempts were made to breed it in captivity, and the national airline, Cyprus Airways, has adopted it as its emblem. You can visit around 60 of these

Icon inside Kykko monastery.

animals in a reserve in the idyllically located village of Stavros tis Psokas, further up Cedar Valley. Also in **Stavros tis Psokas** is the Forest Station, the headquarters of the largest forest division of the Paphos Forest. This was the first of the Cypriot forestry stations to be set up in 1882.

There are two possible ways of proceeding from Paphos or Polis to Stavros tis Psokas and into Cedar Valley: from Paphos, via the village of Kannaviou, and from Polis via Pomos on the north coast to a turn-off called the Lorovouno Junction, south of the enclave of Kokkina.

The southern foothills: On the way from Limassol to Platres or the monastery of Kykko you should take time to explore the southern foothills of the Troodos mountains, with its wide variety of landscapes and pretty villages. Here you can find peace and tranquillity in a shady *kentron*, such as near the famous Royal Oak, an ancient oak tree growing near Trimiklini. On the side of the roads fresh fruits, nuts and figs are sold, all produced in the fertile land of the area.

A wide variety of wines and spirits are made in the Troodos. As well as producing the excellent local wine and distilling the fiery *Zivania*, locals make a range of grape-based liqueurs such as *Palouzé*, *Sudjuko* and *Loukoumi*.

Loukoumades, small doughnuts dipped in syrup, can be bought fresh in **Phini**, a pretty village which is worth visiting on a number of counts. In the local **Folk Art Museum of Phanis Pilavakis** (dedicated to Cypriot folk art), for example, you can find information about the production and use of the large clay *pithoi*. The potters of Phini used to be famous for their skill in producing these storage containers.

Unfortunately, the decline of traditional crafts seems unstoppable. One member of Phini, Philippos Kallis, now nearly 80, is the last of the craftsmen working on another once flourishing trade. Kallis produces stools for the coffee house. His raw materials are selected parts of strawberry trees and golden-leaved oaks. He fells these him-

Courtyard of Kykko.

self in the Troodos forests and carries them home on his back. The stools are both stable and beautiful. Alas, Kallis hasn't yet found anyone to continue the family craft.

Pitsilia is the name given to the slopes of the long eastern Troodos chain with its many forested peaks, the highest being Papoutsa which towers to a height of 5,098 ft (1,554 metres). A total of around 21,000 people live in 49 villages, some of which are tiny. The area has always been inhabited by Greek Cypriots; many originally came here to flee from the Ottoman invaders. Like other remote areas, Pitsilia suffers bitterly from the emigration of its younger working population. Nevertheless a number of serious attempts have been made to reduce the exodus, and to prevent the decline of the houses and meadows. In 1977 the Cypriot government started the Pitsilia Integrated Rural Development Project as a way of improving living conditions in the region. The World Bank, which helped finance the project and acted as a consultant, would like it to be regarded as a model for the whole of the eastern Mediterranean.

At considerable expense and with great technical expertise new, wide arable terraces were laid out, small dams, reservoirs and water supply systems were built, and the road network was improved considerably. The farmers were given loans so that they could invest in the rural economy. A grammar school was built in **Agros**, a gymnasium and a health centre in Kyperounda. New life has since returned to the area, particularly in larger villages such as Agros and Pelendria. Many of the inhabitants, however, work in Nicosia or Limassol, as shown by the convoys of cars every morning and evening.

Agros offers visitors a special treat in the months of May and June, when local farmers unload vast baskets of rose petals in the village, for in an inconspicuous-looking factory on the outskirts rosewater is distilled. This makes an excellent souvenir to take home.

On the northern edge of Pitsilia is the **monastery of Makheras**, a popular

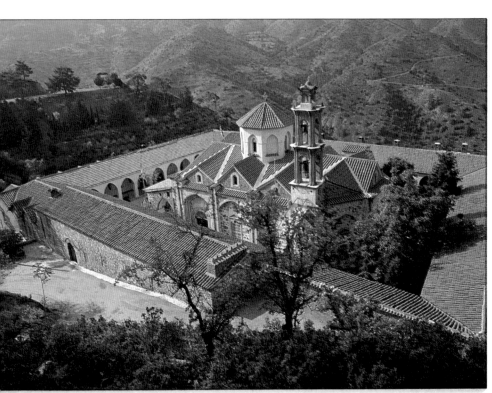

destination for the Cypriots themselves during the summer months, not least because of its shady location. Like so many Cypriot monasteries, the 12th-century building is supposed to mark the site where a miraculous icon was found. Under the gallery on the upper floor, the history of the monastery is recorded in illustrated texts.

The undisputed hero of the monastery is not, however, a devout man of the church, but Gregoris Afxentiou, a secular rebel. Afxentiou, one of the leading men of the EOKA at the time of the anti-colonial struggle for independence, was tracked down by British soldiers to a hide-out in a cave just below the monastery in March 1957. He put up bitter resistance against his enemies, but was killed when his British captors set his refuge on fire. The place where Afxentiou died is now decorated with wreaths and the Hellenistic flag. It has become almost as important a place of pilgrimage as the grave of Archbishop Makarios at the monastery of Kykko. In the monastery of Makheras a special

little museum has been set up in memory of the heroic fighter. Visitors with a taste for the macabre can even see his partly charred remains.

The Marathasa and Solea Valleys: These valleys cut into the northern slopes of the Troodos mountains run parallel to each other. Without doubt, they comprise one of the most beautiful areas on the island, even though the lower reaches of the valley and the local connections to the sea have been cut off by the demarcation line and cannot be reached from southern Cyprus. The patchwork landscape, dotted by tightly-packed gabled houses, is enchanting. Each season has its own particular appeal: in spring, for example, the upper Marathasa Valley becomes a white sea of cherry blossom. Not least of the region's attractions, concealed under rather inconspicuous "barn roofs", are the most important art treasures left behind by the Byzantine rulers.

Kakopetria in the Solea Valley is a particularly popular Sunday destination for citizens of Nicosia, who come specially to eat its famous trout. Parts of the village have been undergoing extensive restoration in recent years in a successful attempt to preserve the traditional local building style.

In the Marathasa Valley, which until a few decades ago was extremely remote, a number of interesting traditions have been preserved. You can still sample the villlage's traditional speciality – wonderful aromatic dried cherries, once enjoyed as far away as Egypt. In **Moutoullas** the mineral water of the same name is bottled, and *sanidhes* and *vournes* are produced from sandalwood. Sanidhes are long planks with hollows (usually 11), in which the bread dough was placed to rise in traditional farming homes. *Vournes* are wooden bowls also used in bread-making. Just a few decades ago such items could be found in every Cypriot household. Only selected parts of pine trunks were used, and the carpenters' demand for wood was so great that they were regarded by the British forestry officials as one of the biggest threats to the forests of the Troodos area.

240

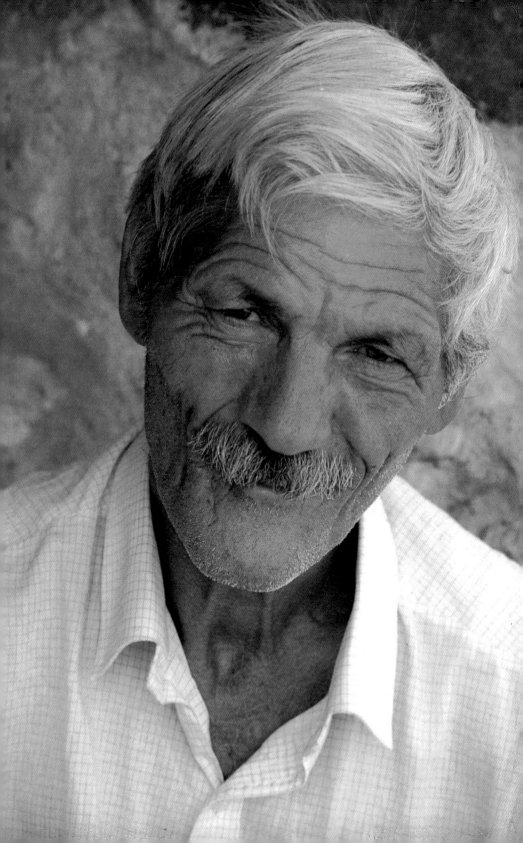

BRITAIN'S GREEN LEGACY

In the ancient world, Cyprus was known as the Green Island, a description undoubtedly awarded on account of its forests. The Apostle Paul reported that he had to pick his way through thick forests on his journey from Famagusta to Paphos, even on the plains. This wealth of trees, together with a favourable geographical location in the eastern Mediterranean, made Cyprus into an important exporter of wood and a centre for shipbuilding. Alexander the Great kept part of his fleet here. The wharfs in Cyprus could produce the largest trading ships from bow to stern.

The island was totally independent of the outside world in terms of know-how and raw materials. According to records, the forests withstood the demand for wood for shipbuilding and copper smelting relatively well, even during Roman times.

The forests were again brought to the attention of a wider world at the beginning of the period of British colonial rule, when a thorough inspection was made of the island's forests. British officials claimed that the Ottoman Empire had virtually destroyed this great natural resource. The plain of Mesaoria was a treeless steppe. Nearly all the fruit trees had been axed: people preferred to forgo their yields rather than turn them over to the tax collectors. The only remaining forests were in the mountain regions.

Sir Samuel White Baker reported from the Troodos mountains in 1879: "If a hurricane had crossed the country and knocked down nine out of every ten trees, the destruction would have been nothing in comparison with the damage the local people have inflicted. They have mutilated those trees which they haven't already cut down. Wonderful trees lie in their thousands rotting on the ground... I was tempted to stop my donkey and arrest the owner... but I couldn't have tied my donkey up... not a single branch was left which would have held her weight."

It seems that the uneducated population, tormented by the tax collectors, had carried out a thorough destruction of the forests. Burning down a forest was considered an acceptable way to obtain arable land or to destroy an enemy's herd of goats. The forest was regarded as no-man's-land. Without any concern for regeneration, the locals exploited the best trees for sap and pitch, bark for the tannery or simply for firewood.

From the beginning of their rule over the island in 1878, the British paid particular attention to the forests. The first Forestry Commission in the British Empire was set up in Cyprus and the first Forestry Officer, G.P. Madon, warned: "We are convinced that the remaining stock of forests on the island will not survive the end of this century unless radical measures are taken to put an end to their destruction."

As early as 1879 the first forestry laws were passed. In stark contrast to all other aspects of colonial administrative practice it was the maintenance and regeneration of the forests rather than their economic exploitation which was the main consideration. No less a person than Earl Mountbatten of Burma has described the forests as Cyprus's most valuable treasure.

The British recognised that the main enemy of the forests was the practice of free-grazing goats. The first census conducted by the British showed that there were 250,000 sheep on the island – two for every inhabitant. In the period of Ottoman rule ownership of "mobile property" in the form of a herd of goats had proved a successful ploy for escaping the exploitative claws of the tax collectors. Everywhere in the forests, mandras (goat pens) proliferated.

For the British administrators, the goats were the incarnation of destruction. G.P. Madon stirred up feelings against the "satanic" animal in a speech in the British Parliament: "Soon we will have just naked rocks... where the thickets currently stand, which the tireless and cruel teeth of the goat denude – these insatiable rodents, which sit on the bushes in order to reach the highest branches. What an appetite they have, these eternally starving wretches. They will complete the work of destruction which humans began! Where the axe of the woodsmen has cut the forest to the ground, the teeth of the goat ensure that nature cannot repair the damage. As soon as the first shoots appear in spring, the goats devour them... every sign of vegetation that shoots up is brought to a standstill through the incessant work of their cruel teeth and their poisoned saliva!"

What followed was a war against the

goatherds. A special "Goat Law" formed the legal basis for banning the herds of goats from the most important forest areas. A number of goatherds were offered alternative employment as forestry workers; while others were paid compensation. Nevertheless, those affected were reluctant to relinquish their traditional occupation, which they regarded as a natural right. There were numerous arson attempts and even a bid to murder one of the forestry supervisors.

It took several generations before the people of Cyprus accepted the measures of the British Head Foresters. The first major success was achieved at the end of the 1930s when the powerful monasteries gave up their right to pasture in the forests, thereby sending an important signal to others. By the 1940s, 96 percent of the Main State Forest – which was particularly carefully looked after and mainly comprised areas in the Troodos mountains and the Pentadaktylos – was free from goat pastures. A whole series of villages of former goatherds had been moved from the forest regions to the coastal area, where they were supplied with free houses and land.

Forestry policies in Cyprus were to become an example for the whole of the Near East. The British left behind 670 sq. miles (1,735 sq. km) of forests, 19 percent of the whole island. Their method of reporting forest fires with a network of "forest telephones", remains a model system even today. Since 1951 knowledge about the care and regeneration of Mediterranean forests has been developed at the Cyprus Forestry College. Foresters from the Third World – from Belize to Yemen – are taught here.

Since taking over from the British, the work of the Cypriot Forestry Commission has not always gone smoothly. During the wars of 1964 and 1974 large areas of forest went up in flames. The Turkish invasion of 1974 alone led to the destruction of 16 percent of the state-owned forests. These areas were reafforested in the period up to 1982. Today, all over Cyprus terraces which had been barren for decades are being replanted. Those who design the forestry policies have also shown themselves open to new knowledge and methods. With the aim of promoting more environmentally-friendly methods, they work without bulldozers. ■

The Forestry College.

Ἅ(γιος) ὁ Βασίλ(ειος) ὁ ἅγιο(ς) Ἰω(άννης) ὁ Χρυ(σό)στο(μος)

BYZANTINE LANDMARKS

Cyprus is a treasure trove of Byzantine art. There are few countries in the Orthodox Christian world where so many masterpieces of Byzantine art – from the 11th to the 18th centuries – can be found within such a small area. The island boasts examples from all epochs of the Byzantine Empire, including the iconoclastic period.

Many of the masterpieces lie in the Troodos mountains, or in the areas around its eastern and western foothills. Only the most important of the many examples will be described here (they are grouped according to the region in which they are located).

The eastern Troodos mountains: The church that is considered to be the masterpiece of Byzantine art on Cyprus is the **Panayia tou Araka church**, with its frescoes from 1192, in the village of **Lagoudhera**. So that it may serve as a model for the other examples of Byzantine art which are listed here, its architectural and iconographic features are described in detail.

The Panayia church of Lagoudhera lies just outside the village to the west. On arriving, you may be surprised and confused to be confronted by a large barn rather than a church. The well-proportioned gleaming white edifices familiar on mainland Greece and the Greek islands are nowhere to be found in the mountains of Cyprus. The weather hereabouts, particularly the heavy snow in winter, created static and construction problems, and so from the 14th/15th centuries sacred domed Byzantine buildings were given barn-like gable roofs for extra protection – as here in Lagoudhera.

The iconographic cycles of frescoes, traditionally painted in the dome, were housed on the raised long walls and on the surfaces of the gables.

The simple cruciform domed church of Lagoudhera contains works of the neo-classical style painted by artists from the Byzantine capital, Constantinople. The name of a painter, Leon Authentou,

is included in the donor's inscription. As befits the importance of this unique work of art, all the most important iconographic themes are represented: in the **sanctuary**, with its semi-circular apse, is the Virgin Mary in majesty with child, flanked by the two archangels, Gabriel and Michael. Below this are seven medallions with the busts of saints (the third from the right is the Cypriot saint Heracleidius).

In the vertical section of the apse are the 12 Early Fathers, including the Cypriot St Barnabas to the right of the middle window, and (under the window on the left), the bust of the Cypriot St Spyridon, who became the patron saint of the island of Corfu at the end of the 15th century. In the vault above the sanctuary is Christ's Ascension, on the northern wall below are St Simeon Stylites Thaumaturge and St Onufrios; on the southern wall is a portrayal of St Simeon Stylites Archimandrite.

On the eastern pendentives of the dome (the triangular supporting vaults between the piers and the drum of the

Preceding pages: fresco in the St Heracleidos monastery. **Left,** Tripioti church, Nicosia. **Right,** St John the Theologian, Kiti church.

dome) is a scene of the Annunciation with the Archangel Gabriel and Mary, whilst between them hangs a medallion depicting the beardless Christ Emmanuel. The western pendentives show the Evangelists Mark and Matthew (left) and John and Luke. On the piers of the drum are 12 life-sized prophets from the Old Testament, while the dome itself is filled with an impressive *Christus Pantokrator* (Christ as the judge of the world) surrounded by medallions with angels; on the east side is a medallion with the "empty throne" (*Etoimasía*) ready for Christ's rule over the world after the Day of Judgement.

In the vertex of the vault are four medallions decorated with the bust of martyrs, below an *Anastasis* (Christ's descent into Hell following the Crucifixion) and the Baptism of Christ. On the lunette is a mural of the Virgin's Presentation in the Temple, below which are life-sized depictions of saints whose expressive faces are unusually realistic for this kind of art: Sabbas, Nicholas, Simeon with the baby Jesus, John the Baptist, *Panayia Eleoussa* (Mary with the Angels).

A beautiful Dormition of the Virgin can be seen on the lunette of the southern recess: Below is the *Panayia Arakiótissa*, which as *Panayia Amolyntos*, the Mother of God with the Instruments of the Passion, has become a model for numerous portrayals of icons. Next to this on the right is a larger than life portrayal of the Archangel Michael, and on the underside of the arches are excellent representations of saints (for example St Antonios on the right). On the south side of the west vault is a portrayal of the Nativity, and below St Peter and various other saints.

Stavros tou Ayiasmati church: The gable roof of this church, situated about 3 miles (5 km) north of the village of **Platanistasa**, in a remote mountain area, has a cycle of frescoes by Philippos Goul from 1494 which is well worth seeing. (Before visiting the church be sure to collect the key from the Kafenion in the village.) One special iconographic feature in the church is the fresco-cycle

Many churches look more like barns.

entitled *The Discovery of the Holy Cross* (in the arched recess of the north wall).

Ayios Saviur tou Sotiros church: This small chapel with just one room in the village of **Palekhori** contains a number of good traditional frescoes from the first half of the 16th century, in particular a detailed iconographic cycle portraying the life of Christ.

Ayios Mama church: This one-roomed chapel in **Louvaras** has a complete cycle of frescoes by Philippos Goul (1495).

The Panayia Amasgou monastery: This barrel-vaulted one-roomed chapel, which also has the additional protection of a barn roof, lies about 2 miles (3.5 km) outside the village of **Monagri**. The key to the church is looked after by the village priest. Inside are fragments of frescoes with very high quality paintings from the 12th and 13th centuries, reminiscent of the large paintings from Lagoudhera and Asinou.

Churches in the northwestern Troodos: The best way to visit all the art treasures in this area is by basing yourself in one of the mountain villages of the Troodos (Platres, Fini or Pedhoulas). However, it is also possible to arrange an outing from Nicosia or Limassol, though this would be lengthy. The route suggested here begins in the north with the Asinou church, then turns south into the mountains (Kakopetria), before ending in the northwest at Kalopanayiotis.

Panayia Phorviotissa church: The church in Asinou is a veritable museum of Byzantine art. The quality of the paintings from various epochs gives a very good impression of the art of Byzantine Cyprus. Again, the key for the church is obtained from the village priest in Nikitari. He accompanies visitors to the church, so a small gratuity is welcomed.

The little one-roomed chapel, dating from the turn of the 12th century, was adorned with Comnenian paintings by artists from Constantinople in the years 1105–06, in accordance with the style of the capital. At the end of the 12th century a **western narthex** (entrance hall) was added with semi-circular apses to the north and south. After the narthex had been built, the **southern portal** was

The raising of Lazarus, depicted in Asinou church.

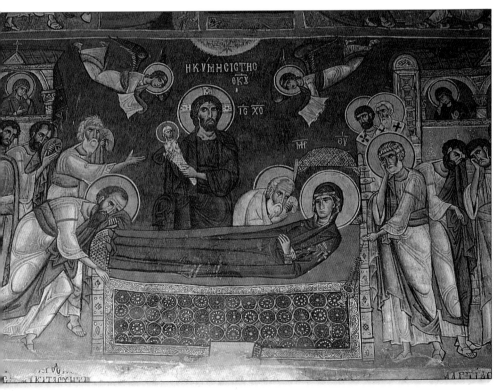

walled up, and towards the end of the 12th century or beginning of the 13th century a picture of St George on his horse was painted on the inside of the portal.

All in all there are five different layers of paintings in the Asinou church, from four different epochs:

Some paintings from 1105–06 are in the sanctuary, for example the Communion of the Apostles and Christ's Ascension. In the nave and on the western wall are portrayals of Christ's Entry into Jerusalem, the Last Supper and the death of the Virgin Mary. The 40 martyrs and various saints are depicted on the north wall.

St George in the southern apse of the narthex dates from the end of the 12th century and the beginning of the 13th century. All the other paintings date from 1332–33, including the Mother of God in the apse and the patron's picture with St Anastasia in the narthex (to the right of St George). A booklet explaining the themes and history of the frescoes is available.

Galata: In the mountain village of Galata, with its plentiful springs, there are no fewer than four Byzantine churches. All are worth visiting, but the two described below are particularly impressive. (Again, the keys can be obtained from the priest; the best place to find him is in the Kafenion near the bridge with the plane trees.)

The **Panayia Theotokos church** is also known as the Michail Arkhangelos church, as a larger-than-life archangel keeps guard over the main portal. The church houses an extremely detailed cycle of Christian works, and the quality of the paintings is very high. The frescoes are the work of the Cypriot artist Symeon Axenti and were painted in 1514.

The **Panayia Podhitou church**, has a number of Italo-Byzantine frescoes from 1502. The influence of the Venetian epoch (1489–1571) is noticeable in the case of the portrayals of the Mother of God and the Communion of the Apostles in the apse. The dramatic portrayal of the Crucifixion in the western gable

The church of Asinou, perhaps the finest Byzantine church in Cyprus.

250

is very moving, although there is nothing Byzantine about it.

Ayios Nikolaos tis Stejis: This church (Nicholas of the Roof) lies some 2 miles (3 km) outside the village of **Kakopetria,** and contains important Byzantine paintings from the 11th to the 17th centuries. The examples from the 11th century include Christ's Entry into Jerusalem and the Transfiguration, which is portrayed in one large composition together with the Raising of Lazarus. The Comnenian style of the 12th century is represented by the Virgin Mary's Presentation in the Temple, the 40 martyrs (exactly as in Asinou), the Day of Judgement and so on. Examples from the 14th century include various excellent works in the nave, particularly the Nativity and the two soldier saints, Theodoros and Georgios.

Michail Arkhangelos church: The gable roofed church of the Archangel Michael is situated in the lower part of **Pedhoulas,** directly on a side street. The frescoes in the nave are the work of a certain "Adam" from 1474. The cycle depicts rarer themes such as Pilate, and Peter's denial of Christ.

Panayia tou Moutoulla church: This tiny chapel is located on the western edge of **Moutoullas,** (to the left of the road when you are coming from Pedhoulas). This is the oldest known church with a gable roof on Cyprus. The frescoes date from 1280. Some are not in very good condition, but the most interesting is the fresco of the donors; the carved doors are also worth closer inspection.

The monastery church of Ayios Ioannis Lambadistou: The monastery, which is no longer inhabited by monks, is situated in the valley on the opposite side of the river to the village of **Kalopanayiotis** (key from the village priest). Its colossal barn roof incorporates a collection of sacred Byzantine architecture spread over three centuries (from the 13th century to around 1500). The extraordinary paintings in the domed Orthodox church of Ayios Heracleides have survived from the first half of the 13th century, from the Early Comnenian Period. Their expressiveness, lines and colours seem to

Decorative panels in the chapel of Panayia Arkhangelos, Galata.

indicate that they were painted by artists from Constantinople. The Entry into Jerusalem is particularly outstanding. Equally accomplished are the Raising of Lazarus, the Crucifixion, and the Ascension in the southern recess.

The christological scenes in the main church come from the period around 1400 and show good examples of traditional painting. The **narthex**, which was built later, was decorated with frescoes in the later style of Constantinople, before the city was conquered by the Ottomans in 1453. According to one of the inscriptions, the painter was a refugee from Constantinople who painted this part of the church shortly after 1453.

The 15th-century **Latin chapel** in the north of the complex is the work of a Venetian. Its frescoes of the Acathist Hymn were done in 1500. The paintings show strong Western influences in terms of their style, though iconographically they follow in the Byzantine tradition.

The west coast and eastern foothills: To the north and east of Paphos, there are three important Byzantine monuments. They make ideal destinations for day trips from Paphos.

Panayia Khryseleousa church: This domed cruciform church with a domed narthex extension lies right in the middle of **Emba** (key from the village priest). It contains frescoes from the end of the 15th century and a valuable iconostasis from the 16th century.

The monastery of Ayios Neophytos: In 1159 a 25-year-old monk by the name of Neophytos settled as a hermit to the north of Paphos. He cut a hermitage in the rock with his own hands, and by about 1200 a sizeable community had evolved around it. Even during his lifetime, people came on pilgrimages here. He was famous far and wide for denouncing the injustices of the Byzantine tax collectors. His bones, removed from his tomb in 1750, are contained in a wooden sarcophagus; his skull is preserved in a silver reliquary.

His rock grotto was painted in two distinct phases and styles at the end of the 12th century. In 1183 artists from Constantinople painted frescoes in the neo-classical style, and then in 1196 the "monastic" frescoes were painted, as was usual in monastic churches at this time. The paintings in the Neophytos Rock-Grotto are among the most important on the island. The few paintings dating from 1503 are of traditional rural character.

In the 16th century a large monastic development was built to the east of the rock-face (it is now inhabited by Orthodox monks). In the **northern aisle** of the monastic church some artistically valuable frescoes from the beginning of the 16th century have survived. In terms of their style and execution these are excellent examples of Italo-Byzantine art.

Ayia Paraskevi church: The church of Yeroskipos, the Sacred Garden of Aphrodite, in **Yeroskipos** is not only a masterpiece of Byzantine sacred architecture, but also one of the most important monuments from the Iconoclastic Period. The church, with its five domes follows the same architectural pattern as Peristerona, and is modelled on the multi-domed 6th-century Justinian church of St John in Ephesus.

In the dome above the sanctuary rare frescoes with Byzantine motifs have survived from the Iconoclastic Period (the first half of the 9th century). Only a few fragments have survived from the frescoes of figures from the end of the 12th century (for example the head from the Dormition of the Virgin on the northern wall, centre aisle). Most of the works from this epoch were painted over in the late 15th century.

The eastern slopes of the Troodos: The Gothic architecture and French inscriptions in the **Ayia Ekaterina** in **Pyrga** are a reminder of the end of the period of Lusignan rule (1191–1489). The chapel was painted in 1421, and the figures in the donor's picture are probably King Janus and his wife Charlotte of Bourbon.

Although the frescoes in the little cemetery chapel of **Ayii Apostoli** in **Perakhorio** are not in very good condition, their extreme age and artistic quality mean they are nonetheless among the most important Byzantine monuments on the island. They were painted between 1160 and 1180 and are examples of the classical Comnenian style.

Icon in the Ayios Neophytos monastery.

NICOSIA

"When, having climbed up the gentle hills, you first catch sight of Lefkosia, with its slender palms and minarets, and the picturesque mountain range in the background on the scorched plains of Cyprus, it is reminiscent of a scene out of the *Arabian Nights*. A jewel of orange gardens and palm trees in an area otherwise devoid of trees, an oasis (by dint of its embankments) – created by human hand. And in the same way that the contrast between the city and its surroundings stands out clear and harsh, the spirit of contradiction can also be felt within the city. Venetian fortifications and Gothic buildings crowned by the half-moon of Turkey; Turks, Greeks and Armenians mingling together colourfully on this ancient land, each other's enemies but united in their love of this piece of earth which is their common home." This was how Ludwig Salvator, the Archbishop of Austria, described the city in *Lefkosia, the Capital of Cyprus* in 1873.

A divided capital: Today, however, Nicosia bears little resemblance to this description. The Ledra Palace Hotel is damaged from shelling, and surrounded by barbed-wire. To the right of Drakos Avenue are the remains of a burnt-out villa, just 100 yards from the Venetian fortress walls of the old city.

The walls are still functioning as a bulwark, 400 years since they were built. They are now part of a heavily guarded border. And for many years the Ledra Palace has served as the barracks for the Canadian contingent of the UN peacekeeping troops. Drakos Avenue is blocked by barbed wire, and carefully painted blue and white concrete walls. Ramps in the road near the provisionally erected post of the Republic of Cyprus force the traffic to slow to walking pace. The UN guard in his shelter greets people casually. There are no special incidents to report from the only crossing between north and south Nicosia in the buffer zone.

In Berlin an asphalt surface, now barely visible, is the only thing left to remind one of the legendary Checkpoint Charlie, the ultimate symbol of the division of that city. In Nicosia the Cypriot equivalent of Checkpoint Charlie looks as though it is here to stay. In fact very few people are allowed to pass checkpoint Ledra Palace, generally only diplomats, UN soldiers and foreigners may cross the border.

Depending on the current state of relations between the two parts of Cyprus, tourists holidaying in the southern Republic of Cyprus are allowed to go north of the "Green Line" until sunset. The only Cypriots for whom the barrier is open from time to time are members of the tiny minorities – Greeks, Turks and Maronites – who live in the "wrong" part of the island.

At first sight, the two halves of the city appear to have virtually nothing in common. Greek Cypriot and Turkish Cypriot soldiers face each other irreconcilably in primitive shelters. The capital of Cyprus doesn't even have a common name: the Greeks call it

Lefkosia, whilst to the Turks it is Lefkosha. Nicosia is the old name given by the European conquerors. The "Green Line" cuts the streets and water pipelines in two, has put the former international airport out of action, and divides the capital of the island into two parts. It is the job of the blue-helmeted soldiers of the UN to ensure that armed conflicts do not arise.

Past glories: At the entrance to Hermes Street in the old city, you can recognise the faded victory slogans of the Olympiakos football team, which once had its home here. *Olympiakos 3 Omonia 2* has been painted on the wall with an unsteady hand, along with the date – 8 June 1961. A hundred yards further on, near a post of the Greek Cypriot National Guard, the buffer zone begins. Unlike in the rest of the island, the division of Nicosia didn't start with the Turkish invasion of 1974, but in 1964. On Christmas Eve 1963 civil violence broke out in the city. The Greek Cypriots demanded that the newly formed Republic become part of Greece, the so-

called *enosis*. The Turks, on the other hand, fought for *taksim*, the division of the island. Neither of the two demands could be realised at the time, and yet the common state divided along ethnic lines. In 1964 a British soldier marked the front which divided the two communities with a green marker: this was the birth of Nicosia's famous Green Line.

Ghia runs a tiny grocery store in Patroclos Street just a few yards south of the Green Line. Here, in the most cramped conditions, you can buy everything from batteries to butter. And yet Ghia has very few customers, and those few she has are poor. The people who live in the dilapidated flats of the old city centre have remained untouched by the economic miracle of the Republic of Cyprus: old people whose pensions are barely enough to live on and families with too many children, who had to flee from the Turkish troops in 1974. Nobody who can afford to do otherwise wants to live in such close proximity to the demarcation line.

The prosperous Greek Cypriot ma-

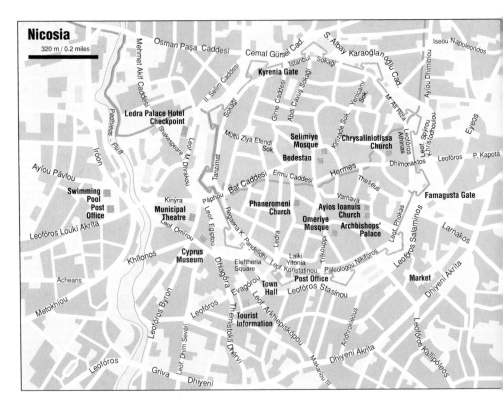

jority live in large apartment blocks or in their own detached houses in the new part of the city. In the old city centre the houses become more dilapidated every year. First the plaster crumbles away, then the roof begins to leak. The inhabitants have no money for the repairs, and the owners no longer care. Many valuable buildings from the Ottoman era now stand empty. In some, only the ground floor is inhabited, because the upper floor is in danger of collapsing.

The city authorities have renovated a small area of the city: Laiki Yitouna, the "traditional neighbourhood", could be a model for the restoration of the old city. The only problem is that virtually nobody lives there: it has been turned into an enclave of expensive restaurants and souvenir shops.

Minarets and church towers rise above the mainly one or two-storey houses of the old city. And palm trees too, hundreds of them, either standing in line along the city walls, or in groups of twos and threes, casting their flat shadow on the narrow streets and courtyards.

Most of the streets are narrow, the shutters of the houses pulled down. From the outside there is little indication of the beauty of the old buildings. Life here has always gone on in those parts of the buildings hidden from the outside. The traditional houses of the Levant face inwards, with arcades and inner courtyards, in which palms or orange trees grow.

Ghia sells mandarins and lemons directly from the trees which stand behind her house. From the Selimiye mosque in the north, the wind blows the *muezzin*'s call to prayer as far as Patroclos Street. For the inhabitants of this area, the minarets of the cathedral of St Sophia, the coronation church of the Middle Ages, visible from a long distance, are an infinite distance away.

Ahmet is a paediatrician and lives in the Turkish Cypriot north of the old city. But very few patients ever come into his tiny practice. According to Ahmet, they simply don't have the money and prefer to go to the chemist to buy their medicine, without a medical

The main square.

diagnosis. Nicosia has its own north-south divide: in contrast to the southern Republic of Cyprus, the Turkish-occupied part is poor. In the south the average income per head is around £4,300 per year; in the north it is just £1,300, and many earn considerably less.

Around 165,000 people live in the southern part of the capital. In northern Nicosia there are just 35,000. Although the stores in the main shopping streets are overflowing with jeans, leather jackets and electrical equipment, most of the purchasers come from the 29,000 Turkish soldiers who have resigned themselves to being based permanently in north Cyprus. On the pavements a flourishing trade is in progress – the goods, wrapped in newspaper, are destined for Turkey. Veiled women and the occasional Kurdish expression clearly indicate that it is now not only Cypriots who live and trade here. The phantom state of the Turkish Republic of North Cyprus, officially recognised only by Ankara, has reeled in at least 55,000 settlers from Anatolia.

Although the citizens in the two halves of Nicosia are not allowed to visit each other, have two different religions, and speak different languages, they have more in common than most of them would like to admit. In the south as in the north the men invariably spend their spare time in one of the small coffee-houses. All Nicosians – like all Cypriots in general – have a passion for extensive company. In the gestures that are used, in the customs of daily life, in the strong sense of family identity – life is much the same everywhere in the narrow streets of old Nicosia . In both north and south the carpenters are busy in their open work-places, and you can watch the chair-makers as they go about their business. Owners sit in front of their small shops and wait for customers, cats patrol their territories. It would be wrong to say that time has stood still in old Nicosia, but the clocks certainly seem to go slower than elsewhere.

City history: Nicosia was founded in AD 965 under Byzantine rule although the area was settled well before that. In **The Archbishop's Palace.**

the 7th century BC the city of Ledra, one of the Cypriot city kingdoms, was sited here. Under Greek and Roman rule Nicosia – which at that time had the name *Leukos* – was an important trading centre. Its upswing from the 9th century onwards was largely due to the fact that the coasts were plagued by pirates. Nicosia had the advantage of lying inland and so remained protected from such attacks.

Under the Lusignans (1192–1489) the city became the seat of residence of the Catholic archbishop and capital of the crusader state of Cyprus. At that time there were around 20,000 people in Nicosia, a considerable number for the time. The population was a colourful mixture: along with the Greek Orthodox majority and the Catholic feudal lords, there were Nestorians, Copts, Armenians and Jews. Gothic churches and cathedrals were built at this time.

A large palace, built in the 14th century, served as the seat of government for the French nobles. Unfortunately little is known about its architecture, not even its exact location. Like many other buildings, the palace fell victim to the Venetian military planners. Between 1567 and 1570 they built a circular fortified wall with 11 bastions. To maintain a free field of fire all the buildings outside the new city boundaries had to be erased. Churches and palaces, cemeteries, domestic dwellings and monasteries were all burned to the ground. The engineers responsible for the wall also diverted the river Pedios (which had previously flowed straight through the city) around the new city wall. The only entrance to the city was through one of the three heavily fortified gates.

The purpose of this bulwark was to repel the Ottoman. Yet this hastily erected fortification, praised as being of the most perfect design, proved to be no serious obstacle at all for the Sultan's troops: after a two-week siege they conquered Nicosia. The Catholic feudal lords were either killed or driven out, and the Ottoman soldiers and settlers from Anatolia moved in.

Favourable impressions: "Nicosia is the capital of Cyprus and lies under the mountains in the middle of a wide plain with a wonderful, healthy climate. As a result of the perfect air temperature and the healthy climate, the King of Cyprus and all the bishops and prelates of the Kingdom live in this city. A large number of the other princes, counts, nobles, barons, and knights also live here. They busy themselves each day with spear-throwing, tournaments and, above all, with hunting." Thus wrote the pilgrim Ludolf von Suchen in 1340.

The walls have been maintained as a symbol of the city. On the bastions, which are named after influential Italian families, the cannons of the defenders once stood. One of them, *Flatro*, remains a prohibited military zone up until today. The Greek and Turkish posts now stand facing each other at this point, separated only by a small UN building in the middle. In all other respects, however, the walls have lost their purpose; during the period of British colonial rule, gaps were cut in the wall, so that streets could connect the old and new parts of the city.

Male pride.

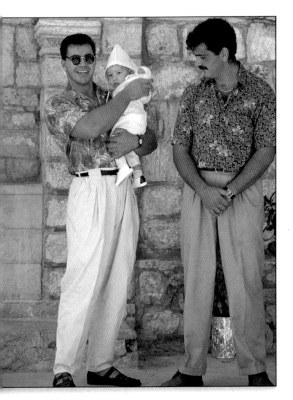

It is only a few steps from the Orthodox Greek Bishop's Palace in the Ayios Ioannis quarter to Taht el Kala with its mosque. The Phaneromeni church is just a few yards from another tiny mosque. And from the church of the Armenians to the Arab Ahmet mosque is also not far. Yet nowadays the mosque in Taht el Kala is closed and the Armenian church lies in the middle of the Turkish military no-go area. The Armenians were driven out of their traditional area and now live outside the city wall in the new city.

The **Omeriye mosque** is the only place in the Greek Cypriot south of the city where the *muezzin* still calls the faithful to prayer five times a day – for the Arabian tourists and the Lebanese refugees. The **Ayios Loukas church** in the north has been turned into a secular cultural centre. Nevertheless, the intricate patchwork of churches and mosques shows just how closely integrated the Christians and Moslems used to be. There are 18 mosques and 13 churches in the 24 districts of the old city. Hardly any of these districts had an ethnically homogeneous population before the invasion. Sunni Moslems, Orthodox Greeks and the small Armenian and Maronite minorities all lived together peacefully.

When the Ottomans conquered Nicosia, they changed only the Gothic churches of the Venetians into mosques: the other places of worship remained untouched. As a result, the splendid **cathedral of St Sophia**, built in the 13th century and once the coronation church of the ruling French nobles, the Lusignans, has been the main mosque of the Moslems for 400 years. Nowadays, the attendance is rather poor, because the Turkish Cypriots are not, as a rule, very religious; on the other hand the settlers from Anatolia attend prayer regularly. The Armenians were even given a Catholic church in the 16th century as a reward for their intervention on the side of the Ottomans.

Foreign conquerors have left their mark all over the city. The entrance to the large Turkish bath in the northern **Lunching in Laiki Yitouna.**

quarter consists of the portal of an earlier Gothic church, of which nothing else remains. And a Venetian column stands at **Atatürk Square**, a sign of former glory. The magnificent house of the Christian dragoman who, under the Ottomans, was responsible for the collection of taxes from the Christian population, is today a museum. Its outward appearance belies its splendour. Ottoman *caravanserais*, churches built by the Lusignans, the Greek Orthodox **Khrysaliniotissa** church in Byzantine style – Nicosia is a vast open-air museum, divided and threatened with decline. Even in the 1950s and 1960s, certain cardinal sins were still being committed by builders – ghastly concrete buildings were put up in a number of streets and a tower-block was erected in the middle of the old city.

Two of the three former city gates have survived: in the north the smaller Kyrenia Gate (formerly the **Porta del Provveditore**) spans a major roadway through the city wall. In the south the massive Famagusta Gate (formerly the

Porta Giuliana) has been restored in the most exemplary fashion. Art exhibitions, concerts and lectures take place here. **The Paphos Gate** – known by the Venetians as the **Porta Domenica** – has been reduced to a simple pedestrian gateway through the city wall.

The largest and indeed most beautiful building in Nicosia is the **Selimiye mosque** which lies in the Turkish part of the city, and which is still known as **Ayia Sophia**, St Sophia, by the Greek Cypriots. This Gothic building, which measures 216 ft (66 metres) by 125 ft (38 metres) is the largest church in the whole of Cyprus.

The construction of the church began under Archbishop Eustorge de Montaigu in 1209 – probably out of the remains of a still older church – and on 5 November 1326 the building was consecrated. At that time the church aisle sparkled with gold and precious stones, but in 1373 the church was plundered for the first time, when the Genoese invaded Cyprus. In 1570 the Ottomans added two narrow minarets in place of church steeples and converted the church into their main mosque.

Nowadays prayer mats cover the old memorial slabs. However, because the building – unlike purpose-built mosques – doesn't face Mecca, the inner furnishings are arranged diagonally so that the faithful can face in the right direction. Despite the fact many of the figures which decorated the church have been removed (in accordance with the rules of Islam), the Selimiye mosque still offers a magnificent example of French High Gothic architecture.

Directly next to the mosque is an expanse of ruins. During the Venetian period the main **church of the Orthodox Greeks** stood here, a Gothic domed building. By the **northern gate** there are six coats of arms of Venetian families and a figure of a saint. **Bedestan**, as the building is called, means market, and indeed this is the market district of Turkish Nicosia.

Just a few steps away is the **Haydar Pasha mosque**, named after the commander of the Ottoman conquerors. The former church of St Catherine, built at

Inside the Selimiye mosque, formerly the cathedral of St Sophia.

the end of the 14th century, is smaller than St Sophia and has only one minaret. The mosque hasn't been in use for a number of years now; restoration work is taking place.

Two **caravanserais** (*khans*) are located in the Turkish part of Nicosia. These buildings, complete with inner courtyard and an arcade passage, are typical of Ottoman architecture. They were intended to provide accommodation for visiting merchants and travellers, with stalls on the ground floor and sleeping quarters on the first. The **small** **khan** has been restored, and the Turkish Cypriot Antiquity Service now has its office here. The **large khan** has been in the process of renovation for a number of years; despite the continuing work it can usually be visited.

Like the Selimiye and the Haydar Pasha, the **Omeriye mosque** also has a Christian past. The former Augustinian church was dedicated to John de Montfort, who accompanied St Louis on the Fourth Crusade but died here in 1249. It was destroyed by Mustapha Pasha during the Ottoman conquest, and a mosque dedicated to the prophet Omar, whose final resting place Mustapha Pasha thought it occupied, was erected on the site. On one side, opposite the old **Turkish steam bath**, it is still possible to trace elements of Gothic style. The tiny **Arablar mosque**, encircled by flowers near the Greek Orthodox **Phaneromeni church**, was formerly a chapel. Some of the churches of the Orthodox Greeks have survived virtually unaltered.

The most beautiful church of all is the **Khrysaliniotissa church** near the **Famagusta Gate** in the carpenters' quarter. In the middle of this dilapidated area is the unexpectedly grandiose **palace of the Greek Orthodox Archbishop**, a modern building completed in 1961. Directly in front of it stands the **statue of the Archbishop and President Makarios** in solitary splendour, measuring around 20 ft (6 metres) high. The statue of the guiding father of all Greek Cypriots was erected a few years ago and was the subject of some controversy. Near the Archbishop's Palace is

a smaller predecessor – the **Ayios Ioannis church**, the cathedral of Nicosia. In the **Old Palace**, part of a former Benedictine monastery from the 15th century, is the small **Folk Art Museum**, whose exhibits comprise mainly everyday items. Also in this building complex is the **Museum of National Struggle** which provides a reminder of the Greek Cypriot guerrilla struggle against the British. Photographs, mementoes, pistols and even a gallows are displayed. The right-hand section of the New Palace houses the Icon Museum, in which around 150 icons illustrate the development of 1,000 years of icon-painting, from the 8th to the 18th century.

The House of the Dragoman Georghakis Kornesios documents the life of the upper classes during the Ottoman Period. Kornesios was one of the tax collectors appointed by the Sublime Porte. The inside of this building, which has been restored with old furniture and carpets, is a testimony to the comfortable life style which Kornesios was able

Rooting around.

to enjoy. Yet even this splendour didn't help Kornesios in the end: in 1804 he was executed in Istanbul on account of his various intrigues.

A walk round Greek Nicosia: Begin this tour at **Elephtheria Square** near the centre of the old city, where the small town hall stands on one of the bastions of the city wall. From here it is only a few steps to **Constantinos Paleologos Avenue**. Opposite the main post office is a small street to the left, and here you will find yourself in **Laiki Yitouna**, a reconstructed area of the old city with shady cafés, good restaurants and many souvenir shops. If you want to know more about the history of Nicosia, visit the new **City Museum**, which is nearby in Hippocrates Street.

A little further to the west you come to **Ledra Street**. This was once the most important area for shopping, although it wasn't always as busy as it is today: during the Greek Cypriot guerrilla struggle it was given the name "murder mile" by the British, because numerous soldiers were ambushed and murdered here.

Nowadays, in terms of shopping, the street has been surpassed by Makarios Avenue in the new city. Ledra Street ends abruptly at the Green Line after a few hundred yards.

Shortly before the Green Line, on the right, you come to the Greek Orthodox **Phaneromeni church**. The small **Arablar mosque** is situated directly behind the church. If you follow the Green Line to the east at a suitable distance – taking photographs is strictly forbidden – and go past the indoor market, you will come to a confusing maze of tiny streets, where you can watch various craftsmen at their trade. Continuing further, you come to the **Archbishop's Palace**. (The House of the Dragoman is situated about 100 away away, in Patriachis Gregorios Street to the south.) If you follow the street to the west you will arrive at the **Omeriye mosque** and the **Turkish bath**.

When you want to go back to the beginning of this tour, follow Trikoupis Street to the city wall, and then go in a westerly direction along a palm-lined

Drinking partners.

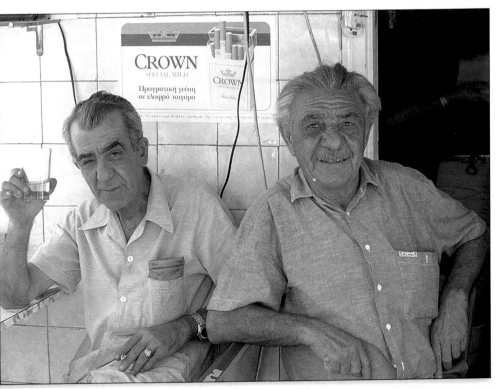

avenue. To the east, the way leads along the wall to the Famagusta Gate. After a further 100 yards you come to Hector Street on the left and then turn right into Khrysaliniotissa Street, which leads to the small church of the same name, a domed building in Byzantine style. (The whole walk lasts 2–3 hours.)

The oldest treasures on the island are in the **Cyprus Museum**, a house built in classical style by the British. It is due to be replaced by a new building, as the house is already bursting at the seams. A representative selection of archaeological discoveries is on display in 14 separate rooms, stretching from the Stone Age (around 7,000 BC) to the time of the Roman Empire. Mycenaean ceramics and tomb monuments, larger than life bronze statues, furnishings fitted with ivory decorations, and coins and jewellery from over 5,000 years give an insight into the island's rich history. One of the most impressive exhibits is the collection of around 2,000 votive figures from the **Sanctuary of Ayia Irini**. Also on display is the famous

Aphrodite from Soli, which has become a symbol of Cyprus. What is missing, however, are the discoveries which the Europeans made in the 19th century and at the beginning of the 20th century. These were taken off the island and now adorn museums all over the world, including the Metropolitan Museum of Modern Art in New York.

Opposite the museum building is the City Garden and the Theatre of Nicosia.

A walk round Turkish Nicosia: Begin this circular tour at the Kyrenia Gate, the old northern gate of the city. At the start of Kyrenia Avenue is the former **Monastery of the Dancing Dervishes**, which is now the **Museum of Turkish Cypriot Arts and Crafts**. From here the busy street leads directly to **Atatürk Square**, instantly recognisable from the metal bust of the founder of modern-day Turkey on one of the roof-tops. In the middle of the square is a **Venetian Column**. At one time the Lion of St Mark sat enthroned at its peak; this has now been replaced by a globe. Also worth mentioning are the administrative buildings, built in classical style by the British, grouped around the square.

If you follow Asmali Street you will soon come to the **small *khan*** (on the left), and then to the **large *khan***. From here it is only a few steps through the shopping centre to the **Selimiye mosque** and the **Bedestan**. Behind the former cathedral of St Sophia is a small building, the **Ottoman Library**. Turning half-left from here you will see the minaret of the **Haydar Pasha mosque** (Church of St Catherine). If you follow Yeni Cami Street to the small mosque of the same name you come back to the city wall. Turn left here into Istanbul Street and then return to the starting point. (The whole tour lasts 1–2 hours.)

From the Turkish north of Nicosia to the Greek Cypriot south is only a few hundred yards, yet they are two completely different worlds. If north Nicosia can justifiably be described as conjuring up memories of an underdeveloped provincial city in the Asian part of Turkey, then the southern half suggests the Greek outlook towards business, and Europe. On the Greek Cypriot side of

A naked Septimus Severus, Cyprus Museum.

the wall, extensive business areas have sprung up in recent years, with tower blocks, large banks, boutiques, antique shops, shopping centres and a chaotic traffic system. Street cafés invite you to come in and while away the time.

Outside the centre, the city is growing in a more or less uncontrolled fashion (with the exception of the Turkish-occupied sector). What were previously independent villages have been swallowed up by the sprawling suburbs. In the outer districts, the Republic of Cyprus has built large settlements for refugees from the war in 1974. Banks, businesses and the subsidiaries of many European firms have been particularly drawn to Cyprus and Nicosia since the demise of Beirut.

The mayor of south Nicosia, Lellos Demetriades, wants to "build bridges in a divided city". Mustafa Akinci, mayor of north Nicosia until February 1990, is also in favour of more contact between the two peoples. There are no official relations, however, between the Republic of Cyprus and the Turkish Republic of North Cyprus. Nevertheless the two city fathers have proved that a form of practical collaboration is possible across the Green Line. Around 10 years ago they began cooperation on a project to develop a joint sewage system. Today the network of channels is finished.

Now the restoration of the valuable buildings in the old city has also begun. It is a race against time, in which the decline of the city is currently the fastest. Money is short, despite help from international sources such as the European Community and the World Bank. Collaboration between the popular "Lellos of Nicosia" and the Turkish Cypriot authorities is naturally continuing. With the help of the UN development plan (UNDP) a common city development plan has been drawn up to avoid planning catastrophes, for example to make sure a situation can't arise where a park is spoilt by the construction of a new factory just over the border. The plan contains alternatives for each eventuality: one with the Green Line firmly in place, and one without.

Admiring glances.

TOUR OF NORTH CYPRUS

Day trips to the north of Cyprus are made more difficult by the various bureaucratic hurdles which have to be overcome. Nevertheless, despite the hindrances and military no-go areas, it is worthwhile making the effort to visit the north. For one thing, the real attraction of the island lies in the wide variety of its landscape and the numerous legacies of different cultures which evolved here over the centuries. It is also interesting to see at first hand how this part of the island has developed since 1974.

Visits to the north from the south are limited to the hours between 8am and 6pm. Bearing in mind these limits, there is really a choice of only two tours: one in a westerly direction, and the other going east.

Western tour – from Nicosia to Vouni: Just over the border (information about the necessary formalities for crossing the border can be found in Travel Tips) one finds oneself in a very different, oriental culture (*see also north Nicosia*). After leaving Nicosia, take the road to Kyrenia. Just before the edge of town, on the right-hand side, is an excellent Turkish Cypriot baker selling unusual specialities. Continuing your journey, cross the **Mesaoria**, the fertile plain between two mountain ranges, the Pentadaktylos, the legendary five-finger mountains in the north, and the Troodos mountains in the south. During early spring this area is covered with a vast carpet of flowers, quickly followed by golden corn, reaped in June. The brown landscapes left after the second sowing gives the area the appearance of a sprawling steppe.

In 1191 a battle took place here which was to play a decisive role in the future of the island. The fleet of Berengaria of Navarre, the fiancée of Richard the Lionheart, ran into a storm off the south coast of Cyprus, whilst her betrothed was fighting in the crusades. Ducas Comnenos, the sole emperor of Cyprus, was on the point of incarcerating Berengaria, when Richard came gallantly to her aid. After their marriage in Limassol, the English king defeated the Cypriot army so decisively on the plains of Mesaoria that the island remained under mid-European rule for the next 400 years.

During this very significant epoch a whole series of splendid buildings were constructed, many of which are still in good condition today. Among them are the Ayios Nikolaos in Famagusta and the beautiful Ayia Sophia (Selimiye mosque) in Nicosia. The fortresses were also reinforced during this period: the first of these, Ayios Hilarion, is reached after a short journey.

This building, on the site of a monastery dating from Byzantine times, is named after St Hilarion, a Syrian hermit who lived during the 6th century. Of the three hill fortresses, this one is in the best condition. The Lusignans used it as their summer residence, for reasons which are easy to understand. It was a place of pleasure as much as defence: in the Middle Ages magnificent jousting

tournaments took place here. Going past the the soldiers' camps and stores, you come first to a 10th-century Byzantine church, then the palace up above. From here there is a magnificent view of the whole of the north coast. The castle belongs to a chain of fortresses running all the way to Syria.

Neither the café located at at the entrance to the fortress nor the snack bar inside keeps to regular opening times.

Kyrenia: Descending slowly from St Hilarion to the sea, you arrive at the next fortress which was reinforced by the Lusignans. This is Kyrenia, once known as the jewel of the Levant. Those who knew this small coastal town before 1974, with its circular harbour, picturesque setting and swinging international social life, may not recognise it these days. It is overrun by Turkish soldiers and a steady process of orientalisation has taken place, attempting to eradicate all trace of the city's Greek history. In the formerly thriving villages of the surrounding area, now fallen into decline, European hippies (mainly English

and German) have set up communities.

Some Turkish Cypriots still claim that the Turkish military presence is essential to protect the area and its population; others believe they are needed primarily for economic reasons – northern Cyprus is heavily dependent on Turkey, the only country which has recognised it as an independent state. The atmosphere is not helped by tensions between the Turkish settlers flown here in 1974, and the indigenous population. Although great efforts are made to hide these tensions, they are felt everywhere. Part of the problem lies in the fact that the Turkish Cypriots are often discriminated against in comparison with their Anatolian counterparts.

Kyrenia was founded by Greeks from Arcadia in the 10th century, and played an important role during the period of the Cypriot city-kingdoms, although hardly anything remains to be seen either from this period or from the Greek and Roman epochs. The architecture of the oft-painted city, with its splendid citadels, harbour area and fortified walls,

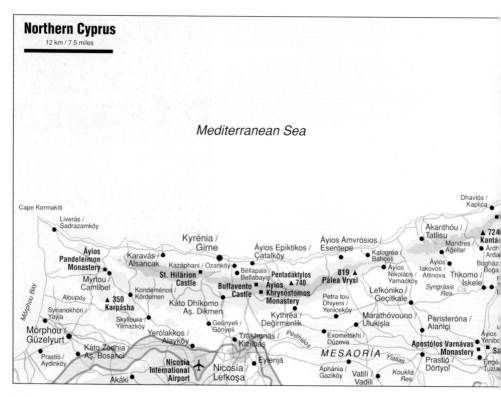

is of medieval Italian and Frankish origin with Turkish elements.

Taking a stroll from the harbour through the city, past the towers on the city walls, past the pretty **House of the Museum of Folk Art** (with Cypriot furniture, woven articles and costumes), and on past the little mosque in honour of Sadik Pasha (whose fleet conquered Kyrenia in 1570), you come to a 12th-century Byzantine domed, cruciform church near the castle. From here you have a beautiful view over the harbour and castle. The other harbour to the east is used mainly for military purposes.

The foundation walls of the **castle**, on the eastern side of the city, were laid out by the Byzantines, but its present form is the work of the Doge's architects. In addition to the bastions and royal living quarters, it is possible to visit the dungeons. It was here that the rebellious nobles and knights of 1310 starved to death. In more recent times Greek Cypriot EOKA fighters were imprisoned here by the British.

The biggest attraction of the castle, however, is the **Shipwreck Museum** which it houses. It contains one exhibit which is unique in the world – a trading ship from the time of Alexander the Great. It was discovered at a depth of 108 ft (33 metres) and salvaged, between 1968 and 1969, by a team from the University of Pennsylvania and the staff of the Director of the Cypriot Antiquity Service Vassos Karagheorgis.

The wreck, which is 48 ft (14.75 metres) long and 11 ft (3.4 metres) wide, is a singled-masted ship with a sail measuring 33 ft (10 metres) by 20 ft (6 metres), and contained 404 amphora filled with wine, oil and almonds. The amphora came from various ceramic workshops, indicating that the ship must have been loaded at a number of different places. Radiocarbon analysis of the 10,000 almonds and the planks on the ship has also revealed important information which, along with the dating of two coins, indicates that the ship must have sunk some time in the middle of the 3rd century BC.

The museum is open from 8am until

When the donkey work is over.

KLÍDHES ISLAND

Cape Apostólos Andréas

Áyios Phílon (Church)

Apostólos Andréas Monastery

Rizokárpaso / Dipkárpaz

Panayía Eleoúsa Monastery

Cape Plakotí
Yialoúsa / Máltepe

s Andrónikos / Yeşilköy

K A R P A S I A

Galinóporni / Kaleburnu

Kanakariá
Áyios Symeón / Avlepe

kómi / onak
Leonárisso / Ziyamet

Galátia / Mehmetcik

anayía s Kyrás

Áyios Theódhoros / Çayirova

Cape Eléa

Mediterranean Sea

gústa / Magósa

1pm and from 2.30pm until 5.30pm.

Visitors wanting to relax by the sea will be delighted by the beaches of the east coast, with their fine sands. A number of bays have snack-bars and the largest of all, **Acapulca**, has a restaurant. Around 3 miles (5 km) beyond Kyrenia a small, badly-signposted road to the left leads to a tiny mosque, the **mosque of the Seven Wise Men (Ömer Türbesi)**. The scenery here is stunning. There is a good view to the House of Mary, described in Lawrence Durrell's *Bitter Lemons*, which should be essential reading for all visitors to Cyprus. Nowadays the house belongs to the Turkish Embassy.

Durrell country: One trip from Kyrenia which you shouldn't miss is to the abbey at **Bellapais**. After driving a little over 2 miles (4 km) to the east, you turn off towards the mountains and pass through a succession of pretty villages and lush greenery. The village of Dogamköyist, formerly Kazaphani, is particularly worth visiting. This is where Lawrence Durrell lived and wrote.

The abbey is one of the most beautiful, and certainly the most atmospheric Gothic buildings on the whole island, its history beginning with the Lusignans. In 1191, when Frankish rule over Cyprus was at its peak under Amaury de Lusignan, monastic life on the island was fostered. The initial Augustinian settlement lasted for only a short period. Hugo I (1205–18) handed the monastery to the Premonstratensians. The fact that its new occupants dressed in white led to it being known as "the white abbey". It soon become the favourite location of the Lusignans. The refinement of the architecture made it seem more like a palace, and it was called "Abbaie de la Pais", which later became Bellapais.

Hugo III (1267–84) donated the Early Gothic monastic church to the monks, bestowing on them various privileges: like the princes, they were allowed to go riding with a gilded sword and golden spurs. The normal principles of monastic life were held in abeyance at this time – according to one of the contemporary reports "the brothers in the monastery **The Kyrenia landscape.**

278

lived like princes, and each of them had more than one wife." During the Venetian Period, however, the monastery was brought to the brink of ruin, and the buildings were in such an appalling state of repair that a well-ordered life was no longer possible. No help was received from Venice and the monastery declined still further, until all the monks were driven out in 1571 following the Ottoman conquest.

There is a fantastic view from the window of the refectory, an imposing room measuring 36 ft (11 metres) by 98 ft (30 metres), whose entrance is decorated with the Lusignan coat of arms. On a clear day you can see as far as the snow-capped mountains of Turkey. In earlier times concerts were held in the cloisters under the trees of the inner court, which are still in good condition. Now Turkish military quarters surround the area; the whole of the Greek population was driven out and interned in 1974–75. Eventually they were transported to the south as part of the mutual exchange of the two population groups.

Given the time restriction, it is hardly worth visiting the hill fortress of **Buffavento** to the east, which has not been particularly well-maintained. The fortress is reached with difficulty along a steep and stony road, and can be scaled only on one side – on the other is another Turkish military camp. The climb takes one hour, but when you reach the top there is a rewarding view.

South of Buffavento lies the legendary **Khrysostomos monastery**, with its famous holy spring. Once a favourite spot for an outing, it is now commandeered by the Turkish military.

A vivid example of military glorification is the concrete victory monument on the way from Kyrenia to Soli and Vouni. It is dedicated to the Turkish Peace Operation of 20 July 1974, and is surpassed only by a hideous display of Greek tanks and other spoils, which can be found a few yards away at the so-called **Landing Point**. The monument also commemorates other dark events in Cypriot history: reliefs on the walls provide a reminder of the cruelties per-

Bellapais.

petrated on the Turkish Cypriots by the Greeks and Greek Cypriots.

The cosy, backwater city of **Morphou** lies in extensive, if unkempt, orange and lemon groves. The sense of neglect is partly due to the uncertainty which surrounds property rights here and partly because the Turkish Cypriots who settled here came from wine-growing areas in the south, and were unfamiliar with the management of citrus fruits. Apart from the little natural history museum, and the **Archaeological Museum** (open from 8am to 2pm), the 12th-century monastery **of Ayios Mamas**, with its Roman marble tomb of the saint and a notable iconostasis, is particularly worth visiting.

The ancient city of **Soli** was founded in 600 BC, when King Philokypros summoned the famous Athenian statesmen and poet Solon to Cyprus and named the new city after him. As a result of its copper mining industry, the city-kingdom quickly flourished. In AD 498 the citizens defended their city bravely but unsuccessfully against the Persians, and were then ravaged in AD 648 by the Arabs. Under British rule Soli suffered the fate of many other ancient cities: many buildings were dismantled, and used as building material in faraway places – in this case the Suez Canal.

The ancient city of Soli comprises three areas worth visiting. High up above, cut into a slope, are the remains of a 2nd-century Roman amphitheatre. Further down to the east are the impressive foundation walls of a 5th-century **Early Christian basilica**, with interesting floor mosaics. To the west is the ancient market place (agora), and the Isis and Aphrodite temples from around 250 BC. The famous symbol of Cyprus, the marble statue of Aphrodite, was also discovered here; it can now be found in the archaeological museum in Nicosia.

For the modern visitor, the unbelievable geographical location of **Vouni**, lying some 820 ft (250 metres) above sea-level, is particularly impressive, even though only the foundation walls remain to be seen. The palace is presumed to have been built in the 5th **The Mesaoria.**

century BC, either by the Persians or by their ally, King Doxandros of Marion (modern-day Polis). Its purpose was probably to control access to Soli. The original oriental architecture was extended under Greek influence following the conquest of Cimon of Athens. The palace finally fell victim to a fire in 380 BC.

Eastern tour – from Nicosia to Kantara: A further day trip to the places and sites mentioned above can be undertaken via two roads which are well sign-posted and go through the fertile land of the Mesaoria Plain. Note, however, that the whole of the Karpas peninsula is closed to day-tours.

Of all the cities in Cyprus, **Famagusta** is the one which has been most badly affected by political developments, but even its earlier history was marked by numerous ups and downs. The city was founded in the 3rd century BC by Ptolemy II, but first achieved prominence when settlers arrived from Salamis, after it fell victim to the Arabs. (This can be deduced from the Greek name which the city bore, and which the Greeks still use today: Amochostos, the city sunken in the sand.) Later, around 1136, the city expanded further when it received an influx of Armenians compulsorily settled here by the Byzantine emperor. Its first real period of ascendency, however, came with the fall of Acre in 1291, an event which benefited the whole of the island. The population grew dramatically as a result and, thanks to its central location, the city became a wealthy trading centre for east-west trade. The Pope indirectly benefited Famagusta when he forbade (under threat of excommunication) trade with the infidel rulers of the Holy Land.

A German traveller to Cyprus at this time, Ludolf von Suchen, gave a vivid description of the splendour of this city, which he believed to be the richest in the world; a city in which the wedding jewellery of a merchant's daughter was "worth more than that of the Queen of France", and in which one citizen, Franziskus Lakhas, frequently entertained the king and his household with

The north boasts some of the best beaches.

evening feasts spread on tables strewn with flowers and precious stones (intended as parting gifts for the guests). It was a city in which loose women were "the most expensive in the world", and could earn a fortune "of at least 1,000,000 gold ducats" at the discreet drop of a handkerchief.

So much splendour and riches was naturally a source of envy, and so it wasn't long before the city fell under the influence of others, particularly after 1372 when it was no longer forbidden to enter the ports of Asia Minor. First there were the Genoese, then the Venetians. During this period the city was provided with new fortifications.

In 1570 Famagusta suffered the first traumatic events in its history. After laying siege to the city for several months, the Ottoman pasha, Lala Mustafa, promised Famagusta's heroic defender, the Venetian commander Bragadino, safe passage in return for handing over the city. Mustafa, however, broke his promise, tortured Bragadino to death and had the Christian inhabitants driven out of the town or murdered.

Those who fled from the city built a new settlement outside the city gates – **Varosha**, the new city, which in this century has experienced both prosperity and catastrophe. With the emergence of mass tourism, an ugly hotel city developed on the beautiful sandy beaches, making it, by 1974, one of the biggest earners of foreign currency on the whole island, with some 10,000 beds. In the summer of that year Turkish soldiers bombarded the city, captured it and then isolated it with cordons, having driven out the 30,000 inhabitants. Since 1974 this ghost town has remained empty and can only be entered by the Turkish military. Gardens grow wild and the houses are slowly decaying from the effects of the sun, wind and sand.

A number of hotels outside the city were unaffected by the invasion and are still in business under Turkish management. The Greek Cypriot owners have yet to receive compensation.

The old part of Famagusta remained Turkish. After its conquest a certain

Far left, Othello's Tower, Famagusta. **Left,** Lala Mustafa mosque, Famagusta.

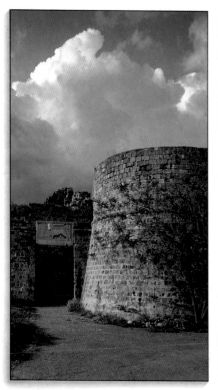

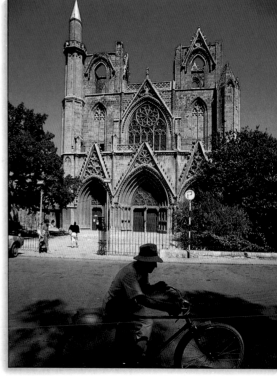

amount of building took place – particularly of mosques. The Gothic churches were converted for the new ruling religion with the addition of minarets. The city is still attractive, but it is impossible not to notice the neglect of its distinguished medieval legacy. That which can't serve tourist purposes is used as car-parks, football pitches, or for anchoring washing lines.

A number of splendid buildings are nevertheless still in good condition. The best way to begin a tour of the city is on the 2-mile (3-km) long, 69-ft (21-metre) high and 23-ft (7-metre) wide city wall of the fortification. A walk around the wall provides interesting insights into the building styles of the Venetians. You can wander from the southeast corner (i.e. from the Land Gate, to which a drawbridge once led) to the northern side, to the architecturally less important Sea Gate.

The most impressive building in the area is the Citadel, which people like to pass off as the setting for Shakespeare's *Othello*, and whose tower is therefore known as Othello's Tower. It is impossible to prove conclusively whether the dark-haired vice-governor Christofero Moro (1506–8), who lost his wife here, was the role-model for the tragic figure, or whether it was one of his successors, de Sessa, who had the epithet "Il Capitano Moro". Nevertheless, this Lusignan building, redesigned in 1492 by N. Foscarini with its famous lion-reliefs and its many dark steps, corners and courtyards, remains a plausible and stimulating stage. This has led to its often being used as a setting for all sorts of films.

In the **old city** you should be sure to take a look at the remains of the **Palazzo del Proveditore**, the palace of the Venetian Governor in which the Turkish poet, Namik Kemal Bey, a fierce opponent of the Sultan, was incarcerated for 38 months between1873 and 1876. His cell can still be visited. Of the sacred buildings, the smaller ones of which are normally closed, the **Sinan Pasha mosque** (formerly the **church of St Peter and St Paul**) most deserves a visit. It was built during the golden age

of Famagusta; a merchant by the name of Simone Nostrano is said to have built it from the profit of a single transaction with a Syrian friend. The building served the Ottomans as a mosque, the English as a potato store, and nowadays is used as the town hall.

A few yards further on is the former cathedral of St Nicholas, now the **Lala Mustafa mosque**, which was built by the Lusignans between 1294 and 1326 and is often regarded as a masterpiece of Gothic architecture. When you stand in front of the high, clearly divided west facade, with the massive tree – believed to be as old as the building – behind you, you gain a real sense of history. It is easy to imagine the splendour of the numerous coronation processions which it has witnessed; the Lusignans from Guy I onwards were crowned "King of Cyprus and Jerusalem" here. Equally vivid is the picture which Titian painted of the sad, young widow of the last king of this dynasty, Catarina Cornaro, victim of the bitter power-struggle between the rebelling nobles and the "advisers" from

Backgammon below the city walls.

her home-town of Venice, who was forced to sign her abdication here.

Inside the cathedral the columns have been painted white and quotes from the Koran hang from the walls. Prayer mats cover the old tombstones.

Ancient city-kingdom: To make an excursion to Salamis, St Barnabas, Enkomi and Kantara, leave Famagusta in a northerly direction, past the delightful sandy beaches – it is possible to swim just about everywhere here – and after about 5 miles (8 km) you come to the turn-off to the remains of the ancient city-kingdom of Salamis. The area covers around 2 sq. miles (5 sq. km) and is framed by beautiful scenery. Much of it has yet to be uncovered. You can drive in with a car, although it makes more sense to explore on foot, particularly in spring, when the mimosa bushes turn the area into a vast carpet of yellow, or in autumn when the pine and cypress trees exude an aromatic scent. At the entrance there is a restaurant.

Salamis is believed to have been founded by the Trojan hero Teykros who, unable to prevent the death of his brother Ajax, was driven out by his father and settled here. What is certain is that, due to its natural harbour, the city was for a long time one of the most important city-kingdoms on the island, until it fell under the rule of the Ptolemies. During the Byzantine Period, it was renamed Constantia, and regained its former importance, before succumbing to the Arab invasions in 700 and then being destroyed by a series of devastating earthquakes.

Directly behind the tourist pavilion is the most interesting excavation, the **Roman Palaestra**, with its inner courtyards surrounded by columns and lined with a wonderful marble floor. Equally impressive is the monumental **Thermal Area** from the 3rd century, with its *frigidarium* (cold bath) and *sudatorium* (steam bath), still decorated with fragments of mosaics, depicting a plump Leda with the swan and Apollo and Artemis fighting against the Niobeans. An amphitheatre and the rows of seats from a Roman stadium are also partially intact.

The largest and most imposing building is the theatre, which dates from the time of Augustus. It originally held 15,000 spectators and was rebuilt in the 1st and the 4th centuries. The rows of seating have been well restored and eight of them are original.

Those who want to delve further into Salamis's history shouldn't miss the chance to visit the nearby **Royal Tombs**, which give a good idea of the intensive contact between the ancient cultures who met here. The tombs are on the street leading to the monastery of St Barnabas. A number of them can be visited. If you are short of time, tomb number 79 is indicative of the typical architectural pattern of all the tombs in Salamis – small burial chambers, a 43-ft (13-metre) wide forecourt, and a 52-ft (16-metre) long *dromos*, a shaft-like lane leading to the burial chamber.

The valuable items that were found in grave number 79 – three thrones, a magnificent wooden bed decorated with ivory and silver, pitchers and amphora with food, weapons, jewellery, four

chariots and the skeletons of 10 horses that were sacrificed – provided useful evidence of burial rites. They date from the time of the Mycenaeans whom Homer described so vividly is *The Odyssey* and *The Iliad*.

The findings from the tombs are in the Archaeological Museum in Nicosia, mainly in the so-called Salamis Room, where they are supported by photographs and reconstructions.

Founder of the Church: The monastery of St Barnabas, a few miles beyond the Royal Tombs, plays an important role in the history of the Cypriot Orthodox Church. Its patron saint, the Apostle Barnabas, was not only the founder of the Church on the island, but also indirectly helped it achieve independence (*Autocephaly*) some 478 years later. Born in Salamis and brought up in Jerusalem, where he became a follower of Jesus, Barnabas toured Cyprus with the Apostle Paul, and again seven years later with Mark. He finally died as a martyr at the stake in Salamis. He was buried with a hand-written copy of St

Matthew's Gospel. Centuries later he appeared in a dream to the archbishop of the time and showed him the location of his tomb. When the hand-written gospel was discovered it seemed so important to the Byzantine emperor Zeno that he declared the Cypriot Church to be autocephalous, i.e. independent from Antioch. Right up until today the local archbishop has enjoyed certain privileges, including the right to carry a sceptre and wear a red coat, and to sign his name in purple ink. A monastery was founded on the location of the tomb in the 5th century; its present building dates from 1757.

Skeletons at home: On the way back to Nicosia there is another worthwhile detour for those interested in archaeology. A mile or so beyond the monastery are the excavations of **Enkomi**. The founders of this Bronze Age city, which was later to outshine Salamis, are thought to have come from the Peloponnese. When archaeologists began to uncover the city in 1934 they initially thought they had discovered a necropolis, as there was a skeleton in every house. It was only later they discovered that the inhabitants of this city buried their dead under their houses, and that this was in fact a real city, whose clear rectangular arrangement, and size of the houses, complete with baths and toilets, is still a cause for amazement. Some interesting clay slates with Minoan inscriptions have also been found here. Today the symbol of the city is the horned god of fertility, found in the museum in Nicosia.

Those who want to enjoy another breathtaking view of the north coast should climb up to the third Lusignan fortress, Kantara, which lies a little further to the north. This was where Isaac Comnenos hid after his skirmish with Richard the Lionheart. From the carpark there is a series of 125 steps and then a shorter flight of 75 to the Queens' Chamber (though no queen has ever been associated with the fortress), where a picturesque picnic spot rewards the visitor. It is the perfect place to enjoy *meze* under the shade of the trees, so make sure you come prepared.

Left, ready to serve. **Right**, northern market.

TRAVEL TIPS

GETTING THERE

BY AIR

Up until the Turkish invasion, Cyprus's international airport was in Nicosia, and indeed this is where the major airlines still maintain their offices. But for the Greek part of the the island the airport at Larnaca has now taken over Nicosia's former role. The national airline Cyprus Airways, which is based here, operates direct flights to London, Birmingham and Manchester. There is another airport at Paphos, which also serves these British cities.

Cyprus Airways, 21, Alkeou Street, Nicosia. Tel: 02/443 054.

There are two airports in the Turkish-occupied part of the island: Ercan lies 16 miles (25 km) to the east of Lefkosa (Nicosia) and Gecitale (Lefkonico) lies some 20 miles (30 km) to the northwest of Magusa/Famagusta. At the moment the Turkish national airline Türk Hava Yolari flies into northern Cyprus from Istanbul, Ankara, Izmir and Adana. In addition to countless offices in Turkey, the airline has an office in Lefkosa/Nicosia at Cengizhan 5 (tel: 020-71382/71061). The Turkish private airline, Istanbul Airlines, also operates services to Cyprus from Istanbul and Ankara. It is not common for European charter companies to fly into the northern part of Cyprus.

It is important to remember that those who enter Cyprus via the north cannot extend their journey into the southern part of the island. The Republic of Cyprus treats direct entry into the occupied territory as an illegal act (*see Travel Essentials*).

BY BOAT

Mediterranean cruise ships stop at Limassol. Boat traffic between Europe and Cyprus is also conducted from the harbour here; there are connections to the islands of Rhodes, to Heraklion on Crete and to Piraeus. The crossing to Piraeus takes about 48 hours. Ticket prices depend upon whether you travel during the peak or off-tourist seasons.

Those who prefer not to travel long distances to Piraeus over land may want to use one of the boat connections to Greece. There are direct passages from Ancona and Venice to Piraeus, and a cruise line connects Bari and Brindisi in Italy with Igoumenitsa and Patras in Greece. (The final leg of the journey to Piraeus from both these latter cities is over land.)

During the main tourist season boat passages are offered, according to demand, direct from Italy. They depart from Ancona or Venice and include a stopover in Limassol, where the Cypriot Tourist Information Centre can provide an up-to-date schedule of boat arrivals and departures.

Other shipping lines connect Limassol with Alexandria in Egypt and Haifa in Israel. The main port for boats heading for destinations in the Near East is in Larnaca. Vessels arrive here from Latakia in Syria and Jounié (about 16 miles/25 km north of Beirut) in Lebanon.

In the northern part of Cyprus Famagusta, on the east coast, is the most important port. From here there are boat connections to Syria and Turkey. The main connection is with Mersin on the southern coast of Turkey.

In addition to these, shipping lines operate between the southern coast of Turkey and Kyrenia or Girne (so named since the Turkish invasion) on the northern coast of Cyprus. The quickest way to cross is by Hovercraft. Between May and October a Hovercraft service operates three times a week, departing from Tasucu, about 7 miles (11 km) southwest of Silifke, Turkey. This passage, usually conducted overnight and usually offered at a 20 percent reduction to students, takes about 8 hours. Tickets can be purchased in Tasucu through the shipping companies Ertürk (in Tasucu tel: 1033) and Liberty (among others).

The company **Turkish Maritime Lines** maintains offices in Lefkosa/Nicosia (92 Girne Cad., tel: 202-715 87; telex: 66138 TRBA TK) and Magosa/Famagusta (tel: 036-654 94; telex: 57103).

BY CAR

As a rule, the aforementioned shipping lines will also transport motor vehicles. Prices vary considerably, depending on whether it is the peak or off-peak season. If you and your car do not remain in the country for more than three months, you will not be required to pay any additional tax or duties; should three months be too short, it is possible to apply at the main customs office in Nicosia for permission to stay in Cyprus for a period of up to 12 months.

In order to be able to drive your car legally on the island you must be in possession of Green Card insurance.

Travel Essentials

PASSPORTS & VISAS

Visas are not required by, among others, nationals of Australia, Canada, Denmark, France, Germany, Ireland, Italy, The Netherlands, New Zealand, Spain, the UK and the US.

Passports must be valid for at least 3 months beyond the date of entry into the Republic of Cyprus; a personal identification card is not considered sufficient. Children and minors must have their own passports if their names have not been entered into their parents' passports.

Any kind of stamp issued in the Turkish Republic of Northern Cyprus and found amongst your travel documents constitutes grounds for denying you access into the southern part of Cyprus. Bear in mind that although it is possible to enter the Turkish northern part of the island directly from Turkey visitors using this route will be prohibited from entering the southern part of the island. Official authorities of the Republic of Cyprus regard direct entry into the occupied territory as an illegal act. A stamp from the Turkish Republic of Northern Cyprus may even cause you difficulties later when trying to enter Greece. *Also see* "Turkish-Occupied Cyprus" at the end of this section (*page 293*).

MONEY MATTERS

The unit of currency in the Republic of Cyprus is the Cypriot Pound (abbreviated CY £) and is referred to as Greek Lira. Although 1 pound is officially divided into 100 cents, the general population still insists on calculating in old-fashioned shillings (1 shilling = 5 cents).

By multiplying a price in shillings by five, you'll thereby come up with the official price in cents. The "Lira", as the pound is popularly known, consists of 20 shillings. Cypriot bills come in denominations of 1, 2, 5, 10 and 20 pounds, coins in ½, 1, 2, 5, 10 and 20 cents.

While there are no limitations restricting the importation of foreign currency, all larger sums (US$1,000 or more) should be declared upon entering the country. The importation or exportation of Cypriot money is limited to CY £50. In any case, it's more advantageous to exchange money on Cyprus than in your own country. At the present time 1 Cypriot Pound equals about £1.20 sterling.

MONEY EXCHANGE

In addition to regular banks (where customers can obtain Cypriot Pounds on their credit cards), most hotel receptions will exchange cash, traveller's cheques and Eurocheques. The maximum amount paid per Eurocheque is CY £100. In line with modern developments in the rest of Europe, there are even a few banks that have machines which you can use for withdrawing cash on your Eurocheque card.

As a rule, banks are open in the morning 8.30am–noon Monday–Saturday; in the tourist centres, however, they frequently maintain special afternoon hours (Tourist Afternoon Service) between 3.30pm–5.30pm (October–April) and between 4pm–6pm (May–September). Currency exchange counters at the Larnaca and Paphos airports are open upon demand, which is to say following the arrival of all foreign flights.

In the northern part of the island the Turkish Lira – the same money in circulation in Turkey – is the official currency. Nevertheless the Cypriot Pound (as well as other common European units of money) is considered "hard currency". Because of this foreign money is often exchanged not only in the banks, but also in shops (and not infrequently for a better rate than what you'd get at the bank). Eurocheques must be issued in the "hard" currency of the tourists' respective country.

CUSTOMS

In addition to the limitations already mentioned regarding the import and export of Cypriot money, the following restrictions apply: Wine 0.75 litres; spirits 1 litre; 50 cigars or 200 cigarettes or 250 grams of tobacco; perfume or *eau de toilette* 0.3 litres. The total value of other goods brought into the country (for instance electronic wares) may not exceed CY £25. Clothing, jewellery, food and medicine destined for personal use are not subject to restrictions.

PETS

All animals must be quarantined for a period of six months prior to entering the country, so it is practically impossible for a visiting tourist to bring along a pet.

HEALTH

There are no specific vaccinations prescribed or required by visitors to Cyprus. Hygienic conditions, including those pertaining to drinking water, medical care and chemist shops are on par with Central European standards. In all cities you'll find hospitals which employ English-speaking doctors. Even tourists who are covered by health insurance (check prior to your journey whether or not you'll need to take out an additional travel policy) will initially have to pay doctor's fees and the cost of medications out of their own pockets, sums which should be reimbursed by the insurance company later. Be sure to ask for and keep all receipts and bills received for any medical treatment and medicine.

As is the case in any southern region it is important to come prepared for strong sunlight; suntan lotion, sunscreen, sun-glasses and protection for your head are all necessary. In order to avoid circulatory difficulties, it is important to compensate for fluid, electrolyte and salt lost through sweating. In other words, make sure you drink enough. Generally speaking, most Cypriot dishes are prepared with sufficient salt.

WHEN TO GO

Many hotels offer reduced prices in off-peak seasons. In the popular swimming resorts the off-peak season last from the 1 November–31 March (with the exception of the Christmas holidays between 20 December–6 January), and in Troodos from 1 October–30 June.

Spring is the best time of year to visit the island. As is characteristic of all countries in the Mediterranean region, winters are mild (even in December water temperatures remain at about 19°C). However, travellers to the interior of the island will need to take warm clothing (see What to Wear). Most rain falls between December and February, when you can expect approximately 9–11 rainy days.

Summers on Cyprus are hot and dry; and although it is an island the humidity is relatively slight and the heat is not considered particularly sultry or oppressive.

Darkness falls earlier and quicker on Cyprus than it does in other Central European countries; twilight lasts for only 30 minutes.

Cypriot clocks run 1 hour ahead of Central European Time. The switch to Daylight Saving Time occurs at the same time as in other European countries.

WHAT TO WEAR

Most tourists tend to visit Cyprus during the warmer seasons of the year. This being the case, aside from the accessories necessary to protect against sunburn (see Health), visitors should pack lightweight, cotton clothing. Those planning to spend time exploring the mountainous interior should bear in mind that even in summer temperatures can drop considerably; and it is advisable to pack a warm sweater and slacks.

Generally speaking, during winter it's necessary to take predominantly warm clothes (in the Troodos Mountains there's sure to be snow). At this time the sun's rays can still be strong enough to warrant wearing a sun-hat or at the very least sun-glasses.

Visitors who are staying in one of the more luxurious hotels will also want to bring some elegant clothes to wear at dinner.

CLIMATE CHART

	Jan	Feb	Mar	Apr	May	Jun	Jul	Aug	Sep	Oct	Nov	Dec
Lowest night temperature °F	43	45	46	54	61	64	70	73	68	59	52	46
Highest day temperature °F	59	61	64	72	79	86	93	93	88	82	72	63
Water temperature °F	63	63	64	68	70	75	79	81	79	75	70	66
Air humidity percentage	70	69	65	67	68	64	60	61	59	64	68	70
Rainy days per month	11	9	6	4	3	1	1	1	1	4	5	9
Hours of daily sunshine	5	6	7	8	10	12	12	12	11	9	6	5
Approximate time of sunset	4.45	5.30	5.45	7.15	7.45	8.00	8.00	7.30	7.00	5.15	4.45	4.30

SOUVENIRS

Typical souvenirs from Cyprus (aside from the local wine and other spirits) include native handmade articles and various Cypriot handicrafts. Many towns are known for a specific product, for example ceramics from Kornos and Phini, embroidery from Lefkara and Omodhos, silver jewellery from Lefkara, basketry from Liopetri and Yeroskipou or woven wares from Phiti. Good quality gold jewellery and leather goods can be very reasonably priced.

In addition to the numerous privately-operated souvenir shops the national "Cyprus Handicraft Centre" maintains branches in the old parts of Nicosia, Limassol, Larnaca and Paphos. In the one at Nicosia visitors can watch various craft items being made. The workshops here are open: 7.30am–2pm Monday–Friday and 7.30am–1pm Saturday.

TURKISH-OCCUPIED CYPRUS

Currently the only way to visit both the Republic of Cyprus and the northern part of the island occupied by Turkey during the same holiday is to arrive in the former and then take a day excursion into the north. It's quite impossible to manage this the other way around as officials in the south refuse to recognise entry documents issued in the Turkish north.

The only border-crossing is located at the "Green Line" (taking photographs here is strictly prohibited) in Nicosia. The border lies directly to the west of the old Venetian city wall at the old Ledra Hotel. The Greek authorities keep a record of the date of passage and the place where the guest is staying. The Turkish control check-point is located approximately 500 ft (150 metres) away. All potential visitors must apply here for a day visa. This costs 1 Cypriot Pound (in other words, in the "hard" currency of the South) and is speedily obtained. Passports are not stamped in this procedure. You will be asked to name the destination point of your excursion.

The Turkish-Cypriot authorities' visa office usually has copies of the free brochure *Special News Bulletin* (written in English), containing interesting travel tips.

The border-crossing is open after about 8am. The Republic of Cyprus requires visitors to return by 6pm at the latest, which means that time is quite limited. It is illegal to spend the night in the northern part of Cyprus if you've entered over this border. Bringing goods that have been acquired in the northern part of the island into the southern part is also prohibited.

The occupied northern section of Nicosia can easily be explored on foot; for destinations located outside the city limits it's advisable to procure a taxi. There are cabs ready and waiting at the border-crossing itself, as well as at the square distinguished by Venetian columns. It's also possible to rent a car from one of the travel agencies located at the Kyrenia

Gate. Furthermore, there are buses and communal taxis which operate throughout the day between the provincial city capitals of Nicosia, Famagusta, Kyrenia and Morphou. Both ticket and rental prices are cheaper in the north than in the south. In contrast to the rules of the road in Turkey, in the northern part of Cyprus vehicles are driven on the left side of the road.

Under normal circumstances the southern authorities permit tourists two excursions to the northern part of the island per stay. But if you can manage to convince the necessary officials of a passionate artistic and/or historical interest regarding the monuments located in the occupied northern territory, chances are good that they'll allow you more than two crossings.

GETTING ACQUAINTED

GEOGRAPHY

Cyprus is located in the eastern part of the Mediterranean Sea about 60 miles (95 km) west of the Syrian coast, 47 miles (75 km) south of the Turkish coast and 203 miles (325 km) north of the Egyptian coast.

It encompasses a total surface area of 3,571.81 sq. miles (9,251 sq. km) of which about 64 percent belongs to the Greek south and 36 percent to the Turkish north.

According to a 1960 religious survey, of the 700,000 inhabitants residing on the island about 77 percent are Greek Orthodox, 18.3 percent are Moslem and most of the remaining 4.7 percent are Armenians or Maronites. Following the settlement of Turks from Anatolia in northern Cyprus after 1974, the percentage of Moslems has increased considerably.

The capital city is Nicosia, with a population of 164,000.

Cyprus first became an independent republic in August 1960; prior to this time the island was a British colony (even to this day Cyprus has remained a member of the British Commonwealth). The Republic of Cyprus also belongs to the United Nations and is an associated member of the European Community.

TABLE OF DISTANCES

	Ayia Napa	Larnaca	Limassol	Nikosia	Paphos	Polis	Troodos
Ayia Napa	–	25	66	53	114	136	101
Larnaca	25	–	43	32	88	110	75
Limassol	66	43	–	50	45	67	32
Nikosia	53	32	50	–	94	117	50
Paphos	114	88	45	94	–	23	76
Polis	136	110	67	117	23	–	100
Troodos	101	75	32	50	76	100	–

GOVERNMENT

The Republic of Cyprus has a democratic constitution which grants a great deal of authority to the country's president. The president is simultaneously chairman of the council of state and is elected directly by the population for a period of five years.

NATIONAL LANGUAGE

In the southern part of the island the official language is Greek, although visitors should have no trouble communicating in English due to the fact that until 1960 Cyprus was a British colony and even today the British maintain military bases on the island.

In Northern Cyprus Turkish officials have declared Turkish the official language. Turkish Cypriots who have been living in the country since before the occupation can, for the most part, understand both Greek and English.

ELECTRICITY

The public electrical supply system is operated on AC 220–240 volts. As a rule electrical outlets correspond to British standards.

BUSINESS HOURS

The Republic of Cyprus: Most businesses are open 8am–1pm Monday–Saturday. During winter (October–April), with the exception of Wednesdays and Saturdays, shops maintain afternoon hours from 2.30pm–5.30pm; during summer (May–September) afternoon hours are 4pm–7pm.
Northern Cyprus: Between 15 May–14 September most businesses are open 7.30am–1pm and 4pm–7pm Monday–Saturday. From 15 September–14 May shops remain open all day from 8am–6pm.

CHRISTIAN WORSHIP

During summer some religious services are held in English in the Republic of Cyprus. For more information contact the clergyman's office in Nicosia (tel: 02/465 694).

HOLIDAYS

THE REPUBLIC OF CYPRUS

1 January: New Year's Day
6 January: Epiphany
19 January: Name Day of the Archbishop Makarios III
25/26 March: Greek Independence Day
1 April: Cypriot National Holiday
1 May: Labour Day
3 August: Anniversary of the Death of the Archbishop Makarios III
1 October: Independence Day
28 October: Greek-Cypriot Day
24 December: Christmas Eve (half-day holiday)
25/26 December: Christmas
31 December: New Year's Eve (half-day holiday)

Sliding holidays: Monday before Lent, Good Friday, Easter Saturday and Sunday (the Orthodox Church usually celebrates Easter a week later than in Central Europe), and the Day of the Assumption.

In addition to the aforementioned holidays, there are also a number of **holidays special to the Orthodox Church** which have no effect on regular business hours and are often celebrated only in certain regions (these include name days of local holy figures and the patron saints of monasteries). These holidays are always celebrated with processions and festivities:

6 January: Coastal regions hold the *Blessing of the*

Sea. As a part of the ceremony, the local bishop plunges a cross into the sea.

17 January: *St Anthony's Day*, the Egyptian father of monasticism and monastic life; celebratory services are held in Nicosia and Limassol.

24 January: *St Neophytos's Day*, a massive procession ending at the cave of this hermit.

1, 2 February: *Jesus Christ's Presentation in the Temple*. Pilgrimage to the Khryssorroyiatissa monastery.

23 April: *St George's Day*. Festive services are held just about everywhere on the island.

29 June: *SS Peter and Paul*. A large, festive service held in Kato Paphos, celebrated by the archbishop and all the other bishops.

15 August: *Death of the Virgin*. Celebrations conducted in the larger monasteries. Festival processions take place all over the island.

14 September: *Erection of the Holy Cross*. Large celebrations (particularly in the Stavrovouni Monastery) in Lefkara and Omodos.

4 October: *Ioannis Lampadistis*. Celebratory service held in the monastery devoted to this local patron saint.

18 October: *St Luke's Day*. Celebrated in Nicosia and Palaechori in particular.

The following sliding Orthodox holidays are also worth mentioning: the *Procession of the Lazarus Icon* through Larnaca, held a week before Easter and the *Flood Festival (Kataklysmos)* also held in Larnaca at Whitsun.

NORTHERN CYPRUS

The official holidays here include:

1 January: New Year's Day
23 April: Children's Day
1 May: Labour Day
19 May: Young People's and Sports Day
27 May: Independence Day
20 July: "Operation Peace" Day (the anniversary of the occupation of the northern part of the island)
19 October: Turkish National Holiday
15 November: Anniversary of the proclamation of the "Turkish Republic of Northern Cyprus".

All museums are closed on 1 January, 19 May, 29 October and 15 November.

In the Turkish northern part of Cyprus Islamic rather than Christian holidays are celebrated. The most prominent among these include the end of the month of fasting, Ramadan (referred to as the "Sugar Festival" *Ramadan Bayram*); the sacrifice festival (*Kurban Bayram*), which takes place about two months after the end of Ramadan; the Muslim New Year Festival and the birthday of the Prophet. Because these holidays are celebrated in accordance with the Islamic, i.e. the lunar calendar, their dates shift 11 days each year.

COMMUNICATIONS

POSTAL SERVICES

Post offices in the Republic of Cyprus are open from 7.30am–1.30pm Monday–Friday and 7.30am–noon Saturday. A letter sent to a country in Central Europe takes about five days. At present, an airmail letter to Central Europe weighing no more than 10 grams costs about 19 cents, a postcard about 16 cents. On top of the normal postal rate there is an extra "Refugee Aid" charge of 1 cent (in the form of an additional stamp).

Because Northern Cyprus is not officially recognised as an independent country, postal authorities in other lands are not permitted to recognise stamps issued by this "country" (a situation which, for instance, Italy takes very seriously).

All mail destined for Northern Cyprus must first make a detour through Turkey. In practice this means that in addition to the address in Northern Cyprus, "Mersin-10, Turkey" must be written on the envelope.

TELEPHONE

The telephone offices (CTA = Cyprus Telecommunications Authority) all maintain different business hours; in larger towns and cities they frequently remain open until evening. Calls may also be placed from regular telephone booths and direct dialling is possible from all telephones. It is not possible to telephone from post offices.

Telephone connections to Northern Cyprus are conducted via Turkey. Because of this you must first dial the Turkish dialling code 0090, followed by 5 (the direct number for Northern Cyprus), then the local dialling code (omit the 0), and lastly the number of the party you are trying to reach.

MEDIA

Newspapers & Magazines: Foreign publications and other sources of information can be purchased in bookstores, hotels, and at newspaper kiosks in both parts of Cyprus.

Two English-language papers are regularly available in the Republic of Cyprus: the *Cyprus Mail* (daily) and the *Cyprus Weekly*. There are three English magazines which cater exclusively to tourists and contain an extensive calendar of events (look in hotel receptions or tourist information offices): *Time Out*, *Seven Days in Cyprus* and *Nicosia this Month*. **Radio & Television:** The Republic of Cyprus broadcasts television news reports in Greek, Turkish and English (6pm).

EMERGENCIES

MEDICAL AID

Throughout the Republic of Cyprus the police, fire brigade and emergency medical aid can be contacted by dialling the number 199. Hotel receptions have access to names and addresses of doctors who speak English.

In Northern Cyprus, however, the system is different; here the police and emergency medical aid have different numbers, contingent upon where they are located:

Nicosia:	Police	tel: 020/713 11
	Emergency	tel: 020/734 41
Famagusta:	Police	tel: 036/635 10
	Emergency	tel: 036/635 28
Kyrenia:	Police	tel: 081/520 14
	Emergency	tel: 081/520 66

GETTING AROUND

TRAFFIC REGULATIONS

In both parts of Cyprus vehicles are driven on the left-hand side of the road – a custom dating back to when the island was a British colony. Despite this, vehicles approaching from the right always have the right of way, provided there isn't a sign in the vicinity stating otherwise.

The maximum speed limit within cities and towns is 30 mph (50 kph); on normal country roads (unless otherwise marked) it's 37 mph (60 kph) and on the motorways 60 mph (100 kph).

When going around bends where visibility is limited it is common practice to warn any oncoming vehicle by tooting the horn. All traffic signs in the Republic of Cyprus are written in both Greek and English.

CAR RENTAL

All it takes to rent a car on Cyprus is a valid national driver's licence; it's not usually necessary to be in possession of an International Driver's Licence. The person renting the car as well as anyone else intending to drive must be at least 21 years of age.

In the Republic of Cyprus there are car rental agencies located at the airport and in larger cities. Many hotel receptions can provide access to an agency. If you choose one of the international car rental companies which maintains an office on Cyprus, reservations can be made in advance from home. The extensive hotel guide put out by the Cypriot Tourist Bureau also contains a list of car rental agencies.

Leasing a car for several days running will ensure a better rate; the longer you keep the car, the less you'll have to pay per day. Vehicles are rented out grudgingly – if at all – for one day at a time. Rates are generally calculated per day and without any mileage limitations.

Regular petrol currently costs more than twice as much as diesel fuel.

MOTORCYCLE & BICYCLE RENTAL

Rental agencies in the Republic of Cyprus often lease motorcycles and sometimes even bicycles too, as well as cars. For information on possible bike tours through the island, contact:
Cyprus Cycling Federation, 5 Vizinos Street, Nicosia (tel: 02/459 056).

BUSES

In the Republic of Cyprus buses do not run on Sundays. During the rest of the week the inner city buses in the larger cities operate between 5.30am–7pm (approximately); during the main tourist season these hours are occasionally extended. Long-distance buses connect city centres, departing at roughly 1-hour intervals. In addition to these, there are also small, private "regional buses" which transport passengers between little country communities and the nearest main town (usually at times corresponding to the beginning and end of a regular work day).

TAXIS

COMMUNAL TAXIS

Communal taxis able to accommodate 4–7 people operate between all the larger towns. Each person pays a predetermined amount which is not contingent upon how many people are actually in the car.

*Mediterranean beauty and zest for life have attracted travellers from all over the world for centuries. Peoples, cultures and continents meet at the Mediterranean Sea. Italy, Spain, Greece, Yugoslavia, Portugal... the Mediterranean area reads like a "Who's Who" of popular travel destinations. And **Insight Guides** are indispensable travel companions.*

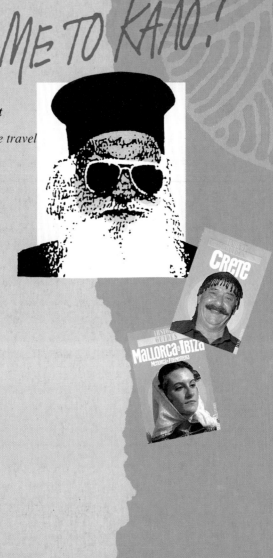

ΜΕ ΤΟ ΚΑΛΟ!

A P A
INSIGHT
GUIDES

Between 6am and at least 4pm taxis connect the large cities of Nicosia, Larnaca, Limassol and Paphos, departing approximately every half hour; after this communal cabs run according to demand. As is the case with regular taxis, communal taxis will pick up passengers from their apartments or hotels if they are within the city limits and if the taxi has been summoned via the taxi control office. Likewise, on reaching the destination, cab drivers will usually deposit passengers at their front doors.

Communal taxis can be taken to and from just about everywhere, with the exception of the airport. New arrivals must use one of the private cabs which wait outside the airport building. Their rates are higher than those of the much cheaper and just as speedy group taxis.

The biggest communal taxi companies in the Republic of Cyprus include Akropolis, Karydas, Kypros, Kyriakos and Makris. The telephone numbers of each of their offices are listed in the brochures available at tourist information centres.

PRIVATE TAXIS

If you're interested in taking a city sightseeing tour via taxi, it's advisable to choose a private one and pay according to the sum accrued on the taximeter (most taxis are fitted with one of these instruments). There are set rates for uninterrupted long-distance trips. Currently the base fare is 35 cents, with an additional 17 cents reckoned per kilometre for a one-way and 13 cents per kilometre for a return trip journey; having the taxi wait for you costs about CY £1.75 per hour. There is no extra charge for one piece of heavy luggage (weighing more than 28 lbs); for each additional piece you'll be expected to pay 20 cents more. Between 11pm and 6am passengers pay an extra "night rate charge" of 15 percent.

If you're taking a sightseeing trip by taxi make sure you come to an agreement beforehand as to how much it will cost, how long it will last, and exactly which sights you will be visiting. At the end of such a private tour the driver will expect to receive a tip.

WHERE TO STAY

HOTELS

The best guide to hotels in the Republic of Cyprus is the annually updated hotel guide issued by the Cypriot Tourist Information Bureau, available free at all tourist information centres. The room rates listed in this guide have been determined by the official authorities and those hotels which try to demand more from their guests than the prices quoted will be reprimanded (if caught). Moreover, each room must be furnished with a list of rates for overnight accommodation and extra services.

The price for an overnight stay in a simple hotel room is the equivalent to about £7 (sterling) per person. During the off-tourist season (*see the section When to Go*) many hotels offer price reductions.

Because official control of overnight lodging is fairly tight, private *pensions* are almost non-existent. This situation is irksome in smaller villages where there are no hotels. (It is no longer possible for tourists to get a room at one of the monasteries without prior arrangement.) This means that excursions must be planned beforehand and must end in larger towns or cities where hotels are available.

Before the invasion of the Turkish army, beach tourism – and thus hotels – was mainly concentrated on the eastern coast south of Famagusta (Varosha) and by Kyrenia. Today the hotel strip at Varosha occupies the no-man's-land buffer zone and has been quite abandoned.

The remaining hotels in the Turkish Zone have been taken over by Turkish management, even though the former Greek operators still claim ownership. In addition there are the hotels which have been run by Turkish proprietors from the start and ones which were built by the Turkish shortly after the invasion. Among these are the Saray and Sabri's Orient in Nicosia, the Celebrity and Acapulco near Kyrenia and the Altun Tabya and Kutup in Famagusta.

In the Northern Cypriot Tourist Information Agency brochure you'll find a complete list of hotels and *pensions*.

CAMPING

At present, there are six licensed campsites in the south of Cyprus. Rates are the same at all of them: currently CY £1 per person each day with an additional charge of CY £1 per caravan or tent.

Each camping area has its own sanitary facilities and a grocery shop or restaurant. With the exception of the campsite located near Troodos, all sites are situated along the coast. The names of the campsites are (from west to east) Polis, Yeroskipos, Governor's Beach, Larnaca and Ayia Napa.

Troodos Camping: Located about 2 miles northeast of the town in the midst of a pine tree forest. Open: from end-April until end-October. Tel: 054/216 24.

Polis Camping: Located along the town beach in a small stand of eucalyptus trees. Open: end-February until end-November; tent rental possible. Tel: 063/215 26.

Yeroskipos (Geroskipou) "Zenon Gardens" Camping: Located about 2 miles east of the Paphos harbour. Open: March–November. Tel: 061/422 77.

Governor's Beach Camping: Located about 6 miles (10 km) east of Limassol. Open: all year round.

Forest Beach Camping: Located about 5 miles (8 km) east of Larnaca. Open: April–October. Tel: 041/224 14.

Ayia Napa Camping: Located west of the town. Open: March until November. Tel: 037/219 46.

Although it is illegal to camp anywhere you happen to find a suitable spot, during summer it is common – among tourists and natives alike.

In the northern part of the island there's a campsite located on the beach about 2 miles (3 km) west of Kyrenia.

YOUTH HOSTELS

Access to youth hostels depends on possession of an International Youth Hostel Card. Currently the price for an overnight stay is between CY £1.75–£3 per person.

Further questions should be addressed to:
Cyprus Youth Hostels Association, PO Box 1328 Nicosia, Cyprus. Tel: 02/442 027 (day) and 02/446 542 (night).

Youth Hostel Addresses:
Nicosia: 13, Prince Charles Street. Tel: 02/444 808
Limassol: 120, Ankara Street. Tel: 05/363 749
Larnaca: 27, Nicolaou Rossou Street. Tel: 04/621 508
Paphos: 37, Eleftherios Venizelos Avenue. Tel: 06/232 588
Troodos: in a pine tree forest near Troodos. Tel: 054/216 49
Stavros tis Psokas: Forest Station Rest House. Tel: 067/223 38.

YACHT HARBOURS & MARINAS

Yachting crews wanting to break their cruise across the Mediterranean Sea can take advantage of the marinas near Larnaca or Limassol. Both are equipped with repair facilities and supplies (petrol, diesel,

electricity, drinking water, laundry and sanitary facilities).

Larnaca: Located in the bay of Larnaca (34° 55'N– 30° 38'E) with 210 mooring slips. Tel: 04/653 110/3; telex: 4500-CYTMAR; telefax: 04/624 110.

Limassol: Located east of the city (34° 42'N–33° 11'E); operated by the Sheraton Hotel; 227 mooring slips. Tel: 05/321 100; telex: 5626-SHERANT CY; telefax: 05/324 394.

Radio Cyprus broadcasts the weather report on channels 15, 24, 26 and 27.

FOOD DIGEST

The prices in nearly all the restaurants in the Republic of Cyprus have been sanctioned by the Cypriot Tourist Information Bureau. Included in the prices listed on every menu is a 10 percent service charge as well as a 3 percent tax which goes to the Tourist Information Authorities. It is customary to leave the waiter a little something extra too. The best place to eat if you're looking for a relatively authentic and inexpensive meal is in one of the traditional tavernas.

Restaurants located on the northern part of the island offer pretty much the same fare and national dishes – with the addition of a few specifically Turkish specialities – as you'll find in the southern part of Cyprus. However, both the wine produced in the South as well as the beers brewed there are not available in the North, where you'll have to choose from an assortment of imported Turkish brands.

Much of the cooking is done in olive oil. And despite the fact that the markets are overflowing with a wide variety of vegetables, in nearly every restaurant the emphasis is on meat dishes.

Vegetarians can opt for a range of vegetable-based side-dishes. Although Cyprus is surrounded by sea, most of the fish on restaurant menus has not been caught locally and is therefore quite expensive.

In line with the predominance of Moslems on the northern part of the island, beef and lamb are eaten rather than pork.

NATIONAL SPECIALITIES

Afelia: pork marinated with coriander.
Greek Salad (Choriátiki salata): salad composed of cabbage, lettuce, celery, cucumber, tomato, pepper, olives, feta cheese and herbs.

Bread: white; an indispensable component of every meal.

Fish: usually deep-fried.

Vegetables: artichokes, asparagus, various kinds of lettuce, avocados, potatoes, mushrooms, aubergine, courgettes and celery.

Güvec (Turkish): vegetable stew with meat.

Halloumi: cheese made from either sheep's or cow's milk which tastes especially good when fried; spiced with peppermint (Turkish: *helim*).

Hiromeri: smoked ham.

Homus: cold chickpea purée.

Kleftiko: lamb simmered in foil.

Keftedes: fried meatballs (Turkish: *köfte*)

Kolokasi: root vegetables.

Kolokithakia: courgettes either stuffed or plain, as a side-dish.

Koukia: broad beans, either as soup or raw in salad.

Koupepia (dolmadakia): stuffed vine leaves (Turkish: *dolma*).

Loundza: ham, especially when served in sandwiches and fried with *halloumi* .

Makaronia tou Fournou (pastitsio): macaroni casserole made with ground meat.

Meze: possible order of dishes: Greek salad, *halloumi*, *loundza*, calamari rings, *sheftalia* and *souvlakia* pieces, *afelia*, *stifado* and lamb chops served with olives, *tahini*, *taramosalata* and *talattouri* .

Fruit: apples, pears, little bananas, grapes, figs, melon, citrus fruits, papaya, peaches, almonds, apricots, pomegranates, strawberries and carob.

Oil: the local olive oil is especially tasty and used liberally – though not excessively – in the preparation of many foods.

Olives: marinated exquisitely with garlic, coriander, lemon and thyme.

Pastourmas: garlic sausage (Turkish: *sucuk*, but with the omission of pork).

Pitta: flat, hollow rounds of bread filled with different *sheftalia* or *souvlaki* and vegetables.

Pilaw: coarsely ground wheat grains and vermicelli cooked in chicken broth and served with a selection of different vegetable side-dishes (Turkish: *bulgur*).

Souvla: lamb roasted on a spit, especially popular fare at family picnics.

Souvlakia: grilled meat kebabs (Turkish: *sis kebab*).

Sheftalia: grilled sausage made of ground meat.

Stifado: beef or rabbit prepared with lots of onions – reminiscent of goulash.

Tahini: sesame sauce with lemon and garlic (Turkish: *terator*).

Talattouri: yogurt prepared with cucumber and peppermint, similar to *tsatsiki* (Turkish: *cacik*).

Taramosalata: cod roe with lemon, potato purée, onions and oil.

Trahanas: coarsely ground wheat grains dried with yogurt and added to soups together with *halloumi*.

TRADITIONAL FESTIVE MEALS

Wedding Meal: *ressi* (wheat with meat), *pastitso*, *kleftiko*, cucumber, tomato, chips for each well-wisher and *kourabiedes* (short-crust pastry filled with almonds).

Easter: lamb Souvla, Easter Soup (made of parts from the head of either a calf or lamb and vegetables, served with garlic bread), eggs dyed red, and *flaounes* (a kind of turnover made from a yeast dough and filled with eggs, cheese and raisins).

Christmas: *wassilopitta* (cake made from a yeast dough, spread with egg and generously strewn with sesame seeds and almonds).

DESSERT

Baklava: puff pastry filled with nuts and soaked in syrup.

Daktila ("finger"): finger-shaped strudel pastry filled with a nut-cinnamon mixture and soaked in syrup.

Glyko tou koutalioú: fruit or walnuts marinated in syrup and served with a glass of water as a welcome titbit for guests.

Honey: very aromatic. Often served with yogurt and almonds.

Kourabiedes: *see* Wedding Meal; this delicacy also available in shops.

Koulourakia: a ring-shaped cookie or rusk biscuit sprinkled with sesame seeds.

Loukoumades: deep-fried balls of choux pastry served in syrup.

Loukoumia: an especially famous culinary speciality from Yeroskipos, near Paphos: cubes of gelatin served in rose water and dusted with powdered sugar.

Palouses: a kind of pudding made from grape juice and flour; it is the basis for *soutsouko*.

Soutsouko: a long chain of almonds strung together, dunked in *palouses* and then dried (very popular).

Sütlac (Turkish): a pudding made of milk, rice and rose water.

BEVERAGES

Visitors to Cyprus will find an abundance of both alcoholic and non-alcoholic beverages. Coffee is prepared as traditional Turkish mocha, which means that it's boiled in a little pot with sugar added upon request and poured into a cup together with the steeped coffee grounds. For those who prefer something a bit less exotic, Nescafé is also usually available.

An especially delicious treat is a glass of freshly-squeezed orange juice, sold by numerous street-side vendors. In addition to beer, a number of excellent wines, local brandies and fruit liqueurs are offered. These are not only significantly cheaper than other, imported spirits, but are also of very high quality.

WINE

Dry white wine: Arsinoe, Keo Hock, Loel Hock, Thisby Medium/Dry, Aphrodite, Amathus, Danae Medium/Dry, White Lady, Palomino, Bellapais, Graves.
Semi-dry white wine: Demi-sec, Blonde Lady, St Panteleimon, St Hilarion, Fair Lady.
Dry red wine: Afames, Othello, Keo Claret, Dark Lady, Buffamento, Hermes, Mirto, Salamis, Semeli, Negro, Domaine d'Ahera.
Rosé: Rose Bellapais, Rosella, Rose Lady, Amoroza, Coeur de Lion, Pink Lady.
Dessert wines: Commandaria St John, Commandaria St Varnavas, Muskato.

HIGH-PROOF ALCOHOLIC BEVERAGES

Ouzo: Keo Extra Fine, Roccos, Christodoulides.
Brandy: V.S.O.P. Keo, Anglias, Peristiane V.O. 31, Loel V.O. 31, Supreme, Five Kings, V.S.O.P. Adonis, V.O. Loel Expert, Etko Cherry Brandy, Keo Cherry Brandy.
Sherry: Keo Medium, Keo Pale Dry, Keo Fino, Sodap Mavra, Etko Emva Cream.
Liqueurs: Apricot Brandy, Filfar Orange Liqueur.

RECIPES

If you'd like to prepare a Cypriot speciality at home to remind you of your holiday, the following recipes are recommended:

KOUPEPIA

Blanch about 30 vine leaves and rinse in cold water (if these are not available, substitute marinated vine leaves from a Turkish or Greek grocer's). You'll need 1 tablespoon each of finely minced peppermint, parsley and onion, ½ pound of diced tomatoes, 1 egg white, ½ pound ground meat (beef and pork). Mix all the ingredients together and add salt and pepper to taste. Sprinkle lemon juice over 2 tablespoons of rice and let stand 5 minutes; add to meat mixture.

Unroll vine leaves and place 1 tablespoon of the meat filling in the centre of each. Roll up, folding in the edges as you go. Place all filled vine leaves in a pot and cover with meat broth; simmer for 40 minutes.

BRANDY SOUR

A refreshing and very popular aperitif to enjoy while watching the sun go down is Brandy Sour. Bring back holiday memories with the following recipe:

Take a long glass and fill it to quarter full with a light brandy. Add a generous shot of lemon juice or lemon syrup. Flavour to taste with a few drops of Angostura and fill the remainder of the glass with soda water. Add ice cubes just prior to serving and garnish with a slice of lemon.

CULTURE PLUS

MONASTERIES

There are 12 Greek Orthodox monasteries still in operation on the island today. All of them are located in the Republic of Cyprus.

Generally speaking, the monasteries do not maintain specific visiting hours. However, prospective guests should respect the midday pause and plan their visits outside this time. Frequently the monks must unlock the churches which visitors come to see. When this is the case, it's customary to leave a small donation for the monastery after you've completed your tour. The most courteous way to accomplish this is not to hand your donation to the monk himself, but to leave it either on the plate used for this purpose at the entrance to the church or near the iconostasis.

Out of respect, visitors should avoid pointing to icons with their fingers or standing with their backs turned towards them. (For further information regarding appropriate behaviour when visiting a monastery, refer to the section *Photography*.)

The most important monasteries are listed here in alphabetical order:
Ayios Georgios Alamanos: 12 miles (20 km) northeast of Limassol, not far from the street leading to Larnaca.
Ayios Heraklidhios: located in the village of Politiko, about 15 miles (23 km) from Nicosia.
Ayios Minas: near Lefkara.
Khryssorroyiatissa: 24 miles (38 km) northeast of the town of Troodos.
Kykko: located in Troodos, northwest of the town.
Makheras: located in the eastern foothills of Troodos, about 25 miles (40 km) south of Nicosia.
Neophytos: 6 miles (10 km) north of Paphos.
Stavrovouni: west of Larnaca; women are not permitted to enter.
Troodhitissa: about 3 miles (5 km) northwest of Platres.

CHURCHES

Due to the fact that many of the most beautiful Byzantine churches are situated in rather remote areas, only a few can be reached directly with public transport.

In order to minimise potential danger or damage

to their interior decorations and contents, most of the churches are kept closed; potential visitors must first collect the key. Usually a local in the coffee house in the nearest village will help. After you've visited the church, it is customary to give a small tip to the person responsible for the keys.

Over the past years nine churches of Troodos have been added to the UNESCO list of the buildings important to the cultural heritage of mankind. These are marked by an asterisk in the following list of Byzantine churches.

Ayia Paraskevi: in the village Yeroskipou, 2 miles east of Paphos.

Ayii Apostoli: in the village Perakhoria, 10 miles (17 km) from Nicosia.

Ayios Ioannis: in Nicosia, directly next to the new palace of the archbishop.

Ayios Ioannis Lampadistou (*): in the village of Kalopanayiotis, in a monastery compound.

Ayios Nikolaos tis Stejis (*): 3 miles (5 km) southwest from the village of Kakopetria.

Michail Arkhangelous (*): in the village of Pedhoulas.

Panayia Angeloktistos: in the village of Kiti, 7 miles (11 km) west of Larnaca.

Panayia Phorviotissa-Asinou (*): near the village of Nikitari, approximately 12 miles (20 km) north of Kakopetria.

Panayia Podhitou (*): near the village of Galata.

Panayia tou Araka (*): near the village of Lagoudera in Troodos.

Panayia tou Moutoulla (*): in the village of Moutoullas.

Peristerona Church: in the village of that name, about 17 miles (27 km) west of Nicosia.

Stavros tou Ayiasmati (*): near the village of Platanistasa.

Tou Timiou Stavrou – Holy Cross (*): near the village of Pelendri, about 15 miles (23 km) north of Limassol.

There are also numerous Orthodox churches located in the northern part of Cyprus that are well worth visiting. Unfortunately, though, since the Turkish invasion of 1974 most of them have been vandalised, and priceless icons, frescoes and mosaics have been stolen or destroyed. Today, most of these churches are, with good reason, permanently closed; some have been converted into mosques and others are currently used as sheep-cotes. The churches and monasteries still open for public viewing are listed under the section "Sights in the Turkish Northern Part".

MUSEUMS IN THE MAIN CITIES

In the list of museums below the following terms are abbreviated: SH (Summer Hours; 1 June–30 September); WH (Winter Hours; 1 October–31 May). Special hours apply to all official holidays.

NICOSIA (South)

Museum of Archaeology, Museum Street. World-class archaeological museum; a comprehensive survey of ancient Cyprus commencing from the New Stone Age. SH: 8am–1.30pm and 4pm–6pm Monday–Saturday; 10am–1pm Sunday. WH: 7.30am–2pm and 3pm–5pm Monday–Friday; 7.30am–1pm and 3pm–5pm Saturday; 10am–1pm Sunday.

Museum of Folk Art, located next to the archbishop's palace. SH and WH: 8.30am–1pm and 2pm–4pm Monday–Friday; 8.30am–1pm Saturday.

The Museum of National Struggle, located next to the Museum of Folk Art. Memorabilia from the period of the fight against the British colonial powers (1955–59). SH: 7.30am–1.30pm and 3pm–5pm Monday–Friday; 7.30am–1.30pm Saturday. WH: 7.30am–2pm and 3pm–5pm Monday–Friday; 9am–1pm Saturday.

Byzantine Museum, next to the archbishop's palace. Contains the largest collection of icons on the entire island. SH: 9.30am–1pm and 2pm–5.30pm Monday–Friday; 9am–1pm Saturday. WH: 9.30am–1pm and 2pm–5pm Monday–Friday; 9am–1pm Saturday.

Levention City Museum Nicosia, Hyppocratous Street. Outline of the city's history commencing from antiquity. Levention Museum in Nicosia. SH and WH: 10am–4.30pm Tuesday–Sunday.

National Collection of Modern Art, in Nicosia. SH: 10am–1pm and 4pm–7pm Monday–Friday; 10am–1pm Saturday. WH: 10am–1pm and 3pm–6pm Monday–Friday; 10am–1pm Saturday.

Omeriye Mosque. SH and WH: 9am–3pm Monday–Saturday.

Famagusta Gate (Culture Centre of the city of Nicosia). SH and WH: 10am–1pm and 4pm–7pm Monday–Friday; 10am–1pm Saturday.

The House of the Dragoman Georghakis Kornesios. SH: 7.30am–1.30pm Monday–Saturday. WH: 7.30am–2pm Monday–Friday; 7.30am–1pm Saturday.

LIMASSOL

Museum of Archaeology, Byron Street. SH: 7.30am–6pm Monday–Saturday; 10am–1pm Sunday. WH: 7.30am–5pm Monday–Saturday; 10am–1pm Sunday.

Limassol City Art Gallery. SH: 8.30am–1pm and 4pm–6pm Monday, Tuesday, Wednesday and Friday; 8.30am–1pm Thursday and Saturday. WH: 8.30am–12.30pm Monday, Tuesday, Wednesday and Friday; 8.30am–1pm Thursday and Saturday.

Limassol Museum of Folk Art, 253 Ayiou Andreaou Street. SH: 8.30am–1pm and 4pm–6.30pm Monday, Wednesday and Friday; 8am–12.30 Tuesday, Thursday and Saturday. WH: 8.30am–1pm and 3pm 5.30pm Monday, Wednesday and Friday; 8am–12.30pm Tuesday, Thursday and Saturday.

Kourion Museum, in the village of Episkopi, 17 km (10.5 miles) west of Limassol. Archaeological finds from Kourion. SH: 7.30am–1.30pm Monday–Saturday. WH: 7.30am–2pm Monday–Friday; 7.30am–1pm Saturday.

Medieval Museum, in Limassol castle, near the old port. SH: 7.30am–6pm Monday–Saturday. WH: 7.30am–5pm Monday–Saturday.

LARNACA

District Museum, at Kalogreon Square. Archaeology of the region. SH: 7.30am–1.30pm Monday–Saturday. WH: 7.30am–2pm Monday–Friday; 7.30am–1pm Saturday.

Pierides Museum, 4, Zenon-Kitieus Street. Extensive private archaeological collection. SH and WH: 9am–1pm Monday–Saturday.

Castle Museum, located along the shoreline promenade in the castle grounds. Finds from Kition and the Hala Sultan Tekke. Excavations from Kition in Larnaca. SH: 7.30am–1.30pm Monday–Saturday. WH: 7.30am–2pm Monday–Friday; 7.30am–1pm Saturday.

PAPHOS

District Museum, Grivas Dhegenis Avenue. Archaeology of the region. SH: 8am–1.30 and 4pm–6pm Monday–Saturday; 10am–1pm Sunday. WH: 7.30am–2pm and 3pm–5pm Monday–Friday; 7.30am–1pm and 3pm–5pm Saturday; 10am–1pm Sunday.

Paphos Castle, SH: 7.30am–1.30pm Monday–Saturday. WH: 7.30am–2pm Monday–Friday.

Byzantine Museum, 26, 25th March Street. SH: 9am–1pm and 4pm–7pm Monday–Friday; 9am–1pm Saturday. WH: 9am–1pm and 2pm–5pm Monday–Friday; 9am–1pm Saturday.

Museum of Ethnography, 1, Exo Vrissi Street, near the episcopal palace. Private collection of archaeological and folkloric objects. SH: 9am–1pm and 4pm–7pm Monday–Saturday; 10am–1pm Sunday. WH: 9am–1pm and 3pm–5pm Monday–Saturday; 10am–1pm Sunday.

Kouklia Excavation Museum. Finds from Old Paphos (Palea Paphos).

OTHER MUSEUMS

Yeroskipos Museum of Folklore, in Yeroskipos, 2 miles (3 km) east of Paphos. SH: 7.30am–1.30pm Monday–Saturday. WH: 7.30am–2pm Monday–Friday; 7.30am–1pm Saturday.

Katsinioros House and Achilleas Dimitri House, in

Phikardou. SH: 10am–1pm and 4pm–6pm Wednesday–Sunday. WH: 10am–1pm and 3pm–5pm

Royal Chapel in Pyrga. SH: 9am–noon and 4pm–7pm Tuesday–Sunday. WH: 9am–1pm and 2pm–4.30pm Tuesday–Sunday.

Kolossi, Castle of the Order of St John, 10 miles (15 km) west of Limassol. SH: 7.30am–7.30pm Monday–Sunday. WH: 7.30am–sunset.

Lefkara Museum. Lace and silver articles. SH and WH: 10am–4pm Monday–Saturday.

ARCHAEOLOGICAL SITES

Hala Sultan Tekkesi, located on the banks of the salt-water lake in Larnaca, not far from the airport. The ruins of an ancient settlement and an important destination for Moslem pilgrims. SH: 7.30am–7.30pm Monday–Sunday. WH: 7.30am– sunset Monday–Sunday.

Kato Paphos. Hellenic and Roman royal tombs; Odeon dating from the 2nd century AD; magnificent mosaics in the "House of Dionysos", "House of Theseus" and "House of Aion"; Panayia Khrysopolitissa Church and Byzantine Basilica. SH: 7.30am–7.30pm Monday–Sunday. WH: 7.30am–sunset Monday–Sunday.

Temple of Aphrodite, Kouklia. SH: 7.30am–7.30pm Monday–Sunday. WH: 7.30am–sunset Monday–Sunday.

Khirokitia. Remnants of a Stone-Age settlement, located 19 miles (30 km) west of Larnaca. SH: 7.30am–7.30pm Monday–Sunday. WH: 7.30am–sunset Monday–Sunday.

Kition. Excavation of the ancient ancestor of present-day Larnaca.

The Royal Tombs in Tamassos/Politiko, near Nicosia. SH: 9am–noon and 4pm–7pm Tuesday–Sunday. WH: 9am–1pm and 2pm–4.30pm Tuesday–Sunday.

Kourion, 12 miles (20 km) west of Limassol and including theatre, temple and church ruins as well as mosaics. Located some distance beyond is the Shrine of Apollon Hylates. SH: 7.30am–7.30pm Monday–Sunday. WH: 7.30am–sunset Monday–Sunday.

Tamassos. Tombs dating from the 6th century BC in the village of Politiko, 15 miles (23 km) outside of Nicosia.

SIGHTS IN THE TURKISH NORTHERN PART

For the most part museums and historical places in the Turkish northern part of Cyprus maintain the same visiting hours, during the summer from 9am–1.30pm and from 4.30pm–6.30pm Tuesday–Saturday; winter hours are between 8am–1pm and 2.30pm–5pm. Some institutions are open on Sunday and holidays (these are marked "Sundays/holidays" in the following list).

Museum hours are affected by a number of Islamic

holidays and by the duration of the entire month of Ramadan (the 9th month of the Islamic calendar).

Nicosia:
Museum of Turkish Cypriots Arts and Crafts
Large and Small *Khan*
Derwisch-Pasha House
Bedesten
Ottoman Library
Famagusta and the surrounding area:
Djambulat Museum
Othello Tower
Salamis (Sundays/holidays)
Royal Tombs
Barnabas Monastery (Sundays/holidays)
Enkomi (Sundays/holidays)
Kantara Castle
Kyrenia and the surrounding area:
Fort with Shipwreck Museum (Sundays/holidays)
Hilarion Castle (Sundays/holidays)
Bellapais Monastery (Sundays/holidays)
Aylos Epiktitos (Sundays/holidays)
Morphou and the surrounding area:
Museum of Natural History and Archaeology (Sundays/holidays)
Ayios Mamas Church (Sundays/holidays)
The Soli ruins (Sundays/holidays)
Vouni Palace (Sundays/holidays)

SPORTS

SWIMMING

There are numerous inviting beaches on Cyprus, some more frequented than others. During summer the beaches on the southern coast are busiest. Ayia Napa, Protaras and Paralimni, as well as the Areale (close to both Larnaca and Limassol) are especially crowded. The largest percentage of tourist hotels are also concentrated in this area.

Originally, the island infrastructure was established further to the west. There are a number of beautiful beaches which are less developed in the area surrounding Paphos and, to an even lesser extent, in the area around Polis. The tavernas and pubs thereabouts are consequently more authentic than those at other, more developed spots and tend to offer more traditional, native cuisine.

The sandy beach of Coral Bay extends from the northwest of Paphos; adjacent to this is a cliff-lined, wildly romantic stretch of shoreline called Cape Drepanon, near Ayios Yeoryios. If you're looking

for relatively untouched, rarely frequented beaches try the Khrysokhou Bay between Cape Akamas (at the western tip of the island) and Polis (located at the centre of the bay shore).

Although nude bathing is strictly prohibited, going topless – both on the beaches and at hotel swimming pools – is tolerated.

In terms of natural beauty, the beaches in the Turkish part of the island beat those in the south. There are splendid bays and sandy beaches around Kyrenia and in the east, in close proximity to Salamis. Many of the best spots have been commandeered by hotels and provided with sanitary facilities (for example, showers and toilets). They charge admission for people who are not hotel guests.

Another inside tip for those in search of unspoilt beaches is the Karpasia Peninsula, jutting out to the northeast, which is graced by many inviting coves and beaches.

WATERSPORTS

During summer watersports enthusiasts will have no difficulty renting the necessary equipment (surfboards, water-skis, pedal boats, etc.) at any of the more popular beaches. It's also possible to rent dinghies.

TENNIS

The larger hotels all have tennis courts. It's much more difficult to reserve a court at one of the island's tennis clubs, but in theory it is possible to book a court even without being a club member provided you are willing to pay a fee.
Nicosia:
Field Club, Egypt Avenue. Tel: 02/447 699.
Eleon Tennis Club, 3, Ploutarchou Street, Engomi. Tel: 02/449 923.
Lapatsa Sports Centre, Deftera (7 miles/11 km southwest of Nicosia). Tel: 02/621 201.
Limassol:
Limassol Sporting Club, 11, Olympion Street. Tel: 05/359 034
Famagusta Tennis Club, 3, Mesarias Street. Tel: 05/335 952.
Larnaca:
Larnaca Tennis Club, 10, Kilkis Street. Tel: 04/656 999.
Paphos:
Yeroskipou Tourist Beach (2 miles east of the harbour). Tel: 06/234 525.

MOTORSPORTS

One exciting annual spectator sporting event that takes place in September is the Cyprus Motor Rally, the results of which have a bearing on the European Championships.

HIKING

AKAMAS PENINSULA

The Akamas Peninsula, situated in the westernmost part of Cyprus beyond the Paphos-Polis Line, not only offers wonderful opportunities for swimming and sunbathing (*see page 303*), but also marvellous possibilities for hiking. This area is named after Akamas, the son of the Greek hero Theseus who, according to legend, surprised Aphrodite bathing in the nude here. Aphrodite fell in love with Akamas, but had to renounce this love because she was already married to Hephaistos. "Aphrodite's Pool" (Loutra Aphroditis), an extremely romantic spring-fed pool said to be the site where the two star-crossed lovers met, is one of the most picturesque spots on the island. Over the past years the Cypriot Bureau of Tourism has established a nature path on the peninsula.

TROODOOS

In summer the Troodos Mountains offer active visitors many inviting hiking opportunities. Even during August, the hottest month of the year, day-time temperatures in this mountainous region do not rise above 80° F (27° C). It is possible to set off along either an undeveloped path or on one of the official trails that have been marked by the Tourist Bureau, among which three are classified as nature paths. The point of departure for any hike is Troodos itself, where you'll find hotels, a youth hostel, restaurants and souvenir shops. The trail named "Makria Kontarka" runs for about 2 miles in a southeasterly direction to a scenic viewpoint; the path "Chromion" runs about 6 miles (10 km) in a northwesterly direction, making its way past Olympos and finally ending at an abandoned chromium mine (thus the name "Chromion") last used in 1974. If you follow the asphalt road at the mine for about 2 miles, you'll eventually find yourself back in Troodos.

To reach the trail called "Kryos potamós" (Cold River), hikers must first gain the road that leads to the former palace of the president, located outside to the southwest of Troodos. From here the path follows the "Cold River" for about 1 mile downhill to the picturesque Kaledonia Waterfalls. At the fish restaurant Psilodendro, about a 45-minute walk south of the falls, you can treat yourself to fresh trout. And if you're too tired to walk the trail back to Troodos, make use of the restaurant's telephone to order a taxi.

Olympos, at 6,505 ft (1,951 metres), constitutes the highest point on the island. It is encircled by a 3-mile (5-km) long path which begins and ends not far from the Prodromos-Olympos crossroads. It is not possible to climb to the top of the mountain as the English operate an air surveillance radar station to keep tabs on the Near East here.

Those planning an extended hike in the Troodos region and therefore planning on staying overnight should bear in mind that in the month of August, the peak holiday season for Cypriots themselves, all accommodation is generally booked solid.

Snow falls heavily in the Troodos during winter (it's not for nothing that the mountain's nickname is "Chionistra" chilblain), and in recent years Mt Olympos has been the recipient of three ski lifts. The ski season lasts from January until mid-March. You can rent all the ski gear you need at the Cyprus Ski Club Hut, or in the village of Troodos itself.

Avid fishermen can take advantage of the reservoirs on the island. A special leaflet issued by the Tourist Information Bureau lists the types of fish found in these waters.

PHOTOGRAPHY

Cyprus provides plenty of interesting subject matter for photographers. Basic rules of courtesy should be observed when photographing people – always ask permission. You're best off buying film or, in the case of video cameras, cassettes, before arriving on Cyprus, as these are quite expensive here.

Taking pictures is strictly prohibited in the areas surrounding military facilities (for example, around the British military bases of Episkopi and Dhekelia, along the approach to Stavrovouni Monastery and, of course, around the military installations associated with the Inner-Cypriot Line of Demarcation). As a rule, visitors are not allowed to take pictures inside museums. However, you can take snaps in the museums' gardens and at outdoor archaeological sites if no excavations are under progress.

Apart from at Stavrovouni, visitors are allowed to take photographs inside monasteries both with or without a flash. The same rules of courtesy apply here as anywhere else: ask permission before snapping pictures of the monks or nuns. Keep in mind that these sacred buildings with their wealth of frescoes and icons are considered holy places. Discretion should be employed at all times. Despite the heat, visitors should take care to be appropriately attired; men without shirts and women scantily clad are not admitted.

As many monasteries, as well as churches and church ruins, are poorly lit, it is a good idea to carry a small torch.

LANGUAGE

Turkish: *oyun havasi görmek istiyoruz*
We'd like to go to a coffeehouse
Greek: *théloume na páme s'éna kafenío*
Turkish: *bir kahvehane'ye gitmek istiyoruz*

What's that?	*ti íne aftó?*	*(bu ne?)*
What's your name?	*pos se léne?*	*(adin ne?)*
When?	*póte?*	*(ne zaman?)*
Where can	*pou ipárchi*	*(burada*
I find...?	*edó...?*	*nerededir...?)*
...Cypriot	*...i kipriakí*	*(...kibris'den*
music?	*mousikí?*	*müzik?)*
Where is	*pou ipárchi*	*(Nerede sahil*
a beach?	*paralía?*	*vardir?)*
where?	*pou?*	*(nerede)*
who?	*piós?*	*(kim)*
why?	*yatí?*	*(nicin)*
yes	*né*	*(evet)*
yesterday	*chtes*	*(dün)*

PLACES & FACILITIES

English	Greek	Turkish
bank	*i trápeza*	*(banka)*
envelope	*to fákelo*	*(mektup zarfí)*
letter	*to ghramma*	*(mektup)*
letter box	*to ghrammatokivótio*	*(posta kutusu)*
money/	*ta leftá/ ta chrímata*	*(para/ bozuk*
change	*/ ta psìlá*	*para)*
petrol	*to pratírio venzínis*	*(petrol ofisi/*
station		*benzin istasyonu)*
police	*i astinomía*	*(polis)*
post office	*to tachidhromío*	*(postane)*
postcard	*i kárta*	*(kartpostal)*
stamps	*ta ghrammatósima*	*(posta pulu)*
telephone	*to tiléfono*	*(telefon)*

USEFUL WORDS & PHRASES

bon appetit	*kalí órexi*	*(afiyet olsun)*
cheers!	*(stin) yá mas!*	*(serefe!)*
excuse me/	*signómi*	*(affedersiniz)*
sorry		
good evening	*kalí spéra*	*(iyi aksamlar)*
good morning	*kalí méra*	*(gün aydin)*
good night	*kalí níchta*	*(iyi geceler)*
goodbye	*chérete*	*(allahais*
		marladik)
hello	*kalí méra*	*(merhaba)*
How are you?	*ti kánete?*	*(nasilsiniz?)*
...very well	*kalá*	*(iyi yim)*
How much is...?	*pósa káni?*	*(kac para?)*
How?	*pos?*	*(nasil)*
I don't		
understand	*dhen katalavéno*	*(anlamiyorum)*
I'd like...	*thélo*	*(istiyorum)*
I'd like to	*thélo na pliróso*	*(ödemek*
pay now		*istiyorum)*
It's cheap	*íne ftinó*	*(ucuz)*
It's expensive	*íne akrivó*	*(pahali)*
It's good	*íne kaló*	*(iyi)*
It's nice	*íne oréo*	*(güzel)*
no	*óchi*	*(hayir)*
okay	*entáxi*	*(tamam)*
please	*parakaló*	*(lütfen)*
thank you	*efcharistó*	*(tesekkür ederim)*
tomorrow	*ávrio*	*(yarin)*

We'd like to see some folk dances
Greek: *théloume na dhoume laikóus chórous*

NUMBERS

1	*éna*	*(bir)*
2	*dhío*	*(iki)*
3	*tría*	*(üc)*
4	*téssera*	*(dört)*
5	*pénte*	*(bes)*
6	*éxi*	*(alti)*
7	*eftá*	*(yedi)*
8	*ochtó*	*(sekiz)*
9	*enniá*	*(dokuz)*
10	*dhéka*	*(on)*
100	*ekató*	*(yüz)*
1000	*chília*	*(bin)*

FOOD

apple	*to mílo*	*(elma)*
artichoke	*i anginára*	*(enginar)*
asparagus	*to sparángi*	*(kuskonmaz)*
aubergine	*i melitsána*	*(patlican)*
banana	*i banána*	*(muz)*
bread	*to psomí*	*(ekmek)*
broad beans	*ta koukiá*	*(bakla)*
butter	*to voútiro*	*(tereyagi)*
cabbage	*to áspro láchano*	*(lahana)*
carrots	*to karóto*	*(havuc)*
celery	*to sélino*	*(kereviz)*
cheese/	*to tirí/*	*(peynir/*
sheep's cheese	*i féta*	*beyaz peynir)*
cherries	*ta kerásia*	*(kiraz)*
chicken	*to kotópoulo*	*(pilic)*
courgettes	*to kolokitháki*	*(kabak)*
cucumber	*to angoúri*	*(salatalik)*
egg	*ta avghá*	*(yumurta)*
fig	*to síko*	*(incir)*
fish	*to psári*	*(balik)*
fruit	*ta froúta*	*(meyve)*
garlic	*o skórdhos*	*(sarmisak)*
grapes	*ta stafília*	*(üzüm)*
green beans	*ta fasolákia*	*(taze fasulye)*

green/
red pepper	to pipéri	(biber)
honey	to méli	(bal)
hors d'oeuvre	to orektikó	(cerez)
ice-cream	to paghotó	(dondurma)
meat	o kréas	(et)
musk melon	to pepóni	(kavun)
navy beans	ta fasólia	(kuru fasulye)
oil	to ládhi	(yag)
olives	i eliés	(zeytin)
onion	to kremídhi	(sogan)
orange	to portokáli	(portakal)
pasta/noodles	ta makarónia	(sehriye)
peach	to rodhákino	(seftali)
pear	to achládhi	(armut)
peas	ta bizélia	(bezelye)
pepper	to pipéri	(biber)
plums	ta dhamáskina	(erik)
pomegranate	to ródhi	(nar)
potatoes	i patátes	(patates)
rice	to rísi	(pilav)
ripe	órimos	(olgun)
Romaine lettuce	to maroúli	(marul salatasi)
salad	i saláta	(salata)
salt	to aláti	(tuz)
soup	i soúpa	(corbasi)
spinach	to spanáki	(ispanak)
strawberries	i fraoules	(cilek)
tomato	i tomáta	(domates)
vegetables	ta chórta/ ta lachaniká	(sebze)
vinegar	to xídhi	(sirke)
watermelon	to karpoúsi	(karpuz)

BEVERAGES

aniseed brandy	i ouzó	(raki)
beer	i bíra	(bira)
bottle	i boukála	(sise)
brandy	to brandy	(keskin icki)
cup	to filtsáni	(fincan)
glass	to potíri	(bardak)
juice	o chimós	(meyva suyu)
lemon	to lemóni	(limon)
medium-sweet	métrios	(sekerli)
milk	to ghála	(süt)
mineral water	i sódha	(maden suyu/ soda)
nescafé	to nescafé	(nescafé)
orangeade	i portokaládha	(limonata)
refreshments	to anapsiktikó	(alkolsüz icki)
sugar	i zachari	(seker)
without sugar	skétos	(seker sis)
sweet	glikís	(cok sekerli)
tea	to tsai	(cay)
Turkish/ Greek coffee	o tourkikós kafés	(kahve)
water	to neró	(su)
wine	to krasí	(sarap)

ARCHITECTURAL WORDS

fresco	i tichoghrafía	(fresk)
church	i eklisía	(kilise)
mosaic	to psifídhoto	(mozaik)
mosque	to tsamí	(cami)
temple	o naós	(tapinak)

DIRECTIONS

right	dhexiá	(sagda)
left	aristerá	(solda)
straight on	ísa	(dosdogru)
go back	píso	(geri)

Where does this road go?
Greek: *Pou pái aftós o dhromos?*
Turkish: *Nereye bu yol gidiyor?*
From where/when does the bus go?
Greek: *Apó pou/póte févghi to leoforío?*
Turkish: *Otobüs nerede/ne zaman gidiyor?*
How much is a ticket/the entrance fee?
Greek: *Pósa íne to isitírio/to ísodhos?*
Turkish: *Bilet/giris kacadir?*
When does the archaeological museum open?/ where is…?
Greek: *Póte íne anichtó to archeologhikó mousío?/ Pou ine...?*
Turkish: *Arkeoloji müzesi ne zaman acik?/ ...nerede?*

MOTOR VEHICLES

petrol	i venzíni	(benzin)
oil	to ládhi	(yag)
tires	to lásticho	(lastik)
insurance	i asfália	(sigorta)

Can you repair it, please?
Greek: *sas parakaló na dhiorthósete aftó?*
Turkish: *lütfen bunu tamir edin?*
I'd like to rent a car/motorbike/bicycle
Greek: *thélo na nikiáso éna aftokínito/mía motosiklétta/éna podhílato*
Turkish: *bir otomobil/motosiklet/bisiklet kiralamak istiyorum*

GENERAL TERMS

ashtray	to tasáki	(kül tablasi)
matches	ta spírta	(kibrit)
cigarettes	ta tsigára	(sigara)
battery	i bataría	(pil)
film	to film	(filim)
spoon	to koutáli	(kasik)
fork	to piroúni	(catal)
knife	to machéri	(bicak)
teaspoon	to koutaláki	(cay kasik)
plate	to piáto	(tabak)
soap	to sopoúni	(sabun)
newspaper	i efimerídha	(gazete)

FURTHER READING

Thubron, Colin. *Journey Into Cyprus*. In 1972 Colin Thubron trekked 600 miles through Cyprus. He said, in retrospect, "The nervous cohabitation which I witnessed in 1972 was, I now realise, the island's halcyon time – and this is the record of a country which will not return."

Hepworth Dixon, W. *British Cyprus*. First published in 1887. Classic travelogue.

Durrell, Lawrence. *Bitter Lemons*. What Durrell called "a somewhat impressionistic study of the moods and atmosphere of Cyprus during the troubled years 1953–6." Durrell went to live in the village of Bellapais, with the express intention of writing about the island and thus completing his trilogy of "island" books.

Hitchens, Christopher. *Cyprus*. Political work examining the Greek/Turkish struggle on Cyprus and blaming it on the policies of the British, Greek, American and Turkish governments.

USEFUL ADDRESSES

TOURIST INFORMATION OFFICES ABROAD

Belgium: Cyprus Tourism Organisation, 83 Wetstraat, 1040 Brussels. Tel: 02/230 5984.

France: Office du Tourisme de Chypre, 15 Rue de la Paix, 75002 Paris. Tel: 01/42 61 42 49.

Germany: FremdenvErkehrszentrale Zypern, Kaiserstrasse 13, D-600 Frankfurt/Main. Tel: 069/284 708.

Greece: Cyprus Tourism Organisation, 36 Voukourestiou, Athens. Tel: 361 0178.

Italy: Ente Nazionale per il Turismo di Cipro, 6, Via S. Sofia, 20122 Milano. Tel: 02/58 30 33 28.

The Netherlands: Cyprus Verkeersbureau, Prinsengracht 600, 1017 KS Amsterdam. Tel: 020/ 62 44 358.

United Kingdom: Cyprus Tourist Office, 213 Regent Street, London W1R 8DA. Tel: 071/734 9822.

USA: Cyprus Tourism Organisation, 13 E 40th Street, New York, NY10016. Tel: 212/683 5280.

TOURIST ORGANISATIONS IN CYPRUS

REPUBLIC OF CYPRUS

CTO postal address: PO Box 4535, Nicosia, Cyprus. Telex: 2165-CYTOUR CY.

Nicosia: Laiki Gitonia, tel: 02/44 4264; 18, Th. Theodotou Street, tel: 02/44 33 74

Limassol: 15, Spirou Araouzo Street. Tel: 051/627 56.

Larnaca: Demokratias Square, tel: 041/543 22; Làrnaca International Airport, tel: 041/543 89.

Paphos: 3, Gladstone Street, tel: 061/328 41; Paphos Airport, tel: 061/368 33.

In addition, the following CTO centres are also open during the summer:

Ayia Napa: Tel: 073/217 96.

Platres: Tel: 054/212 16.

NORTHERN CYPRUS

Northern Cyprus does not maintain any tourist information offices in European countries. Information is available by writing to:

The Ministry of Tourism and Social Assistance, Nicosia, c/o Mersin-10, Turkey.

Information Bureaux in Northern Cyprus: Enformasyon dairesi, Mehmet Akif Cad., Nicosia. **Tourism ve Enformasyon Bürosu**, Fevzi Cakmak Bulvari, Famagusta.

EMBASSIES & CONSULATES

Australia: High Commission, 4, Annis Komninis Street, 2nd Floor, Corner Stassinos Avenue, Nicosia. Tel: 02/473 001.

Canada: High Commission, 4 Queen Frederoca Street, Suite 101, Nicosia. Tel: 02/459 830.

France: Embassy, 6, Ploutarchou Street, PO Box 1671, Engomi, Nicosia. Tel: 02/465 258.

Germany: Embassy, 10, Nikitaras Street, PO Box 1795, Nicosia. Tel: 02/444 362.

Italy: Embassy, 15, Themistocles Dervis Street, Margarita House, Nicosia. Tel: 02/473 183.

United Kingdom: High Commission, Alexander Pallis Street, Nicosia. Tel: 02/473 131.

USA: Embassy, Dositheos and Therissos Street, Lycavitos, Nicosia. Tel: 02/465 151.

Because Northern Cyprus is not recognised by European countries as an independent country, no reciprocal exchange exists between ambassadors or consuls. Consequently, there are no official representatives in foreign countries.

ART/PHOTO CREDITS

INDEX

V – W

Y – Z